Counting By Race

COUNTING BY RACE

Equality from
the Founding Fathers
to *Bakke* and *Weber*

TERRY EASTLAND
& WILLIAM J. BENNETT

Basic Books, Inc., Publishers   *New York*

To Our Families

Library of Congress Cataloging in Publication Data

Eastland, Terry.
 Counting by race.

 1. Race discrimination—Law and legislation—United
States—History. 2.Afro-Americans—Legal status, laws,
etc.—History. 3. Equality before the law—United
States—History. 4. Affirmative action programs—Law
and legislation—United States. 5. Discrimination in
medical education—Law and legislation—United States.
6. Bakke, Allan Paul. I. Bennett, William John,
1943-   joint author. II. Title.
KF4755.E35   342'.73'085   79-7337
ISBN: 0-465-01434-8

Contents

Contents

Preface

THE PURPOSES of this book are two: first, to inquire into the history of the idea of equality of all men in America; and second, to present an argument on a question of public policy, specifically on the issue of equality present in the case of *Regents of the University of California* v. *Allan Bakke*.

The historical portions of the book focus on the origins and developments of two ideas of equality, which we call the idea of "moral equality" and the idea of "numerical equality." We do not pretend to have treated the primary materials—the written documents, speeches, debates, and court cases in which these two ideas of equality are found—in any exhaustive sense; rather the purpose has been to consider these documents and speeches and debates and cases specifically as they relate to the two ideas. The conviction that has motivated this historical inquiry throughout is that ideas are important and that they have a life of their own.

Some of the most important historical materials for our study are court cases. As Tocqueville pointed out, it is typical of American life that disputes touching the most fundamental aspirations and purposes of individuals find their way to lawyers and are often decided as lawsuits. But ours is not a legal textbook, nor a book written for lawyers or legal students. While faithful to the facts in each case cited, the use we make of the cases is in service of larger points regarding the two ideas of equality. This is a book for the general public.

The historical inquiry concentrates throughout on blacks and their aspirations for equality. We have so narrowed the focus, recognizing that blacks are not the only racial and ethnic group whose members have been denied fulfillment of the promise of equality. Lengthy chapters—indeed lengthy books—could be written detailing the discriminations against, and successes of, Chicanos, Asian-Americans, and American Indians in this country. But insofar as the issue of equality arose in slavery with blacks and has been most conspicuous historically in the case of blacks, we have chosen to direct attention to their history. The claims of equality put forth today by other minority group leaders are patterned on the claims of black citizens.

Finally, still concerning the historical part of the book, it may be useful to summarize the ways in which history is relevant to the *Bakke* case. In that case, as we explain in chapter 1, the idea of numerical equality collides with the idea of moral equality. History shows the origins and development of both moral equality and numerical equality as distinctive ideas. History shows as well that whatever may be said about it, whether for or against it, moral equality is *our* idea of equality; ours in the sense that it is the one which historically has guided thinking Americans. Finally, it is from American history that much of the moral appeal of the idea of numerical equality derives. The denials, the equivocations, and the postponements of moral equality to blacks and other minority groups suggest to many that minorities deserve such compensation as may be provided by many of the special admissions programs to graduate and professional schools.

Chapter 8 puts together the historical inquiry with the facts and circumstances of the *Bakke* case. We emphasize here what we note in that chapter, that our observations regarding numerical equality apply only to the issue of "counting by race," as we call it, that characterized the program at issue in *Bakke*. Readers may wish to draw conclusions in other, related areas such as school busing and affirmative action in industry, but we do not do so. And, furthermore, we enjoin those who would draw conclusions to refrain from doing so until they have collected the facts on the public policy dispute in question. Principles, in the absence of facts, do not decide specific cases.

As this book was going to press, the Supreme Court rendered its decision in the *Weber* case. Here, in a different but no less important context than that in *Bakke,* the ideas of moral equality and numerical equality were at issue, and yet the case attracted little comment. We felt the need to examine the facts of *Weber* and discuss the significance of the case vis-à-vis the two ideas of equality. Hence we have added an epilogue on *Weber,* which begins on page 197.

At the end of the book is a compilation of suggested readings. We have listed only those items of either greatest importance or maximum interest. The intention of the list is to guide the reader to sources that can inform him well on the matters discussed in the pertinent chapter. The suggested readings by no means comprise a comprehensive bibliography. Readers wishing more sources may consult the Notes.

This book could not have been written without the help of—and thus we wish to thank—Midge Decter and Julia Strand of Basic Books; Libba Dupree, Susan DeFrancesco, and Teresa Wortham of the National Humanities Center; and Joseph P. Duggan of Greensboro, North Carolina.

We would like to remember the example of the late Charles Frankel, a humanist who sought for the humanities what he himself always achieved—as he put it, "an imaginative understanding of public issues." That has been our goal.

> Terry Eastland
> *Greensboro, North Carolina*
> William J. Bennett
> *Raleigh, North Carolina*

July 9, 1979

Counting By Race

We have seen the mere distinction of color made in the most enlightened period of time a ground of the most oppressive dominion ever exercised by man over man.

—*James Madison,*
Address to the Constitutional Convention,
June 6, 1787

Chapter 1

Bakke and Two Ideas of Equality

IN the fall of 1968, its first year of existence, the medical school at the University of California at Davis registered for classes a total of some fifty students; of these none were black, Chicano, or American Indian, and three were Asian-American. The faculty did not consider itself or its admissions processes biased against individuals belonging to these groups, conventionally known as "minorities"; but in view of the fact that minority students comprised merely 6 percent of the initial class, it reasoned that something had to be done to ensure the admission of a higher percentage of minorities in the future. So in 1969 Davis instituted an affirmative-action plan, specifically a special admissions program, whereby minority applicants could be considered separately from other applicants and according to different—in effect, lower—academic standards; Davis did this voluntarily—on its own, that is, without government coercion or suasion. Immediately the faculty achieved the desired results, as some eight minority students entered Davis in the fall of 1970. With a doubling of the class size to one hundred the next year, Davis also doubled the number of places set aside exclusively for minority students to sixteen.

In the fall of 1972, Allan Paul Bakke, a thirty-two-year-old mechanical engineer who had decided to pursue a career in medicine, applied to Davis. The following spring he was rejected, a fact that did not sit well with him, inasmuch as he had compiled an excellent grade-point average while an undergraduate at the University of Minnesota and had achieved distinguished marks on the Medical College Admissions Test (MCAT). Bakke learned of the special admissions program and thought that, because of it, he was a victim of reverse discrimination. In his view, the exclusive reservation of sixteen seats in a class for minority applicants meant that he, a white, had been allowed to compete not for all one hundred places but only eighty-four.[1] Deciding to make an issue of the situation, were he again rejected, Bakke applied to Davis for the fall class of 1974. He was rejected this second time, and in due course he entered a lawsuit in the Yolo County Superior Court, charging the University of California with having discriminated against him because of his race.

Allan Bakke v. *Regents of the University of California* would pass through the California courts and go, by the fall of 1977, to the Supreme Court of the United States. The preceding is, of course, a history of only the origins of *Regents of the University of California* v. *Allan Bakke,** as the case would finally be recorded, and admittedly this history is brief. But it is sufficient to allow the probing necessary to determine the significance of the case.

To begin with, it is necessary to ask why the Davis faculty decided to change its admissions procedures so that more minority applicants could be admitted. The faculty was commit-

Regents of the University of California v. *Bakke,* 98 S.Ct. 2733 (1978).

4

ted to the idea of treating every applicant fairly, but it believed that minority applicants, as a group, could not compete with whites according to conventional admissions criteria, which leaned heavily on the MCAT and college grade-point average (GPA).[2] Minorities simply did not do as well as whites on the MCAT, nor did they perform as well in the undergraduate classroom. The reason for this, in the faculty's view, was obvious: Decades, even centuries of racial prejudice and oppression against blacks, Chicanos, Asian-Americans, and American Indians had resulted in the educational depression of their descendants. So, to treat minority applicants equally, the faculty thought, they could not be treated in the same way as whites; rather, because of the historic discrimination against the various racial and ethnic groups to which they belonged, minorities had to be treated differently from whites. Thus, in the faculty's view, equal treatment *meant* different treatment and different treatment *was* equal treatment.

Equality of treatment can be a synonym for equity, so it may seem that the Davis program, from the faculty's point of view, was simply a matter of justice. But it is clear that far more was involved.

In 1968, 2 percent of the students in the nation's medical schools were black, yet blacks comprised nearly 12 percent of the total population. Similar disparities defined the situation for the other minority groups in question. Moreover, very few members of these minorities had ever attended medical school or become doctors. It was the presumption of the University of California that, in the absence of the historic discrimination and prejudice against minorities, more blacks, Chicanos, Asian-Americans, and American Indians would have been practicing medicine. That is, if history had been

5

otherwise, minorities would have been able to compete on par with everyone else, winning places in the nation's medical schools and ascending to positions of prestige and influence in American society; hence there would not have been the need to alter the existing admissions procedures.

Davis looked forward to the day when it could abandon its special admissions program. It believed that day would come when minority applicants as a group were doing as well as nonminority applicants on the MCAT and were achieving grade-point averages comparable with anyone else's. But, for the time being—for this transitional period—it was necessary, as the university later would explain, for the Davis faculty "to shorten the distance between the concept of formal equality of opportunity and the actuality of real inequality of opportunity."[3] Shortening that distance meant for Davis that sixteen seats in each class should be set aside, to be filled only by minority students.

In 1965, President Lyndon B. Johnson had delivered a commencement address at Howard University. In that speech, Johnson said, in part:

You do not take a person who, for years, has been hobbled by chains and liberate him, bring him up to the starting line of a race and then say, "You are free to compete with all the others," and still justly believe that you have been completely fair.

Thus it is not enough just to open the gates of opportunity. All of our citizens must have the ability to walk through those gates.

This is the next and more profound stage of the battle for civil rights. We seek not just freedom but opportunity—not just legal equity but human ability—not just equality as a right and a theory, *but equality as a fact and as a result.* [Emphasis added.][4]

Johnson's language fairly describes what the faculty at Davis attempted to do: to achieve "equality as a fact and as a result." And the only certain evidence of progress toward this equality lay in the numbers—in the admission of a substantial number of minority students to the medical school.)

Davis did not put a fine point on just how many minority doctors there should be in the ideal society; and in its brief to the Supreme Court, the University of California eschewed characterization of the Davis program as one that sought an exact proportionality of minority doctors to the number of minorities in the population at large.[5] So what might constitute an adequate "representation" of minorities in medicine was never really defined. Yet, in view of the frequency with which the University of California and its supporters adduced figures indicating proportional disparities,[6] it seems clear that adequate representation could only be achieved when minority doctors constituted a percentage of all doctors that paralleled, if only somewhat, if only very roughly, the percentage of minorities in the total population. Here, then, is where an idea of equity turned into an idea of equality, because compensating for the historic discrimination against minority groups meant restoring those groups to the positions in society that, it was believed, they otherwise would have held,[7] the number of these positions being at least a crude approximation to each group's presence in the general population.

"Equality can be measured," Jesse Jackson told the American Enterprise Institute in May 1978. "It can be turned into numbers."[8] That is what the special admissions program at the Davis medical school did as it counted its applicants, and counted them by race. The program was grounded in what may be called a "numerical equality."

Allan Bakke, of course, thought all this was wrong. Because he was white, he had been allowed to compete, he believed, for only eighty-four of the one hundred places in the

Davis medical school. Nonwhites, on the other hand, had been allowed to compete for all one hundred places, and they had been assured of winning sixteen of these. Bakke thought this division along racial lines unfair, especially in his case. After all, he was, he thought, an excellent applicant as the objective indices go, and yet others—the specially admitted— were admitted not by virtue of the indices but in spite of them and because of their race—"by a separate criterion," as he called it in a letter to Dr. George Lowery, dean of the Davis medical school.[9]

Bakke believed he could see that "special criterion" in the differences in aptitude-test scores and grade-point averages between those admitted through the regular admissions process and those admitted through the special admissions process. The average GPA of those regularly admitted for the class entering in the fall of 1973 was 3.49, while that of the specially admitted was 2.88. The average GPA in the sciences of those regularly admitted was 3.51, and that of those specially admitted, 2.62. The average percentile in which the regularly admitted scored on the verbal section of the MCAT was 81, the specially admitted, 46; the average on the quantitative section for the regularly admitted was 76, the specially admitted, 24; the average on the science section for the regularly admitted was 83; the specially admitted, 35; the average on the general information section for the regularly admitted was 69, the specially admitted, 33.[10] The respective figures for those regularly and specially admitted for the fall of 1974 revealed similar differences.[11]

Meanwhile, Bakke had his own figures in hand, and he knew how he compared. He had an overall GPA of 3.51; in the sciences, 3.45. And his percentile scores on the MCAT tests were, in the verbal, quantitative, science, and general information sections respectively, 96, 94, 97, and 72.[12] In light of all this, it is understandable that Bakke thought he had been unfairly treated, that he thought he had reason for litigation.

And Bakke was not just thinking of himself. "Reverse discrimination is as wrong as the primary variety it seeks to correct," he wrote in a letter to the San Francisco office of the Equal Employment Opportunity Commission.[13] And because it is wrong, Bakke believed, it is wrong whoever is affected by it. So he worked not only to secure himself admission but also to resolve the issue so that others would not encounter the possibility of being denied admission to a university because of their race.

It is clear that Bakke's position involved not just a complaint of unfairness on the part of the Davis Medical School, but also an idea of equality—that of what may be called moral equality. Bakke believed that every person should be considered as an individual, not as a member of some racial or ethnic group to which he belongs or says he belongs. Considered as an individual, Bakke further believed, every person should be allowed to have his claims evaluated on the same basis as any other person's. Bakke did not argue a right to be admitted to medical school, nor was his suit against the university a statement that Davis should evaluate all applicants by the criteria of the aptitude tests and the undergraduate grade-point averages. Rather, he argued that he should have his claims for admission evaluated on the same basis as anyone else's, and that to do otherwise is wrong.

Focusing on the individual, Bakke believed that "societal advancement" should not be "based upon racial proportionality"; he believed there should be "no guarantee that any individual or group will be represented in a given professional school or in a given profession."[14] Bakke's position was clearly in conflict with an "equality of results," if by that is meant a guaranteed finish for certain (or even all) participants in a competition. Bakke's position, insisting on equal treatment, implied that the outcomes or results for each individual very well may be unequal. Thus was the issue joined.

It is a thesis of this book that the *Bakke* case was supremely a conflict between two ideas of equality, one the idea of numerical equality, as represented by the academic institution, the University of California, and the other the idea of moral equality, as represented by the individual, Allan Bakke. It was a conflict that for a decade had seemed inevitable. Had the participants not been the University of California and Bakke, they would have been others. In 1974, a similar case, in which Marco DeFunis charged the University of Washington Law School with discriminating against him, a white, by admitting minority applicants with less distinguished qualifications,[15] went to the Supreme Court but was there rendered moot.

—Toward the end of the decade that began, in 1954, with *Brown* v. *Board of Education,* a case in which the Supreme Court ruled that "separate-but-equal has no place in the field of education," many Americans seemed to have accepted the idea that skin color and ethnicity ought not to be relevant in any public or private consideration of the worth of an individual. Ben Martin, a professor of politics at the University of Missouri at Kansas City, has observed that politicians and media leaders took an influential lead "as they appealed to elementary notions of equity, stressing individual merit as the standard of personal worth and making equal treatment and equal opportunity matters of simple fairness."[16] Racial discrimination was formally outlawed by the Civil Rights Act of 1964, and it seemed to many that in a color-blind society, minority individuals would advance socially and economically by virtue of their own talents and abilities. There were, to be sure, those charitable impulses that saw private citizens doing their best to guarantee that black and other minority Americans got a fair shake—as when, for example, they applied for a job. These impulses were federalized, so to speak, first by President John F. Kennedy and then by President Johnson, in executive orders specifying that "affirmative action" be taken. The concept then referred to taking such measures as would ensure that tests to discern employment qualifications were free of racial or cultural bias; or that a recruitment net was flung far and wide so that anyone conceivably interested might find his way into the applicant "pool." Clearly, there was no mention in this fledgling concept of "affirmative action" of any equality that could be "turned into numbers."

In the middle and late 1960s, however, the achievements by blacks and other minorities were not materializing to the degree many people had hoped. The presumption began to insinuate itself into society in general that, as it would be articulated in the government's *amicus* brief in *Bakke,* the United States must "restore victims of discrimination to the position they would have occupied but for the discrimination" against them or their "forebears."[17] Gradually the government agencies responsible for carrying out the mandates of the Civil Rights Act (CRA) of 1964 and the executive orders pursuant to that act began to construe that statute and those orders in ways that would effect, as Johnson had put it in 1965, "equality as a fact and as a result."

For example, the Equal Employment Opportunity Commission (EEOC) created by the CRA began placing the burden of proof on employers whose work forces did not divide into what the EEOC deemed the appropriate percentages for whites, blacks, and other minorities; that is, employers had to explain why minorities were "underrepresented" or "underutilized." The EEOC began to infer racial discrimination against minorities from the mere fact of "underrepresentation" and "underutilization," and employers were directed to establish numerical "goals" to be accomplished within certain "timetables" for the hiring of minorities. As early as 1969 the EEOC had taken the position that "any discussion of equal employment opportunity programs is meaningful only when it includes consideration of results—or lack of results—in terms of actual numbers of jobs for minorities and women."[18]

By the early 1970s every government agency responsible for administering affirmative action understood that the concept entailed a concern for an equality of results that could be measured numerically. Universities and colleges receiving federal funding, for example, began to be instructed by the Department of Health, Education, and Welfare (HEW) to hire new faculty members in accordance with the racial and sexual composition of the pool of professors or prospective professors available. That is, if 10 percent of the doctorates in English were black, then a university was supposed to reflect that ratio in its hiring practices over a specified number of years or face the prospect of losing federal grant money. As the 1970s wore on, the numerical approach was apparent in other ways, as when, in 1977, Congress passed a $4 billion public works law that required 10 percent of the money for each construction project to be spent on purchases from minority contractors.

All of these were government efforts to achieve an equality

that could be turned "into numbers." But by no means were the efforts limited to the government. Gradually, in the decade begun in 1967, private employers not under contract to the government began to think of affirmative action in terms of remedying past discrimination by hiring and promoting minorities in proportion to their representation in the general population. And the voluntary efforts carried out along the most unified front, perhaps, were those undertaken by the nation's institutions of higher education, including the professional schools.

"To treat our black students equally, we have to treat them differently," said Vanderbilt Chancellor Alexander Heard.[19] Administrators at universities similar to Vanderbilt thought they were entering a transitional era, one in which, as the aphorism went, to get past racism, we must first take account of race.[20]

This was the notion of compensation upon which numerous admissions policies began to be based, and joined to it, as at Davis, was the idea that adequate compensation for the groups discriminated against could only be given by enrolling a significant number of minorities. "Although minorities constitute a significant part of our population," the American Bar Association said in 1967, "they comprise only a small percentage of the legal profession";[21] this was the explanation for the association's endorsement of a national program to increase the number of minority students in law school. In the late 1960s the Association of American Medical Colleges formally recommended that medical schools admit greater numbers of minority students.[22]

In the quest for minority students, the admissions procedures at the nation's professional schools differed. Some had a "two-track" system, as at the Davis Medical School, whereby nonminorities were considered by the regular admissions committee and minorities (for the most part) by a special admissions committee. Most schools, however, lumped all applicants together, the same admissions committee considering the lot. Still, most every school had one key procedure in common—that of "counting by race." In "counting by race," the schools admitted a certain number of students because of their race or ethnic background, not because they possessed—the majority of them did not—academic qualifications equivalent to those of the nonminority students admitted.[23]

An implication of "counting by race" was obviously that, in the competition for a finite number of places in the professional schools, nonminority applicants having superior academic credentials would nonetheless be rejected; a displacement would occur. And it was only natural to assume that some of those who thought themselves displaced would consider the situation unfair and indeed contrary to the consensus on race that seemed to have emerged in the early 1960s.

Hence the cry of "reverse discrimination" began to be heard in the early 1970s, and it increased in volume as the decade progressed. It seemed only a matter of time before one of the cries of reverse discrimination would be organized into a lawsuit, only a matter of time before the battle between the idea of moral equality and that of numerical equality would be formally joined. This was the *Bakke* case, and it was, as the Equal Employment Advisory Council (EEAC) observed in its brief in *Bakke,* the first case in which the Supreme Court had to address the validity of an affirmative action program under which the administering entity made the "decision to allocate limited educational or employment opportunities solely on the basis of race in order to rectify an underrepresentation of minorities."[24] The *Weber* case, in which an employee of Kaiser Aluminum had charged the company with having discriminated against him, a white, by promoting blacks with less seniority and fewer qualifications ahead of him, in accordance with its own voluntary affirmative-action plan, would have fit the description given by the EEAC of the *Bakke* case, had it gone to the High Court before *Bakke* did. The Court accepted the *Weber* case for review the year after *Bakke,* so it was largely a chronological fact that invested *Bakke* with distinction and attracted the interest of so many Americans.*

More than sixty *amicus curiae* briefs were filed in *Bakke,* and for more than a year any news about the case seemed to rate first-page status in the newspapers. Magazines and television carried in-depth reviews of the issues involved. Everyone seemed to be affected. Not only those who had taken voluntary actions, whether in the field of education or employment, to admit or hire more minorities, but also those in government agencies charged with administering the nation's equal opportunity laws, thought that very possibly, in this case, the Court might render such judgments or enunciate such principles as would either affirm or deny or otherwise affect their efforts. And all of those who might have some relationship with these efforts—whether minorities, on the one hand, or nonminorities, on the other—had interests at stake. It is inaccurate, however, strictly to identify minorities as siding with the university and nonminorities as siding

---

* Class also explains the great interest in *Bakke.* "The [putative] injury done Brian Weber," wrote Carl Cohen, professor of philosophy at the University of Michigan, "was at least as great as that done Allan Bakke." But the number of blue-collar workers Weber could be said to represent was, if far larger than the number of professional-school students and those interested in professional schools, far less articulate. See Cohen, "Why Racial Preference Is Illegal and Immoral," *Commentary* 67, no. 6 (June 1979): 40–41. See also our Epilogue on *Weber,* p. 197.

with Bakke,[25] for ultimately the conflict was one of ideas. How the Supreme Court would rule in *Bakke* would say much about the direction equality would take in American society.

It is, to reiterate, a thesis of this book that the *Bakke* case was supremely a case about the nature and meaning of the idea of equality in American life, supremely a case about a conflict between the idea of numerical equality and that of moral equality. These ideas have long histories in American life, and it is a second thesis of this book that to understand and assess *Bakke*, it is necessary to be acquainted with these histories. Thus, the task remaining in this chapter is to justify the investigation of critical moments in the history of the idea of equality—an investigation that occupies the bulk of this book. And toward that end, it is first necessary to ask: What does one do with a case involving equality? How should such a case be decided? How, indeed, should the Supreme Court have decided the *Bakke* case?

More lawyers than ever before supplied the Supreme Court with advice on this question; the *amicus curiae* briefs, as we have noted, numbered more than sixty. It is necessary to the legal task, of course, to frame an issue in terms of what seems constitutionally or statutorily or otherwise pertinent; and the *Bakke* case, having been decided by the California Supreme Court on the basis of the Fourteenth Amendment, was framed by the vast majority of the *amici* as a Fourteenth Amendment case. But the Fourteenth Amendment does not immediately suggest its meaning,[26] whereas, by contrast, the Thirteenth Amendment does. The Thirteenth Amendment says, simply, that "neither slavery nor involuntary servitude, except as a punishment for crime whereof the party shall have been duly convicted, shall exist within the United States, or any place subject to their jurisdiction." On this there can be little debate: Slavery cannot exist in the United States. But can racial discrimination of any kind exist in the United States? How should the Fourteenth Amendment—which, in pertinent part, says that no state shall deny to any person the equal protection of the laws—be interpreted? Apart from its apparent meaning, there is a more difficult question of interpretation with this amendment.

Most of the *amici* interpreted the amendment in one of three ways:

1. As forbidding discrimination of any kind on the basis of race, whether of the traditional kind against minority persons, or of the more recent, "reverse discriminatory" kind against nonminority persons.
2. As either mandating or permitting discrimination in favor of blacks and other groups similarly situated.
3. As being "open-textured," that is, open to the interpretations the American people think it ought to bear, in accordance with the society's changing ways and mores, and thus, presumably, its changing ideas of equality.

All of Bakke's supporters fell into the first category, and most of those supporting the university into the second and third.

Bakke's supporters wanted the Court to interpret the Fourteenth Amendment so that what may be called the "non-discrimination" principle—that is, that there should be no discrimination against or in favor of anyone on account of race or ethnicity—would prevail. "It is . . . axiomatic under [the Equal Protection Clause] that a State body may not act in any way to discriminate for or against a person because of his race," said the Young Americans for Freedom.[27] Similarly, the American Federation of Teachers said: "The constitution and the entire philosophical history of our country cries out against discrimination of any kind, in favor of or against anyone. Discrimination on the basis of background is improper in every respect, be it privately or judicially imposed."[28] More elaborately, the American Anti-Defamation League argued:

Does equal protection by the State, commanded by the Fourteenth Amendment, mean one thing as applied to whites and another when applied to non-whites? Since whites and non-whites by definition exhaust the universe, to what are the rights of non-whites to be equal, if not the rights of whites? To what are the rights of whites to be equal, if not to those of non-whites? Equality denotes a relationship between or among those who are to be treated equally by the government. And the Equal Protection Clause means that the constitutional rights of a person cannot depend on his race, or it means nothing.[29]

From this last it is clear that the nondiscrimination principle was closely related to the understanding of equality held by the *amici* on Bakke's side. There could be no equality, in their view, unless there was affirmance of the nondiscrimination principle.

Those *amici* in the second and third categories took precisely the opposite position. They believed there could be no equality unless there was affirmance of a principle of discrimination *in favor of* minority groups. Some of these *amici* —those in the second category—took this to be the meaning of the Fourteenth Amendment. "The unmistakably clear, central purpose of the Fourteenth Amendment is the protection of discrete and insular minorities," said the American Civil Liberties Union.[30] "The central purpose of the Fourteenth Amendment was to guarantee equality for blacks . . .", said the Asian-American Bar Association.[31] Other *amici* supporting the university took the position that the Fourteenth

Amendment was empty of substantive meaning; that, therefore, it had to be given meaning; and that that meaning
should be in accordance with what the society at any given
time perceives as most vital. The Supreme Court itself has
expressed this view of the amendment: "[T]he Equal Protection Clause is not shackled to the political theory of a particular era. In determining what lines are unconstitutionally
discriminatory, we have never been confined to historic notions of equality. . . . Notions of what constitutes equal treatment for purposes of the Equal Protection Clause *do*
change."[32] In line with this understanding of the amendment
was the National Council of Churches: "The requirements of
equal protection do not prohibit a state from considering the
needs of the society and the needs of minorities in distributing the valuable resources of a professional education";[33] and
the American Bar Association: "The Equal Protection
Clause does not prohibit all classifications based upon
race."[34]

These, then, were the three principal views of the Constitution, and in each of them was reflected the idea of equality
the Constitution supposedly embodies. The appeal to the idea
of equality and to the understanding of equality that should
govern interpretation of the Fourteenth Amendment was actually an appeal to the meaning of equality in the American
experience. For whatever disagreements the *amici* and other
parties on both sides had among themselves in *Bakke*, they
were all agreed that equality as an ideal has a special status
in American history, and that the meaning of equality as an
ideal is what should govern interpretation of the Fourteenth
Amendment.

It is history and American political philosophy, then, that
must be consulted in order to understand how it is that all

the proponents and advocates in this case took equality so seriously. The parties to the litigation and their various defenders were all heirs to ideas about equality. Why they were and why these ideas had such overriding importance to this case is the story of this book. All parties were agreed that the meaning of equality in the American experience should govern what ought to have decided this case and, moreover, what ought to decide similar cases in the future. Cases like *Bakke* turn on the meaning of equality in American history that, it is believed by all, the Constitution in relevant part embodies. Does equality mean moral equality, the idea on which Bakke's supporters implicitly stood? Or does equality mean numerical equality, the idea on which the university's supporters implicitly stood? Or, still further, does equality in the American experience mean nothing at all—that is, is equality something that changes, having no constant meaning?

So we come to the need to consider the history of an idea, the idea of equality. Has anyone else done this satisfactorily? How about the lawyers who advised the Court in *Bakke*? It turns out that they do not give much help. The briefs in the *Bakke* case are full of efforts to distinguish between this "test" and that by which racial classifications are said to be valid or invalid under the Fourteenth Amendment; one reads of "rational relationship tests," "compelling interest tests," "intermediate balance tests," and yet others. It is possible to get lost in the sea of tests, to forget where one is going, to forget that considerations of equality are paramount anyway in the briefs' discussions of any "test." Only three times is the Declaration of Independence mentioned, the document that unleashed the idea of equality into American history and whose study is necessary to any understanding of it. And absolutely no mention at all is made of Abraham Lincoln, who not only took the step, at once libertarian and equalitarian, of freeing the slaves, but also debated the subject of equality with Stephen A. Douglas on the prairies of Illinois—a debate that would seem to have attracted (but in fact did not) some attention in the debate over *Bakke*.

The briefs in *Bakke* concentrated their discussions on the Fourteenth Amendment, thus neglecting the larger context in which the idea of equality must be understood—a context supplied in large part by the Declaration and Lincoln. And the briefs picked their way from the Fourteenth Amendment, which was ratified in 1862, to the present, taking due note of critical cases but neglecting the crucial analytical connections regarding the idea of equality that identify its development. That the briefs concentrated on the Fourteenth Amendment and that they considered legal precedent was appropriate and necessary; and given the legal task, it was perhaps inevitable that the briefs in *Bakke* failed to offer a perspective of the case larger than that possible through legal considerations. Nevertheless, it was here that a case like *Bakke* would have benefited from a discussion that was concerned with the history of ideas, with the development of American political thought, and with the significant events in American history; and it would seem that the nonlegal literature on *Bakke* would have supplied this need. But in fact it was vexed with discussions of "affirmative action," "quotas," "goals," and the like. The nonlegal literature consulted American history, but the purpose in doing so was less to ascertain its relevance in the discussion of an idea than to determine its relevance to sociology. The legal literature and the nonlegal literature in *Bakke* thus comprise an unsatisfactory bibliography for the *Bakke* case. The lack of a discussion of the meaning of an idea—the idea of equality in its historical and analytical complexity—was typical of the current trend to ignore the importance of the humanities in considering public policy.

Interestingly, the literature on the general subject of the idea of equality in American history is not extensive. It is instructive to look up the subject "Equality" in a library card catalogue; one finds roughly two dozen books on the subject. Of these only several in any systematic way attempt to trace the history of the idea of equality. Certainly the best work to date is J. R. Pole's *The Pursuit of Equality in American History*, published in early 1978.[35] Pole's work covers much of the waterfront: He pursues many of the equalities in American history—for example, the equality discussed during the Revolution as between Americans and Englishmen, religious equality, racial equality, and sexual equality. There is something dissatisfying about Pole's pursuit of these and other equalities, however, should one wish to use his account to try to comprehend the historical setting of *Bakke*. It is, as sociologist Nathan Glazer pointed out in a book review, that Pole neglects to give a sufficiently rigorous analytic framework that would show the traditions of equality out of which a *Bakke* case would and indeed did come and was decided in the very year Pole's book was published.[36]

Mention should be made of Glazer's own book, *Affirmative Discrimination*, a study of ethnic inequality and public policy.[37] Glazer understands such cases as *Bakke* in terms of a conflict between the idea of equality of opportunity and that of equality of results; and perhaps that is a good enough distinction, if it is the past fifteen or so years that one has in mind. Those are the years Glazer's book covers; there remains the need for a study of the ideas of equality that have resulted in the *Bakke* case—a study that will take one so far back as 1776. It is the purpose of this book to make that study, for it is our contention that only by understanding the history of both the idea of moral equality and the idea of numerical equality is it possible to assess adequately the Court's decision in *Bakke* and to comprehend the similar conflicts that, it now appears, will continue in American history.

The book is organized as follows: Chapters 2 through 6 concern the idea of moral equality. Chapter 2 deals with the emergence of the idea of moral equality in American history in the form of the proposition that, because all men are created equal, no man can be the slave of another. Chapter 3 deals with the development of this proposition by Lincoln, as he placed the principle of equality at the heart of self-government. Chapter 4 concerns the steps taken toward equality after the Civil War, and chapter 5 deals with the frustration of the idea of moral equality that occurred at the end of the nineteenth century. Chapter 6 concerns the ultimate acceptance at law of the idea of moral equality, a fact that came to pass not until 1964, with the Civil Rights Act. Chapters 7 and 8 deal with the idea of numerical equality. Chapter 7 deals at length with the origins and development of the idea of numerical equality, which is not treated until this chapter because it did not make its appearance in American history until very recently). Chapter 8 discusses the tradition of numerical equality, specifically in regard to such special admissions policies as were practiced at Davis. And chapter 9 takes up the question of what the Supreme Court did in *Bakke* in light of the two traditions of equality.

Chapter 2

Are We Men?

Moral Equality
at the Founding

THE IDEA of moral equality to which Allan Bakke appealed includes the proposition that, because all men are equal, no man should be discriminated against or benefited because of his race and no man because of his race should have his claims evaluated on a basis different from another man's. This proposition is closely related to another proposition, one that emerged with the republic's beginnings—that, because all men are created equal, no man should be the slave of another. The origins of the idea of moral equality that was to be accepted in the twentieth century are thus to be found two centuries earlier when that most abject form of racial discrimination, slavery, was an institution, and an issue. But uncovering these origins is not, as we shall see, the simple exercise of thinking that by declaring the self-evident truth that all men are created equal Thomas Jefferson and the Colonial Congress meeting in Philadelphia in 1776 intended to affirm the equality of all men—black and white—and thus to deny that any man—black or white—should be the slave of another.

For in fact the principal concern of the Colonial Congress was to assert the rights of *English* Americans *as* Englishmen. Few things seemed so obvious to Jefferson, who drafted the Declaration of Independence, and to the fifty-five others who signed it, than that they ought to have the same rights and privileges that Englishmen, in their particular tradition dating from the Magna Carta, then enjoyed. The "colonies," as Richard Bland, a Virginia lawyer, put the issue, ". . . have as natural a right to the privileges and liberties of Englishmen, as if they were actually resident within the Kingdom."[1] Yet these privileges and liberties, the colonists believed, were being denied them by the Crown; they believed they were being forced to live in a condition of inequality—"slavery," as some of them even called it.

At the same time, of course, there *were* slaves—some 325,000 of them, of African descent, and by the very definition of their status they were living in a most wretched condition of inequality. But it was no part of the congressional purpose, in the particular words "all men are created equal," to assert that the rights of everyone in America—and thus the African slaves—are equal to those of Englishmen. In 1776 Americans did not feel the necessity to extend the rights of Englishmen to Africans; they believed Negroes to be a "brutish sort of people,"[2] unfit to assume and exercise the particular Anglo rights and privileges secured piecemeal and painstakingly over the centuries. Indeed the colonists had made it an act of treason, often punishable by death, to flee from slavery and live as a free man.

Thus an editor seeking to tighten the language of the Declaration justifiably might have changed "all men" to "all white Americans and Englishmen." Yet the Declaration did say that "all men"—without qualification—"are created equal," and these words soon came to be understood as meaning, literally, *all men*—blacks, whites, any men. Significantly, Jefferson himself believed the words "all men are created equal"—language Congress accepted without change. The words he chose to assert the rights of Americans as Englishmen thus rang for him another meaning as well. The connotation of "all men," for Jefferson, was universal and individualist,[3] and the way in which all men are equal was in regard to their moral faculty. He believed there were intellectual and physical differences among men and among the races, but what made man uniquely man, he also believed, was his possession of moral sense, which makes man accountable to himself and others, capable, therefore, of self-government and of consenting to social obligation.[4] For Jefferson, the moral faculty was man's highest faculty, and so equality in respect to moral sense was the most important way in which all men could be equal;[5] Jefferson's thinking was influenced by the Stoics, who had spoken of a city of wise men where all, rich and poor, are equal; by Cicero, who conceived of a law of nature in which all men are born free and equal; by John Locke and his theory of equality in "the state of nature"; and by Francis Hutcheson and others of the Scottish Enlightenment.[6]

Jefferson, of course, was not the only American who knew of the Stoics, Cicero, Locke, and those of the Scottish school. The ideas of these thinkers pervaded the colonies. Nor were they the only egalitarian influences. There were the abolitionist convictions of the religious, notably the Quakers; there was a celebrated judicial verdict—the *Somerset* case (1772) in England—against slavery; and there were the experiences of masters with their slaves that persuaded slaveowners against slavery and in favor of freedom. Not surprisingly, various societies sprang up, animated by the ideas of equality and liberty, and a number of pamphlets and books were written, arguing from the same ideas. Discussions and debates on slavery—some formal, as one at Harvard College in 1773—were common.

These were the times, and they invested the preamble to the Declaration of Independence with a meaning beyond its immediate aim of asserting the rights of white Americans as Englishmen. "All men" came to be understood as referring to all men, without exception or distinction based on race. And the more the Declaration was cited as referring to all men, the more it came to mean just that, and the more it came, moreover, to reinforce sentiments for equality. On the basis of the Declaration as a document about equality, slaves fled their masters during the Revolution, and abolitionists, meanwhile, found new motivation for pressing their case.

This is by no means to say that most Americans *believed* that all men are created equal. The pertinent distinction is between the meaning of a proposition and assent to a proposition, and many Americans, mostly those in the southern colonies, plainly did not assent.[7] Nor can it be maintained that sentiment in favor of equality developed so that the Negro's condition might be bettered. Just as the Declaration was written without an intention to establish equality for blacks, neither was the Constitution, in 1787, as we shall see. Nevertheless, despite the often ambivalent denial in word and deed that all men are created equal, there is no doubt that few Americans, North or South, disputed, as the eighteenth century wore on, that this famous proposition meant just what it said. And the Declaration was understood in this sense, not because of the intentions of Jefferson or Congress, but because of the sentiment for equality that circulated throughout young America and the ideas about equality that were discussed and debated. Thus, to study the origins of the idea of moral equality in American history is to inquire into the ideas, attitudes, and experiences of Americans in the era before, during, and after the Declaration of Independence was written.

Antislavery sentiment was as old in America as the institution of slavery,[8] and it first arose from religious belief. The first organizational resolution against slavery was composed in 1688, in Philadelphia, where the Germantown Mennonites declared that the maintenance of slavery was inconsistent with Christian principles. Not until the middle of the eighteenth century, however, did the religious objection to slavery gather force, primarily because of the Quakers. In 1757, the Pennsylvania Quakers, in concert with the London Meeting for Sufferings, decided to inquire into Quaker involvement in the slave trade; the following year they decided to banish from business meetings, and to refuse the offerings of, all members who bought or sold Negroes.[9] Quakers were among the first Americans to free their slaves.[10]

In due course appeals to Christianity were joined by philosophical arguments. In his "Rights of the British Colonies Asserted and Proved," written in 1764, James Otis, the Massachusetts lawyer and pamphleteer, asserted that all men, black and white, were born equal, and then argued: "Does it follow that 'tis right to enslave a man because he is black? Will short curled hair like wool instead of Christian hair . . . help the argument? Can any logical inference in favor of slavery be drawn from a flat nose, a long or short face?"[11] Thus Otis denied that any morally interesting conclusion, such as slavery, could be drawn from premises found in physical nature. He termed the slave trade a "most shocking violation of the law of nature,"[12] and, in 1765, together with Thomas Cushing, later the Massachusetts delegate to the Continental Congress, Samuel Adams, and John Hancock, he represented the city of Boston in its request "for a law to prohibit the importation and purchasing of slaves."[13]

In 1772, on the eve of the American Revolution, Lord Chief Justice William Murray Mansfield offered what Albert P. Blaustein and Robert L. Zaugrando have called "the most significant and far-reaching decision on slavery ever handed down by an English court."[14] His decision, in what was known as the *Somerset* case, was to become well known to the colonial bar.*

Born in Africa, James Somerset, a Negro, had been brought to America in 1749 and sold to a Charles Stewart. Stewart was a customs officer, and on business in England in 1769, he brought Somerset along as his personal servant. There Somerset fled for his freedom but was recaptured by Stewart, who consigned him to a third party for sale in Jamaica. But Granville Sharp, one of the first great English abolitionists, intervened on Somerset's behalf; he successfully prevailed upon Lord Mansfield to issue a writ of *habeas corpus* for Somerset. Thus the issue of Somerset's freedom was joined.

Mansfield deferred his decision for a year, during which time he repeatedly urged Stewart to moot the matter by voluntarily liberating Somerset; but Stewart refused. In the end, Mansfield had no choice but to decide the case himself. He

---

*The following discussion of *Somerset* v. *Stewart* relies primarily upon William M. Wiecek, *The Sources of Anti-Slavery Constitutionalism in America, 1760–1848* (Ithaca, N. Y.: Cornell University Press, 1977), pp. 20–39.

narrowed the issues to two. The first was whether contract for sale of a slave was good in England; he concluded it was. The second, more difficult issue, was whether any "coercion can be exercised in this country on a slave, according to the *American* laws?" Mansfield spoke to issues of "conflict of laws" and the opposition of "positive" and "natural" law; it was in the latter discussion that *Somerset* gained its lasting significance. "The state of slavery," said Mansfield, "is of such a nature, that it is incapable of being introduced on any reasons, moral or political, but only [by] positive law, which preserves its force long after the reasons, occasion, and time itself, from whence it was created, is erased from memory: it's so odious, that nothing can be suffered to support it but positive law."[15] And what of positive law? Mansfield concluded it was impossible to establish, as a certitude, the existence of any pertinent positive law. And so he released Somerset, and by the decision the remaining slaves in Britain obtained their freedom.

In England and America the decision was interpreted as capaciously as possible by abolitionists. There was talk of how the air of England was too free for a slave to breathe, and of how now every man would be "entitled to the full protection of the laws."[16] And the decision influenced the courts. The effect of the *Somerset* decision, as one modern commentator, Robert Cover, has said, was to give "institutional recognition to anti-slavery morality." To the pleasure of abolitionists, a "natural law" against slavery could now be argued to be part of common law.[17]

The issue of natural law having been raised, it is not surprising, perhaps, that the formal debate accompanying commencement exercises at Harvard in 1773 addressed whether

30

or not slavery was agreeable to the law of nature. The opponent to slavery argued:

... For what less can be said of that exercise of power, whereby such multitudes of our fellow-men, descendants, my friend, from the same common parent with you and me, and between whom and us nature has made no distinction, save what arises from the stronger influence of the sun in the climate whence they originated, are held to groan under the insupportable burden of the most abject slavery, without one chearing beam to refresh their desponding souls; and upon whose dreary path not even the feeblest ray of hope is permitted to dawn, and whose only prospect of deliverance is—in death. If indeed the law protects their lives, (which is all that can be said even here, and more—shame to mankind!—more than can be said in some of our sister colonies) the only favor these unhappy people receive, from such protection, is a continuation of their misery, the preservation of a life every moment of which is worse than non-existence.[18]

Antislavery sentiment was increasing not only in New England but farther south. In Philadelphia, Anthony Benezet, a Quaker, tirelessly argued against slavery; in 1762 he wrote a book against the slave trade.[19] Eleven years later Benjamin Rush, who was to distinguish himself at the Constitutional Convention, said that several years ago Benezet "stood alone ... in opposing Negro slavery in Philadelphia; and now three fourths of the province, as well as of the city, cry out against it."[20] Rush himself published a tract "designed to show the iniquity of the slave trade"; he was a sponsor of "The Society for the Relief of Free Negroes Unlawfully Held in Bondage"; and, perhaps most important, he led by example. Rush refused 100 guineas a year to practice medicine in South Carolina, "where wealth has been accumulated," he said, "only by the sweat and blood of Negro slaves." Rush, who was white, served many blacks throughout his years of medical practice and never charged a fee to those of slender means.[21]

On the eve of the Revolution, those who opposed slavery stepped up their campaign. The Reverend Samuel Hopkins of Rhode Island, for example, went from house to house urging masters to liberate their slaves. Hopkins relentlessly pursued his goal. When a slave-owning friend told Hopkins that his slaves were happy with their lot, Hopkins asked to see one of the slaves. He inquired of him whether, indeed, he was happy. The slave replied that he was and that he had a good master. Hopkins then asked the slave whether he would be more happy if he were free. The man quickly replied: "Oh, yes, Massa—me would be much more happy." The slaveowner freed the man on the spot.[22]

So it was, then, that Jefferson drafted a document that would be read by Americans aware of arguments, and having had experiences, that persuaded them against slavery or at least showed them that slavery might be wrong. The connection between liberty and equality was intimate. If it were true that slavery was wrong, then it followed that blacks and whites ought to be equal at least in respect to having freedom over their own lives. And if it were true that all men are created equal, then it followed that no man ought to be the slave of another. In 1778 Benezet remarked that "nothing can more clearly and positively militate against the slavery of the Negroes" than the libertarian ideals of the Declaration.[23] Jefferson, the very author of the Declaration, received a letter from Benjamin Banneker, a Negro mathematician and astronomer, that asked him to reconcile his " 'created equal' language" with his practice of "detaining by fraud and violence so numerous a part of my brethren, under groaning captivity."[24] Jefferson continued to hold slaves, but not everyone did. For, as Moses Coit Tyler, an historian of literature, said, it had become "very hard for us to listen to the preamble to the Declaration of Independence and still remain the owners and users and catchers of slaves."[25]

As for blacks themselves, they took the language of the Declaration literally. From the outset of the Revolutionary War, the individual slave's major loyalty was not to a place nor to a people, but to a principle. Insofar as he had freedom of choice, he was likely to join the side that made him the quickest and best offer in terms of those "unalienable rights" of which the Declaration had spoken. Those slaves who fought on the American side won "freedom with their flintlocks," as "manumission orders" granted freedom to slaves who served in the army. That the war did not bring liberty to all slaves, however, enraged many blacks, including the black abolitionist David Walker. "Are we men!!" he declared:

... Are we MEN? Did our creator make us to be slaves to dust and ashes like ourselves? Are they not dying worms as well as we? ... How we could be so *submissive* to a gang of men, whom we cannot tell whether they are as good as ourselves or not, I never could conceive. . . . America is more our country than it is the whites—we have enriched it with our blood and tears. The greatest riches in all America have arisen from our *blood* and tears—and will they drive us from our property and homes, which we have earned with our *blood?*[26]

In an appeal to the state a group of Massachusetts Negroes stated that "every principle which impelled America to break with England 'pleads stronger than a thousand arguments in favor of your humble petitioners.' "[27] And in 1779 a group of Negroes requested of the state of New Hampshire that it pass a law conferring liberty upon them "that the name of slave may not more be heard in a land gloriously contending for the sweets of freedom."[28]

The abolitionists repeatedly made use of the Declaration of Independence in making their case during the war and afterward. William Lloyd Garrison, in his newspaper, *The Liberator*, stressed that because he "assent[ed] to the 'self-evident truths' maintained in the American Declaration of Independence, 'that all men are created equal and endowed by their Creator with certain inalienable rights' " he would "strenuously contend for the immediate enfranchisement of our slave population."[29] Preparatory to that, of course, was the need to abolish slavery, and the abolitionists met with their first success on March 1, 1780, when Pennsylvania became the first state to abolish it, thus extending "a portion of that freedom to others which has been extended to us."[30] Significantly, Benjamin Franklin figured in this result. Franklin himself had freed his slaves before the outbreak of war, mainly because of the influence of the Quakers, of Anthony Benezet, and of Granville Sharp in England; he remained until his death a strong opponent of slavery. In 1785 he became president of the Pennsylvania Society for Promoting the Abolition of Slavery and the Relief of Free Negroes Unlawfully Held in Bondage. And in 1790, he performed his last public act by affixing, for the society, his signature to a memorial presented to the first Congress on February 12, 1790. This memorial asked Congress "to countenance the restoration of liberty to those unhappy men, who alone, in this land of freedom are degraded into perpetual bondage"[31] Franklin was not the only prominent American involved in the abolitionist movement; there were also John Jay, Luther Martin, the Maryland delegate to the Constitutional Convention, Alexander Hamilton, historian Jeremy Belknap, geographer Jedediah Morse, and lexicographer Noah Webster.[32]

Are We Men?

The Massachusetts cases of *Walker* v. *Jennison* (1781), *Jennison* v. *Caldwell* (1781) and *Commonwealth* v. *Jennison* (1783)—the Quock Walker cases, as they were called—were not so important as the *Somerset* case to America's understanding that slavery was wrong and that, as the Declaration declared, all men are created equal; but the cases were nonetheless important, as now a judicial body, rather than a legislature as in Pennsylvania, ended slavery as a legalized institution in Massachusetts. In *Commonwealth* v. *Jennison*, in the Supreme Judicial Court of Massachusetts presided over by Chief Justice William Cushing and heard before jury, Nathaniel Jennison, a white man, was charged with committing assault and battery on Quock Walker, a black man. Jennison's defense was that, because Walker was his slave, he had the right to retrieve him when he had run away and to use such measures as were necessary to do so. Cushing, however, was unimpressed; he found Jennison guilty. And, in his charge to the jury, the only recorded item in the case that survived, Cushing took issue with the assumption planted in Jennison's defense, namely, that there was nothing wrong with owning a slave. Though the province long recognized the presence of slaves and slavery, Cushing could discover no positive law recognizing it. "Nowhere do we find it expressly established," he told the jury. More important, he continued:

whatever sentiments have formerly prevailed in this particular [slavery] or slid in upon us by the example of others, a different idea has taken place with the people of America, more favorable to the natural rights of mankind, and to that natural, innate design of Liberty, with which Heaven (without regard to color, complexion, or shape of noses—features) has inspired all the human race.[33]

Cushing then referred to the Massachusetts Constitution, framed in 1780, specifically that part which says the "people

35

of this Commonwealth . . . [had declared] that all men are born free and equal—and that every subject is entitled to liberty, and to have it guarded by the laws as well as life and property—and [which] in short is totally repugnant to the idea of being born slaves." "I think the idea of slavery" Cushing continued,

is inconsistent with our own conduct and Constitution; and there can be no such thing as perpetual servitude of a rational creature, unless his liberty is forfeited by some criminal conduct or given up by personal consent or contract.[34]

At the end of the Revolutionary War, David Walker wrote: "We need not now turn over the libraries of Europe for authorities to prove that blacks are born equally free with whites; it is declared and recorded as the sense of America."[35] Walker was referring to the preamble to the Declaration, and because it was the sense of America that "blacks are born equally free with whites," one might expect that the course of history was friendly to this meaning of equality. As it turned out, however, though the meaning of the Declaration was plain, its truth was not always conceded, was not always lived in fact. When the Founding Fathers wrote the Constitution in 1787, they denied the truth that "all men are created equal." Slavery was "more clearly and explicitly established under the Constitution" than it had been under the Articles of Confederation in 1781.*[36]

At the Constitutional Convention in Philadelphia in 1787, debate centered on how slaves should be counted for purposes of representation and taxation, on the slave trade itself, and on provisions for the return of fugitive slaves. On these issues, the Deep South Bloc of South Carolina and Georgia

*The following discussion of the Constitutional Convention relies primarily upon Wiecek, *The Sources of Anti-Slavery Constitutionalism*, pp. 62–83.

was formidable, less by its strength of numbers and influence than by its clarity, its unequivocal position, the advantage of knowing its mind when others did not.[37] For example, on the question of the slave trade, General Charles Cotesworth Pinckney, the delegate from South Carolina, said: "While there remained one acre of swampland uncleared in South Carolina, I would raise my vote against restricting the importation of negroes."[38] Those not from South Carolina and Georgia were ambivalent. Often as not, principle was recognized but was defeated, as in the case of Patrick Henry.

Years earlier, having read Benezet's attack on the slave trade, Henry had seen the contradiction between Christian principles and enlightenment values, on the one hand, and the practice of slavery, on the other. Yet this was Henry speaking: "Would any one believe that I am Master of Slaves of my own purchase! I am drawn along by ye general Inconvenience of living without them: I will not, I cannot justify it."[39] At the convention, Henry was again "drawn along." "As much as I deplore slavery," he said, "I see that prudence forbids its abolition."[40] So too was James Iredell of North Carolina, later an Associate Justice of the Supreme Court, "drawn along": "[Abolition] will be an event which must be pleasing to every generous mind, and every friend of human nature; but we often wish for things which are not attainable."[41] And so was George Mason, author of the Virginia Declaration of Rights, the most determined foe of slavery, "drawn along": "It will involve us in great difficulties and infelicity to be now deprived of slaves."[42]

The great "difficulties" were economic—the South depended greatly upon slave labor—and political. By 1787, the unity that had marked the fervor of the colonists during the revolution had largely dissipated: States refused to meet requisition payments and failed to honor laws and regulations of other states. The young country, in short, was drifting apart, and the states were now in convention because of, as George Washington called it, "a half-starved, limping government that appears to be always moving upon crutches, and tottering at every step."[43] The threat of a boycott by the southern bloc hung over the convention, and so accommodation, to many minds, was essential.

On the issue of the representation and taxation of slaves, the convention decided to allow every slave to count as three-fifths of a person; thus Article I, Section 2, Clause 3, of the Constitution of the United States read in part:

Representatives and direct Taxes shall be apportioned among the several states which may be included within this Union, according to their respective Numbers which shall be determined by adding to the whole Number of free Persons, including those bound to Service for a Term of Years, and excluding Indians not taxed, three-fifths of all other Persons.

On the issue of slave trade, the convention decided that not until 1808 could Congress even consider its prohibition; thus Article I, Section 9, Clause 1, read:

The Migration or Importation of such Persons as any of the States now existing shall think proper to admit, shall not be prohibited by the Congress prior to the year one thousand eight hundred and eight, but a Tax or duty may be imposed on such Importation, not exceeding ten dollars for each person.

And on the issue of fugitive slaves, the convention decided that such slaves will be delivered on the claim of the party owning the slaves; thus, according to Article IV, Section 2, Clause 3:

No person held to Service or Labour in one State, under the Laws thereof, escaping into another, shall, in Consequence of any Law or Regulation therein, be discharged from such Service or Labour, but shall be delivered up on Claim of the Party to whom such Service or Labour may be due.

It is worth noting the language used in each of these three sections of the Constitution. None makes mention of "slaves" or "slavery"; each refers to "person" or "persons." The reason for this was that many delegates to the Constitutional Convention were aware, as Anthony Benezet had said, that the libertarian ideas of the Declaration militated against slavery; they knew that slavery was wrong. It had indeed become hard for them to listen each year to the Preamble to the Declaration of Independence and still remain the "owners and users and catchers of slaves." Like James Otis, they could see that if all men are created equal, then nothing morally significant could be deduced from the fact of a person's skin color. They recognized, as Lord Mansfield had, that only custom or positive law could sustain slavery, that natural law could not. And they knew the answer to David Walker's question, "Are we men?" Blacks indeed were men, and all men are created equal. "Slaves" would have been recognized in the Constitution and "slavery" sanctioned had the meaning of the Declaration not expanded beyond the narrow, original purpose of asserting the rights of white Americans as Englishmen, had there not been the wealth of ideas and experiences speaking against slavery and in behalf of an equality that embraced all men.

Here, then, in the proposition that because all men are created equal, no man can be the slave of another, was the earliest form of the idea of moral equality. At least this much is what the Declaration meant, but it would take a great war before this meaning was honored as truth, with the freeing of all slaves, and it would take the genius of Abraham Lincoln to develop the idea of moral equality by more fully explicating the phrase "all men are created equal."

Chapter 3

As I Would Not Be a Slave, So I Would Not Be a Master

Lincoln and the Idea of Moral Equality

PROFESSOR HARRY V. JAFFA has remarked that the "long political duel between Stephen A. Douglas and Abraham Lincoln was above all a struggle to determine the nature of the opinion which should form the doctrinal foundation of American government."* Indeed, in Jaffa's estimate, "no political contest in history was more exclusively or passionately concerned with the character of the beliefs in which the souls of men were to abide."[1] Lincoln believed that the doctrinal foundation of American government lay in what he considered the principle of equality; he thought that the character of the belief in which the souls of men should abide was indi-

*For the discussion of Lincoln that occupies the bulk of this chapter, we depend upon and draw extensively from the historical and philosophical analysis of Lincoln's thought in Harry V. Jaffa's *Crisis of the House Divided: An Interpretation of the Issues in the Lincoln-Douglas Debates* (Seattle: University of Washington Press, 1959).

cated in the famous words of the Declaration of Independence—"that all men are created equal."

Given this, one might suppose that much of the literature on *Bakke*, supremely a case concerning the nature of equality in American society, would have at least mentioned the Lincoln–Douglas debates, if not engaged them in searching dialogue. But not only was this not the case, few writers on *Bakke* seemed aware of the heritage of ideas that come from Lincoln and specifically the debates. Yet it is in those debates that Lincoln recovered and developed the idea of moral equality that was present in the first years of the republic but that had become increasingly obscured as the nation had struggled through the first half of the nineteenth century, half slave and half free.

In his development of the idea of moral equality, Lincoln interpreted it anew, arguing not only that equality and slavery were incompatible but also that the very idea that all men are created equal defined the nature of republican government. If this were all Lincoln contributed to the development of the idea of moral equality, studying him would certainly be justified. But in fact Lincoln did more, and so he becomes all the more pertinent. For example, he expanded on the implications that flow from the proposition that all men are created equal. Not only should slavery not exist, but also free men—which is to say, all men, black and white—should treat each other on the same basis. Too, Lincoln demonstrated that the argument in behalf of the idea of moral equality depends both on the facts of inequality and on principle. This is a point that very few seemed to realize in the modern debate over the issues of equality raised in *Bakke*.

To see all that Lincoln contributed to the idea of moral equality, it is first necessary to be acquainted with the period

commencing in 1787 with the passage of the Northwest Ordinance and concluding in 1857 with the *Dred Scott* decision.
The Northwest Ordinance prohibited slavery in the Northwest Territory, thus establishing the precedent that Congress
had the authority to keep slavery out of the territories. The
pertinent part of the ordinance read: "There shall be neither
slavery nor involuntary servitude in the said territory, otherwise than in the punishment of crimes whereof the party
shall have been duly convicted."[2]

In 1820 Missouri gained admission to the Union as a slave
state; it did so as a part of a compromise in which slavery in
the territory ceded by France, which lay north of 36 degrees
and 30 minutes, was prohibited—prohibited, in fact, "forever." The Missouri Compromise thus was consistent with
the Northwest Ordinance, for here again Congress had used
its authority to outlaw slavery in a territory. Many thought
the compromise had, moreover, settled the entire issue of
slavery expansion, but this judgment would prove incorrect.
John Quincy Adams was, as it turned out, clearly prescient.
"I take it for granted," he said, "that the present question is
a mere preamble—a title page, to a great, tragic volume."[3]

So it was that in the debates regarding the annexation of
Texas more than two decades later, indirectly at stake was
the extension of slavery over the North American lands then
owned by Mexico. The issue became directly focused in the
famous Wilmot Proviso. When in 1846 President James Polk
asked Congress for $2 million to "buy" California and the
other Mexican provinces, David Wilmot, a Pennsylvania
Democrat, attached an amendment to the request. The "Wilmot Proviso" stipulated that "as an express and fundamental
condition to the acquisition of any territory from the Republic of Mexico by the United States, by virtue of any treaty

which may be negotiated between them, and to the use of moneys wherein appropriated, *neither slavery nor involuntary servitude* shall ever exist in any part of said territory."[4] (Emphasis added.) The emphasized words were taken purposely from the Northwest Ordinance of 1787, and thus the amendment was consistent with the spirit of outlawing slavery evident in both 1787 and 1820. But the Wilmot Proviso never passed Congress, and when the Treaty of Guadalupe Hidalgo, which ended the Mexican War, was signed in 1848, the United States secured the Mexican provinces without any restrictions on slavery.

The Wilmot Proviso contended for the idea that freedom should be national and that slavery, if it should exist at all, sectional. The defeat of the proviso in Congress did not spell the death of this idea, which the South viewed as threatening its existence and the balance of power in the Union. The South believed, in fact, that Congress had no power to prohibit slavery in the territories and, moreover, that Congress should protect slavery, as it was an institution of property. In John Calhoun's view, Congress had acted unconstitutionally in 1820 by prohibiting the expansion of slavery north of Missouri.

In 1849, California applied for statehood. The prospect of California as a free state rankled the South, which toughened its opposition to the idea that freedom should be national and slavery, if at all, sectional. "I trust," said Calhoun, "we shall persist in our resistance [to the admission of California] until the restoration of all our rights, or disunion, one or the other, is the consequence."[5] Calhoun was prophetic, but disunion was delayed by more than a decade, as Henry Clay effected a timely series of resolutions that were called, collectively, the Compromise of 1850. By one of the resolutions, California was admitted as a free state. By another, it was established that the states to be formed from the territorial governments of Utah and New Mexico might enter the Union with or without slavery, as their constitutions should prescribe.

It was this resolution that Stephen A. Douglas, Illinois Democrat and chairman of the Senate Committee on Territories, comprehended as establishing "the principle of nonintervention by Congress with slavery in the States and Territories."[6] Douglas placed this principle at the center of a bill he introduced regarding the territories of Kansas and Nebraska. The legislation called that part of the Missouri Compromise forbidding slavery forever in the territories "inconsistent" with the principle and for that reason "inoperative and void."[7] But if the Missouri Compromise was inconsistent with the Kansas-Nebraska Act, so, it would seem, was the Northwest Ordinance of 1787. Was this the result Douglas intended? Precisely. Douglas wished to deny that Congress had the authority to regulate territorial affairs, including slavery. And his Kansas-Nebraska Act, passed in 1854, did just that.

The act permitted the "people" of the territories of Kansas and Nebraska to decide for themselves whether or not they would enter the Union as slave or free states—this, because Douglas believed that the "principle of popular sovereignty" alone defined the nature of democratic government. All issues, including that of slavery, were to be decided by the people, according to Douglas; only numbers—as defined by majorities—could be decisive. Thus, as the act itself said: "It [is] the true intent and meaning of this act not to legislate slavery into any Territory or State, nor to exclude it therefrom, but to leave the people thereof perfectly free to form and regulate their domestic institutions in their own way, subject only to the Constitution of the United States."[8] Despite the bill's reference to a "people," neither Kansas nor Nebraska was lawfully open to settlement until 1854; thus neither territory had a "people." The Kansas-Nebraska Act was actually a recipe for civil war on the plains,[9] but this prospect apparently meant nothing to Douglas; what mattered to him was that the principle of popular sovereignty be honored.

But this principle was to suffer at the hands of the Supreme Court in the *Dred Scott* decision in 1857.[10] The Court did say, as the Kansas-Nebraska Act had stipulated, that the Missouri Compromise was unconstitutional. But it also said (echoing Calhoun) that Congress did *not* have the power to exclude slavery from any part of the unorganized western territories. Thus, even if a people should vote down slavery, it would still exist, because it was now the duty of the federal government to protect the property of citizens, here the property being slaves. The *Dred Scott* decision ratified Calhoun's belief that slavery was national, while freedom was only sectional. *Dred Scott* also declared that no slave or his descendant is, or can be, a citizen of any state.

The seventy years between the Northwest Ordinance and the *Dred Scott* decision supply the background for understanding the remarkable battle between Lincoln and Douglas that was pitched on the plains of Illinois during the summer and fall of 1858. As the two men fought for a seat in the United States Senate, they addressed the practical question of whether federal authority could, and whether it should, be employed to keep slavery out of the new territories in the West. These practical questions were hinged to a great theoretical question: Was slavery consistent with the nature of republican government?[11] Douglas thought it was and that it could be voted in by the white citizens of the territories if they decided they wanted it, because he believed that the principle of popular sovereignty defined the nature of American government. Lincoln thought slavery was not consistent with the nature of republican government and that it could not, by right, be voted in by the white citizens of the territories, because he believed that the principle of equality defined the nature of American government. These two very different principles—Douglas's of popular sovereignty and Lincoln's of equality—had very different implications for the definition of American government.

Douglas believed the principle of popular sovereignty defined republican government because he considered it the sufficient condition of political freedom. Indeed, he considered it the main reason for the revolution. The colonists had revolted because they had been denied the right to govern themselves; they had been told by the Crown how their own institutions ought to be ordered. If the colonists had fought for self-government, Douglas reasoned, why should it be denied to the people of the territories? The principle of popular sovereignty, as Jaffa has observed, was conceptually this basic to Douglas's theory of republican government: "He once said that the principle of the Kansas-Nebraska Act originated when God made man and placed good and evil before him, allowing him to choose for himself." Not only man's humanity but his political freedom, believed Douglas, lay in his power to choose.[12]

Douglas never wavered from his principle. When in 1858 the Senate accepted the fraudulent Lecompton constitution for the state of Kansas, a proslavery document drawn up exclusively by proslavery forces, Douglas insisted that all the people of Kansas have the opportunity to reject it. Kansas indeed went on to reject that constitution, and it eventually became a free state; but these consequences—or *any* consequences, for that matter—were less important to Douglas than the *principle* involved. Douglas often said that he was no more desirous of seeing slavery continue to exist and expand than not; but he˙said he was never prepared to admit that a people could be denied the right to decide whether they wanted slavery by the imposition of a principle upon them that would render slavery illegal and thereby make "popular sovereignty" subordinate to something else.[13]

Lincoln thought Douglas's position was seriously wrong. Republican government, in Lincoln's view, entailed the extirpation of slavery because it required recognition of the generative and nurturing power of the principle of the equality of all men. Lincoln believed this principle was higher than that of popular sovereignty; indeed, he believed that the principle of equality was higher than any other: *It* defined republican government.

In asserting the principle of equality, Lincoln said he was only returning to the beliefs of the Founding Fathers while turning against the beliefs of many of his own time, in particular those of the Supreme Court. Lincoln believed that the Court's judgment in the *Dred Scott* case that "no Negro slave . . . and no descendant of such slave can ever be a citizen of any state" was based upon a misapprehension of the meaning of the Constitution and other founding documents. To say, as *Dred Scott* did, that Negroes were beings "of an inferior order" and "had no rights which the white man was bound to respect" was to deny the clear language of the Declaration. "The entire records of the world," Lincoln said at Galesburg in October 1858, ". . . may be searched in vain for one single affirmation, from one single man, that the negro was not included in the Declaration of Independence."[14]

Lincoln understood the words "all men are created equal"

as a statement unable to be denied by any empirical fact—by any evidence of degradation or ignorance. Especially could it not be denied by the fact that Negroes were not then enjoying, nor had they enjoyed before, the rights they otherwise would have possessed as free men. Obstacles to the fulfillment of a promise did not, in Lincoln's view, detract from the validity of the promise itself.[15]

In debating with Lincoln, Douglas relied upon the ruling in *Dred Scott* to the effect that slavery could be established in the territories. That ruling, articulated in the majority opinion written by Chief Justice Roger B. Taney, depended upon his appeal to the sense of the Founding Fathers; Taney understood them as expressly affirming the right of property in a slave in the Constitution. But Lincoln said that Taney was wrong in fact, for the Constitution did not expressly affirm the right of property in a slave. Indeed, the "fixed and universal opinion" from 1776 to 1857, according to Lincoln, was that the Negro was included in the phrase "all men are created equal." During one of the debates, Lincoln remarked that Taney was the first and Douglas the second ever to deny that the Declaration included the Negro among the phrase "all men."[16] Lincoln did not mean that Taney and Douglas were the first to deny the truth of the Declaration of Independence, but that they were the first to deny its *meaning*. Lincoln thus distinguished Taney and Douglas from Calhoun, who denied the truth but not the meaning of the Declaration.[17]

Taney and Douglas were by no means the first to deny the meaning of the Declaration; nor was it quite the case that the universal opinion from 1776 to 1857 was that the Negro was included in the phrase "all men are created equal." But Lincoln's points survive his exaggerations and historical inaccuracies. The Congress that met in Philadelphia in 1776 intended to assert the rights of white Americans as Englishmen; thus the phrase "all men" included white Americans and Englishmen. But, as we have seen, this narrow meaning did not enter the public domain as the popular meaning, and it is fair to say that soon after the Declaration was written until 1857 the fixed opinion was indeed that the Negro was included in the phrase. The great majority of those living during the Revolution and afterward knew, as Lincoln said, that the Negro was a man and that there was no moral argument that could, or ought to, have persuaded him to be a slave. "I tremble for my country when I reflect that God is just,"[18] Jefferson, himself a slaveholder, once said. "The Almighty has no attribute which can take side with us in such a contest."[19]

Certainly there were those who thought the Negro a "brutish kind of man" and in some ways "closer to an animal than white men"; but all the language of proximity and closeness did not amount to a view that the Negro is not a man. The language of the Constitution bears reconsideration here. On every occasion when the word "slave" could have been used and the institution of slavery thus explicitly recognized, the word "person" instead was used. Historian Allan Nevins has remarked that the Founding Fathers had hopes and expectations that slavery would end but that the expectations were much more equivocal than the hopes.[20] This is true, but it is also true that hopes and ambivalence and bad faith *were* present, and these would not have been present had the debates been about animals. Hopes would not have been present without the recognition that the Negro was a man, and everyone involved knew this.

In asserting that all men are created equal, Lincoln meant

more than equality in some mythological state of nature.[21] His notion of equality had obvious practical significance. "As I would not be a *slave,* so I would not be a *master,*" he said. "This expresses my idea of democracy. Whatever differs from this, to the extent of the difference, is not democracy."[22] Lincoln believed that because all men are equal, no man should be the master of another; clearly, for him, the price of American freedom and indeed of all civil liberties depended upon fidelity to the principle of equality. Equality for Lincoln was, therefore, not simply a starting point for society but its very goal, for nowhere could there be peace while some men were masters over others.

Lincoln recognized that the fear of slave uprisings was motivation enough to treat slaves, if not to regard them, as equals; turmoil, conflict, one crisis of the house divided would remain so long as some men would deny freedom to others, and there would be unrest, unhappiness, resentment, and violence so long as the creed of inequality flourished. But Lincoln did not believe that equality ought to be justified in terms of self-protection or prudence, or the need for domestic tranquility or any other result. He believed that equality was a claim made and justified in its own terms, to a self-governing people. The principle of equality, for Lincoln, defines a self-governing people; it is their hallmark.[23]

Here rested the important differences between Lincoln and Douglas. For Lincoln, "the sheet anchor" of republican government was that no man is good enough to govern another without the other man's consent.[24] If equality is the sheet anchor of government, then the relation of master and slave— the fact of slavery—is a total violation of self-government. The American government, according to Lincoln, is in principle incompatible with slavery, no matter what one might say about popular sovereignty. And of this, Lincoln himself once said:

> I cannot but hate it. I hate it because of the monstrous injustice of slavery itself. . . . It forces so many really good men amongst ourselves into an open war with the very fundamental principles of civil liberty—criticizing the Declaration of Independence, and insisting there is no right principle of action but *self-interest.*[25]

Lincoln thought these "really good men" had fallen away from an earlier wisdom. The denial that Congress had any power to regulate slavery in the territories was only a recent phenomenon; that so many good men could deny Congress's power was evidence of a regression in the understanding of the pernicious character of slavery. Certainly the Continental Congress understood that character, or else it would not have asserted its authority over slavery in 1787. The crisis of the house divided had come about as the Wilmot Proviso was debated, the Compromise of 1850 effected, the Kansas–Nebraska Act passed, and the *Dred Scott* case decided. Increasingly had large numbers of Americans turned their backs on the ancient truth upon which, in Lincoln's view, their rights depended.[26] The principle of equality—the "sheet anchor" of republican government—was not being ripped away for the sake of what was proffered as the fundamental good—the principle of popular sovereignty—but for what was in fact only a subordinate good.

Lincoln did not involve himself in any controversies regarding the intellectual capacities of blacks.[27] He recognized that to say one race was more talented in one area than another was, eventually, to prove too much; for surely the whites living in America were inferior, in certain respects, to other peoples elsewhere. To enter this thicket of controversy, then, was pointless and, furthermore, beside the point. According to Lincoln, Negroes were equal to whites in the fundamental moral sense that no man is good enough to govern another. And, too, they were equal in respect to the certain unalienable rights of the Declaration. "I hold," said Lincoln on August 21, 1858, at Ottawa, Illinois, "that . . . there is no reason in the world why the Negro is not entitled to all the natural rights enumerated in the Declaration of Independence. . . . I hold that he is as much entitled to these as the white man."[28]

The point for Lincoln was that the claims of black men, whatever they were, ought to be determined on the same principles as those of white men. He drew this conclusion from the propositions that all men have an equal claim to just treatment and that the Negro is a man.[29] Thus, the test of right for Lincoln was not how something agrees with the majority's passions or with its view of its self-interest or with what is at some times consented to by the majority, but how it agrees with what is due to a man, because he is a man.

Significantly, equality did not extend, for Lincoln, to just blacks and white Americans of primarily Anglo-Saxon heritage; he was aware that the vast numbers of immigrants into American life on terms of general equality could occur only in and through what Jaffa has called "the religious cultivation of the universal creed of the Declaration."[30] Thus, on July 10, 1858, Lincoln said in a speech in Chicago:

We hold this annual celebration to remind ourselves of all the good done in this process of time of how it was done and who did it, and how we are historically connected with it; and we go from these meetings in better humor with ourselves—we feel more attached the one to the other, and more firmly bound to the country we inhabit. In every way we are better men in the age, and race, and country in which we live for these celebrations. But . . . there is something else connected with it. We have besides these men—descended by blood from our ancestors—among us perhaps half our people who are not descendants at all of these men, they are men who have come from Europe—German, Irish, French and Scandinavian—men that have come from Europe themselves, or whose ancestors have come hither and have settled here, finding themselves our equals in all things. If they look back through this history to trace their connection with those days by blood, they find they have none, they cannot carry themselves back into that glorious epoch and make themselves feel that they are part of us, but when they look through that old Declaration of Independence they find that those old men say that "We hold these truths to be self-evident, that all men are created equal," and then they feel that that moral sentiment taught in that day evidences their relation to those men, that it is the father of all moral principle in them, and that they have a right to claim it as though they were blood of the blood, and flesh of the flesh of the men who wrote that Declaration, and so they are. That is the electric cord in that Declaration that links the hearts of patriotic and liberty-loving men together, that will link those patriotic hearts as long as the love of freedom exists in the minds of men throughout the world.[31]

While class and caste oppressions have existed in fact in America, they have never since been defended or defensible, as a matter of right, because of Lincoln's success in opposing Douglas as a leader of "American political opinion."[32] Lincoln saw importance in "political opinion." He knew that a government failing to embody that opinion was not legitimate, because it did not have the "consent of the governed" demanded by the Declaration of Independence. He knew that the opinion of the governed could deny that all men are created equal; and he knew that in recent years American opinion had been moving in that direction—hence the crisis of the house divided. Lincoln saw it as his task to persuade public opinion to the notion that the Declaration embodied. So it was that he said: "Our government rests in public opinion. Whoever can change public opinion, can change the government, practically just so much." Lincoln sought to change public opinion by saying what public opinion *ought* to be. "[It] always," he said, "has a 'central idea' from which all its minor thoughts radiate. And the 'central idea' in our political public opinion, at the beginning was, and until recently has continued to be, 'the equality of all men.' " [33]

For Lincoln, free government was not a process or a procedure, as Douglas thought. Rather it was substantive, in this way: Free government is government of, by, and for, not just any people, but *a people dedicated to the proposition that all men are created equal.* [34]

Lincoln thus challenged the proposition Douglas offered in defense of the principle of popular sovereignty—that the central idea of the republic is either that all states are equal or that all (declared and therefore mainly white) citizens are equal, because of which idea one group of citizens cannot rightfully impose its view on any one, or all, of the others. To this Lincoln directly spoke: The central idea of the Republic is not "that 'all States as States, are equal' nor yet that 'all citizens as citizens are equal,' but . . . the broader, better declaration, including both these and much more, that "all *men* are created equal.' " [35] Constitutional equality could not be maintained, according to Lincoln, by denying human equality. Douglas's principle of popular sovereignty did not deny human equality, but it allowed the possibility that human equality may be denied. Because it admitted that possibility, the principle could not define the true nature of self-government. Self-government could have no meaning, for Lincoln, unless human equality were maintained—unless, in the specific case, the Negro was recognized for what he is and for what he had always, until recently, been recognized to be: a man. Lincoln asked:

If the Negro *is* a man, is it not to that extent a total destruction of self-government, to say that he too shall not govern *himself?* When the white man governs himself that is self-government; but when he governs himself and also governs *another* man, that is more than self-government—that is despotism. If the Negro is a *man,* why then my ancient faith teaches me that "all men are created equal" and that there can be no moral right in connection with one man's making a slave of another.[36]

Lincoln's importance to the development of the idea of moral equality cannot be underestimated.* His main insight was that the principle of equality was logically necessary to the idea of self-government. Self-government, by definition, requires the assumption that all men possess free will, that all men are morally autonomous, capable of choosing right and wrong. In this sense, all men are created equal, and thus

---

*Lincoln's consistency, whether he really believed in his claims of equality for the Negro, has often been questioned. Critics, sympathetic and unsympathetic alike, point to statements of Lincoln to the effect that he was not in favor of "perfect social and political equality" with the Negro, and that the Negro, in his view, was not likely ever to be the equal of the white man—the critics point, in short, to statements indicating Lincoln might have limited himself to an "abstract" repudiation of slavery while believing no more in the equality of blacks than did others of his time. (See Richard Hofstadter's essay on Lincoln in the *American Political Tradition* [New York: Knopf, 1948], pp. 93–136.) The best answer to this objection is Professor Jaffa's brilliant chapter 17 in the book from which we are drawing. The essential points of rebuttal are these: First, the weight of the evidence in plain view to all emphatically argues that Lincoln's sentiments and convictions were directed firmly against slavery and toward equality for the Negro. Weighing pro and con, taking the man in the totality of his acts and the words in the totality of his speeches, one must conclude that Lincoln was clearly a believer in Negro equality. Second, while everything that Lincoln did and said might not appear to be progressive from the point of view of the 1970s, indeed it was in his own time. It would have been foolish, indeed suicidal, for Lincoln to exhort his fellow citizens to approve of interracial marriage or the appointment of Negroes to juries. Nevertheless, Lincoln took steps far ahead of those taken by most in his time, steps that would lead ultimately to the end of slavery and the recognition of moral equality in American political life. Third, it must be noted that whatever Lincoln's view might have been in his heart of hearts, a view that cannot be known by any one, his arguments, as we have been presented them, stand by themselves. These arguments are grounded in the Declaration of Independence and in the very rationale of self-government of a free and moral people.

for one man to deal with another, because of his race, in ways that deny or diminish his intrinsic worth as a moral agent is to deny the very basis upon which self-government is possible. Hadley Arkes, a professor of political science at Amherst College and one of the few writers in the debate on *Bakke* who read and understood Lincoln, put it well:

As Lincoln sought to teach us, there are certain substantive things such as slavery, that a democratic people may not choose, because those substantive ends would be inconsistent with the fundamental premises that give majorities their right to decide.[37]

Slavery, of course, is the most humiliating denial of a man's dignity and self-esteem, and it was the one great evil that Lincoln sought to extirpate; "When [Douglas] invites any people willing to have slavery, to establish it," said Lincoln, "he is blowing out the moral lights around us."[38] But there are other, if less abject, ways that a man's autonomy may be denied and the "moral lights" blown out—other "substantive ends" that a democratic people may not choose, as Hadley Arkes would say—and these would be apparent in the institution of Jim Crow that would develop in the twilight of Reconstruction. If you begin by taking the Declaration seriously, as Lincoln did, as the fundamental meaning of the American experience, then you will come to see, as the nation's courts and legislatures did, that you cannot deny any man equal treatment before the law because of his race, that you cannot tolerate discrimination toward any man because of his race, that you have to recognize that every man has an equal right to be treated fairly, that just treatment is a matter of intrinsic worth, that "a man's rewards from society ought to be proportionate to the value of his work and not to any subjective liking or disliking" resulting from considerations of his race or ancestry.[39]

It is useful to pause at this point in the study of the idea of moral equality to consider more fully the character of the argument Lincoln employed on behalf of the principle of equality. We have remarked that Lincoln saw the principle of equality as logically necessary to the idea of self-government: One cannot have self-government without a commitment to equality. The idea that "all men are created equal" could not, for Lincoln, be denied by any evidence of degradation or ignorance on the part of black men and women; nor by the fact that at the time most Negroes were slaves. Nor could it be denied by any greater good that might accrue to the country or even to Negroes as a race. If it could have been shown that Negroes were happier or psychologically better adjusted because of slavery, Lincoln would have argued that to enslave a man, whatever his consequent psychological condition, is nonetheless to deny his moral autonomy and thus the foundations of republican government. And, of course, the opinions of the majority could not affect the validity of the words of the Declaration. Wrote Arkes: "The truth of the Declaration ... did not depend for its validity on the approval or disapproval of majorities. That is why Lincoln had to reject Stephen Douglas's policy of solving the problem of slavery through the device of 'popular sovereignty.' "[40]

Fundamentally, because the character of the statement that all men are created equal is moral, one is justified in calling the idea of equality that originated in the Declaration and was developed by Lincoln the idea of *moral* equality. Lincoln was perhaps never more correct than when he called the Declaration the "father of all moral principle." Although Lincoln did not survive the Civil War, his idea of moral equality did. It was reflected in a series of measures that, together with the Declaration, would provide a stronger moral claim on this idea for succeeding generations of Americans.

Chapter 4

Here Is the Difficulty: The Negro Is a Man!

Abolition and Citizenship

ON JANUARY 1, 1863, President Lincoln ordered that "ALL PERSONS HELD AS SLAVES within said designated States and parts of States ARE, AND HENCEFORWARD SHALL BE FREE!" But Lincoln was not certain that the Emancipation Proclamation was constitutionally justifiable, so Congress, in late 1864, gave slavery a "constitutional burial" by abolishing it with the Thirteenth Amendment. The pertinent part of the amendment provided, simply, that "neither slavery nor involuntary servitude, except as punishment for crime whereof the party shall have been duly convicted, shall exist within the United States, or any place subject to their jurisdiction." This was grand, historical language, intentionally borrowed from the Northwest Ordinance of 1787 and in the spirit of the failed Wilmot Proviso of 1846. The Thirteenth Amendment significantly affirmed the libertarian tradition dating from 1787 and denied the more recent doctrine of Stephen A. Douglas and Chief Justice Taney, that a state or territory could, if it wished, vote in slavery. In accomplishing the latter, the Thirteenth Amendment introduced a profound and revolutionary change in the relation of the United States to the individual states: For the first time the federal government would have not a passive but an active interest in the civil status of the individuals residing within each state.*

It can be said that Lincoln set an agenda, in terms of ideas, in his debates with Douglas. The Thirteenth Amendment, consistent with Lincoln's idea of moral equality, certainly placed in the Constitution the most pressing consequence—the abolition of slavery—that should flow from the proposition that all men are created equal. Other consequences—corollaries of the idea of moral equality—can be said to follow from this proposition, though it would take more than a century before they would be realized. These include the following: that, regardless of their skin color, all men should be treated alike in courts of law; should be permitted the exercise of the suffrage; should have access to any store or restaurant or hotel or any other public place; that regardless of race, all men should be permitted to marry whomsoever they might wish; should be able to send their children to the school of their choice; and finally, that no opportunity, no path in life, shall be denied any man because of his race. Stephen Johnson Field, appointed to the Supreme Court in

*Charles Fairman, *Reconstruction and Reunion 1864–1888*, vol. 6, part 1 of *History of the Supreme Court of the United States* (New York: Macmillan, 1971), p. 1156. Writes Fairman: "Never before had there been authority for federal intrusion between the State and its inhabitants in respect of the civil status of the latter; henceforth there would be warrant for entering to make sure that in fact 'neither slavery nor involuntary servitude' existed. It was not merely authority to disallow State action found to contravene the prohibition; it was a power to actually interfere in order to bar the proscribed relationship between persons. To State-rights dogmatists, this shattered the premise which they regarded as fundamental to the Union." In making every individual equal in respect at least to freedom, the Thirteenth Amendment may be regarded as federalizing at least in part the idea of moral equality.

COUNTING BY RACE

1863, did not tie down these propositions so neatly, but he was saying the same thing when he remarked that "the theory upon which our political institutions rests is, that all men have certain undeniable rights—that among these are life, liberty, and the pursuit of happiness; and that in the pursuit of happiness all avocations, all honors, all positions are alike open to everyone, and that in the protection of these rights all are equal before the law."[1]

The decade following the Civil War did not witness the honoring in constitutional amendment and federal statute of the "theory upon which our political institutions rest"; it did not see the full reification of the idea of moral equality. During this time two constitutional amendments were proposed by Congress and ratified by the states; two major pieces of civil rights legislation were passed by Congress; and several minor civil rights bills and enforcement measures were also enacted. And yet all this activity left untouched a number of areas, including public education, where blacks, if they went to school at all, went to schools reserved specifically for them; and marriage, where blacks and whites were forbidden by law in most states to intermarry. Nevertheless, despite this, and despite the palpable sentiment against equality that C. Vann Woodward and other historians have uncovered in the area where most it was needed—the North—if an age of true equality were to dawn, the constitutional amendments and major civil rights legislation of the period in question are significant.[2] The Fourteenth and Fifteenth amendments and the Civil Rights Act of 1875—the most important measures of this period—reflected the idea of moral equality. Though they would be diminished in force by the Supreme Court in the final years of the century, they would become the chapter and verse cited by many in the twentieth century who prodded the nation to comprehend the full meaning of the Declaration of Independence and of Lincoln's Emancipation Proclamation.

During debate on the Thirteenth Amendment, Representative Robert Mallory of Kentucky recognized the task ahead, vis-à-vis the freedmen, when he asked whether the abolition of slavery by a constitutional amendment would settle all the "great questions springing up in relation to that institution"?[3] One of the questions that had sprung up only recently—in *Dred Scott*—was whether or not Negroes could be citizens of the United States.

Because *Dred Scott* had denied that Negroes were or even could be citizens, Congress felt the need to reverse the decision, to affirm that they were indeed citizens. So Section 1 of the Civil Rights Act of 1866, its most important part, began by declaring "that all persons born in the United States . . . are hereby declared to be citizens of the United States."* The late Alexander Bickel, Sterling Professor of Law at Yale University and one of the nation's most respected constitutional theorists, commented that, the original Constitution being "innocent" of the concept of citizenship, "this was the first authoritative definition of citizenship in American law." It was moreover, as Bickel also pointed out, the first time a

*Just how important was seen by Senator Lot M. Morrill of Maine. Said Morrill, during debate in the Senate on the legislation: "If there is anything with which the American people are troubled, and if there is anything with which the American statesman is perplexed and vexed, it is what to do with the negro, how to define him, what he is in American law, and to what rights he is entitled. What shall we do with the everlasting, inevitable negro? is the question which puzzles all brains and vexes all statesmanship. Now, as a definition, this amendment [to Section I, to establish the citizenship of the native of African descent] settles it. Hitherto we have said that he was a nondescript in our statutes; he had no *status*; he was ubiquitous; he was both man and thing; he was three fifths of a person for representation and he was a thing for commerce and for use. In the highest sense, then, . . . this bill is important as a definition . . . " (Fairman, *Reconstruction and Reunion*, p. 1181).

set of rights were bound up in the idea of citizenship.[4] Those rights were specified in the balance of the first section.

Citizens, of every race and color, without regard to any previous condition of slavery or involuntary servitude . . . shall have the same right, in every State and Territory in the United States, to make and enforce contracts, to sue, be parties, and give evidence, to inherit, purchase, lease, sell, hold, and convey real and personal property, and to full and equal benefit of all laws and proceedings for the security of person and property, as is enjoyed by white citizens, and shall be subject to like punishment, pains, and penalties, and to none other, any law, statute, ordinance, regulation, or custom, to the contrary notwithstanding.[5]

By "all persons," Senator Lyman Trumbull of Illinois, the author of this legislation, meant "white men as well as black men." And the point of the bill, he said, was that "all persons . . . shall be entitled to the same civil rights."[6] What were these civil rights? The evidence is overwhelming that by "civil rights" Congress meant only such "fundamental rights" as were enumerated in the bill itself, and not social and political rights. Thus James F. Wilson, who managed the bill in the House of Representatives, said: "I understand civil rights to be simply the absolute rights of individuals, such as—'the right of personal security, the right of personal liberty, and the right to acquire and enjoy property.' " The Negro, said Wilson, should not "be subjected to obligations, duties, and pains" from which other citizens are exempted. All this, he said, "is the spirit and scope of the bill, and not one step beyond."[7] Where might the bill have gone? Into the courthouses or the schools. But Wilson specifically stated that the bill did not secure Negroes the right to sit on juries or the right to attend an unsegregated school. Too, the bill might have gone into the voting booth or even into that most intimate relationship, marriage. But the sense of Congress was

Trumbull's, who said that the bill "does not propose to regulate political rights of individuals; it has nothing to do with the right of suffrage, or any other political right."[8] And as for miscegenation, the bill was understood by all not to reach it.

The Civil Rights Act of 1866, then, was limited in the steps it took to secure equality for blacks. But even a few steps can be important ones, and the important steps were these: The legislation did declare that Negroes were citizens of the United States and of the respective states in which they resided; and the legislation did declare that Negroes were to have the same "fundamental" rights as whites.

When doubts arose as to the constitutionality of the legislation, Congress decided to embody in the first section of the Fourteenth Amendment the Civil Rights Act. The language was:

All persons born or naturalized in the United States . . . are citizens of the United States and of the State wherein they reside. No State shall make or enforce any law which shall abridge the privileges or immunities of citizens of the United States; nor shall any State deprive any person of life, liberty, or property, without due process of law; nor deny to any person within its jurisdiction the equal protection of the laws.[9]

Constitutionalizing the Civil Rights Act was not the chief business of the Thirty-ninth Congress as it drew up the Fourteenth Amendment. Other things concerned it, including apportionment, disqualification of former confederates, and war debts; and the main problem was to find a new basis of apportioning seats to Congress. Charles Fairman, professor of law emeritus, Harvard Law School, has pointed out that on this last issue Congress did a poor job—so poor that only three years later members of Congress were to comment on the "incongruities, looseness, and haste" that characterized the section dealing with apportionment.[10] Therefore it is not surprising to find that Congress did a poor job in the drafting of Section 1, which it regarded as not nearly so important.

The framers of Section 1 thought that Congress, not the courts, would have the power of enforcement; they rejected language by Representative Thaddeus Stevens of Pennsylvania that would have required questions regarding Section 1 to be carried to the Supreme Court. Scant attention in either chamber was paid to the three phrases "privileges and immunities," "due process of law," and "equal protection of the laws." Both chambers took the language to mean what, and only what, the Civil Rights Act meant. It is true, as Fairman has said, that this identification does not necessarily mean that the framers thought Section 1 of the Fourteenth Amendment had no larger significance. But, as he has also noted, "when speaker after speaker says that and nothing more, one surmises that nothing more specific was present in their thoughts."[11]

One who did think it meant more was Senator Daniel Clark of New Hampshire. Clark wanted Negroes to have the right of suffrage, and he denied that to give them the right to vote was a gift or a boon. "The black man has just as much right to his vote as the white man has to his; and the white man has no more authority to confer or withhold it than the black man."[12] Clark based his view on his understanding that the black man's rights had been equal from the beginning— from the Declaration of Independence in 1776. It was therefore not a question of the black man being "given" something; the right to vote was simply his by virtue of his equal standing in the polity. Clark believed that without the vote the Negro could not have access to his other rights:

Man derives the right from his manhood and the quality of his manhood with his fellow-man. . . . Does anyone say . . . that this is negro equality? So it is—political equality—no social. This last is not the creature of legislation, or political organisation, but of taste, propriety and fitness. In some of the States the negro has now, and has for a long time had, the same political rights as the white man. The law makes no distinction for or against him, but he is left to acquire that position in society to which his abilities and behavior entitle him.[13]

Thus for Clark political equality would enable the Negro to make his way in American society, as his abilities enabled him. And the Negro should have political equality, he said, because it derived from the fact that in man's common humanity each man is equal:

Here is the difficulty. The negro is a man! and however degraded, inferior, abject, or humble, it is our duty to elevate and improve him, and to give him the means of elevation or improvement; and the Senator from Kentucky may assert and prove that there are 36, or 56, or a 106 points of difference between him and the white man, but until he shows that he is not a man, the negro will be entitled to be treated by us as a man, and to demand and enjoy the same political privileges as other men.[14]

The Fourteenth Amendment was presented to the country as embodying the Civil Rights Act of 1866. Those opposing the amendment talked only in generalities; it is presumed that if they had any specific objections, they would have raised them. So the meaning of the amendment was considered self-evident by Congress; and as Congress perceived it, so did the politicians in the nation's statehouses. Yet in retrospect we know, as Fairman has said, that the meaning of the amendment had not been clearly understood even by its framers. "A form of words," says Fairman, "had been made supreme law."[15] It would be the judiciary, not Congress, that would take the major role in enforcing Section 1; and it was this section, not the rest of the amendment, that would become its most important part. Congress had no notion it was drafting an amendment that would become the point of reference for future generations in their efforts to achieve equality.

Still, the Fourteenth Amendment was important in itself, constitutionalizing as it did the Civil Rights Act of 1866, which had overturned *Dred Scott* and had at least granted Negroes equality with whites in respect to "fundamental" rights—such as that to hold property, to sue, and so on.

The Fourteenth Amendment had not touched suffrage, but the Fifteenth Amendment would: that, and only that. "The right of the citizens of the United States," read the amendment, "to vote shall not be denied or abridged by the United States or by any State on account of race, color or previous condition of servitude."[16] The language was simple on its face and certainly consistent with the idea of moral equality. And with the ratification of the Fifteenth Amendment the nation implicitly committed itself—for the first time—to a great ideal: that discrimination because of race has no place at the ballot box. It does not diminish this ideal to note a problem with the amendment as drawn up by Congress and to note the lackluster attitude in the North toward equality in the suffrage. The problem with the amendment, as Oliver Morton of Indiana noted in the Senate during debate, was that it would be obeyed literally. States would find ways around it. "Colored men shall not be disfranchised for the three reasons of race, color, or previous condition of slavery," said an agitated Morton. "They may be disfranchised for want of education or for want of intelligence. . . . [States] may, perhaps, require property or educational tests, and that would cut off the great majority of colored men from voting in those States, and thus this amendment would be practical-

ly defeated in all those States where the great body of the colored people live."[17] As for the spirit toward equality in the
suffrage at the time the amendment was ratified, only seven
northern states had, by 1869, voluntarily acted to permit the
Negro to vote. No state with a large Negro population outside the South had done so. Moreover, except for Minnesota
and Iowa, where only few Negroes lived, every postwar ref-
erendum on Negro suffrage had been rejected.[18] Indeed, only
four votes could be found in the Senate for a bill that would
guarantee equal suffrage to all states, North and South.[19] In
short, commitment toward equality for the Negro at the polls
was lacking where it most was needed—in the North—if an
effective amendment was to be drafted. The radicals in Congress, who wanted positive and firm guarantees, federal protection, and national control of suffrage, lost out to the mo-
derates and conservatives, who wanted a limited, negative
amendment that would not confer suffrage on the freedmen,
much less guarantee it.[20]

Of the major pieces of postwar legislation, the Civil Rights
Act of 1875 stands as perhaps the finest reification of the idea
of moral equality, despite the rather curious origins of the
bill. First drafted by Senator Charles Sumner of Massachusetts in 1870 as a bill "supplementary" to the Civil Rights
Act of 1866, it was designed, admirably enough, to expand
federal protection to equal rights in railroads, steamboats,
and so on, and to provide equal rights in education. Such a
bill would encounter opposition in Congress, and it did,
meeting with repeated difficulties. After Sumner fell ill and
died in 1874, however, his bill suddenly came to life—though
not because his colleagues deemed it deserving on its own
merits. Sentimentality prevailed. Champions of equal rights
rarely heard from, historian Bertram Wyatt-Brown has ob-

served, "sprang up to defend the bill's constitutionality and its reasonableness."[21] Meanwhile, the Republican Party, which had led the fight for equality but was now sunk in scandal, tried to right itself in support of the bill.[22] But in the Senate such Republicans as Henry Pease of Mississippi fell asleep, Hannibal Hamlin of Maine squirted tobacco juice on the Senate carpet, and James Winright Flanagan of Texas snored—all while debate on the bill was being heard. The Senate passed the measure before the 1874 elections, but *Harper's Weekly*, a Republican paper, could only manage to note that the bill would not hurt the Republicans' chances at the polls. When the Republicans lost heavily, President Ulysses S. Grant pointed bitterly to the Senate's action. When the House passed the bill, the Republican Grant threatened to veto it. However, he signed it into law on March 1, 1875, and the nation thus committed itself to an impressive proposition, one point for point consistent with the idea of moral equality. The preamble to the Civil Rights Act of 1875 said that Negro equality was "the appropriate object of legislation." The act read, in its pertinent parts:

That all persons . . . shall be entitled to the full and equal enjoyment of the accommodations, advantages, facilities, and privileges of inns, public conveyances on land or water, theaters, and other places of public amusement; subject only to the conditions and limitations established by law, and applicable alike to citizens of every race and color, regardless of any previous condition of servitude.[23]

The undoubted purpose of the legislation was to protect Negroes from racial discrimination in the exercise of their civil rights. And the federal government's reach extended into the states. The idea that a person could not be denied access to hotels, inns, restaurants, and other public places had been federalized by the Civil Rights Act of 1875, despite its origins.

The Fourteenth Amendment overturned *Dred Scott* by contradicting Chief Justice Taney's conclusion that the Negro is not nor could be a citizen of the United States. With this amendment thus came the unprecedented ideals of American citizenship and state citizenship for everyone without regard to race.* With it, too, came an advance upon the Thirteenth Amendment, which had obliterated the color line in respect to that most fundamental right—personal liberty. The Fourteenth Amendment obliterated the color line, so far as state action is concerned, in respect to the "fundamental" rights inhering in freedom—such rights as that to sue, to buy property, and to engage in contracts. With the Fifteenth Amendment came the unprecedented ideal that no man shall be discriminated against in respect to his exercise of the vote; it thus obliterated the color line in respect to the ballot. And the Civil Rights Act of 1875 obliterated the color line in public places.

C. Vann Woodward has pointed out that passion for equality, though it had become a minor aim of the war, diminished as the years of Reconstruction progressed.[24] It is of course true that prejudice against Negroes reigned during this period, and it is hard to imagine how the idea of moral

---

* Professor Harry Jaffa has remarked, using Lincolnian language, that because of the Fourteenth Amendment "anyone who ... attempted to justify depriving Negroes of the privileges of citizenship would set a precedent which might be used against himself. ... The recognition of the Negro's claim to the privileges of citizenship, by the most solemn legislative process known to the Constitution, the amending process, has created a moral claim to political equality which the Negro could not claim by the principles of the Declaration of Independence alone." The Fourteenth Amendment thus may be regarded as federalizing the idea of citizenship for every individual within each state.

equality—requiring, as it does, the proposition that color is morally irrelevant—could have been completely reified—reified so that schools could have been desegregated, that marriage between the races could have been allowed, and so forth. Perhaps the wonder, in retrospect, is that certain steps reflecting the idea of moral equality were taken at all. These steps were important because legally they were unprecedented; they put into law great ideals, those compatible with the Declaration and Lincoln's understanding of equality, ideals that, one hundred years later, would prove instrumental in the nation's final acceptance of the idea of moral equality. But in the interim much happened, and the next chapter in the story of the idea of moral equality is that of its dismal frustration.

Chapter 5

Even a Jim Crow Bible
Moral Equality Denied

NEGROES should be segregated from whites, restricted in their freedom of movement, and denied the vote: This was the answer American society gave to the question raised after the ratification of the Thirteenth Amendment, of what the freedmen's status should be. *Jim Crow* is the term associated with this second-class status, and yet Jim Crow did not emerge—American society did not finally answer the question of the Negroes' status—until late in the nineteenth century. Jim Crow affirmed the doctrine that color is morally pertinent; in particular it affirmed that the color of a black man's skin indicates his inherent inferiority and unworthiness for equality of treatment. The idea of moral equality, by contrast, denies that color is morally pertinent; it affirms that because all men are created equal, no man's freedoms should be diminished on account of his race. The rise and spread of Jim Crow is the story of the frustration of the idea of moral equality.

The reasons for such a complex phenomenon as Jim Crow are many, of course, but chief among them were decisions by the Supreme Court of the United States. In 1873 the Supreme Court, considering its first Fourteenth Amendment case, construed the privileges and immunities clause in such a way as to say that only the privileges and immunities of *national* citizenship were protected. National citizenship, the Court said in the *Slaughter House Cases,* included only such matters as, for example, access to seaports and travel to the District of Columbia.[1] Inasmuch as the largest number of rights for anyone were those incidental to state citizenship, the privileges and immunities clause was thus constructed in a way hardly reflective of the idea of moral equality. With the *Slaughter House Cases,* as Richard Bardolph has pointed out, the Court began developing several principles of constitutional construction in regard to the postwar amendments. The Court decided that the amendments did not touch the behavior of individuals, but only those measures taken by the states themselves or their agents; that if a law was not *prima facie* discriminatory, then the Court would not presume to calculate whether the effects of the law weighed more heavily upon blacks than whites; that the police power of the states had priority over considerations like fundamental equality; and, finally, that although racial discriminations might be outlawed in certain instances by law, racial distinctions were not.[2] These principles of constitutional construction would be apparent in the Court's reasoning throughout the balance of the nineteenth century.

In *U.S.* v. *Reese,* decided in 1876, the Supreme Court declared that the Fifteenth Amendment did not guarantee citizens the right to vote but only a right not to be discriminated against by the states on account of race, color, or previous condition of servitude.[3] The Court's decision was read as allowing ways other than patent racial discrimination to disenfranchise the Negro. Very quickly those means—literacy tests, residency and registration requirements, and grandfather clauses, for example—began to be employed, as Oliver Morton had predicted. Between 1876 and 1884 Negro voting dropped by one-third in Louisiana, one-fourth in Mississippi, and one-half in South Carolina. In 1890 Mississippi, with its adoption of the so-called Mississippi Plan, became the first state to adopt systematic changes in its constitution designed specifically to disenfranchise blacks. By 1910 South Carolina, Louisiana, North Carolina, Alabama, Virginia, Georgia, and Oklahoma had changed their constitutions in many of the same ways and for the same reason as Mississippi had, and the remaining members of the old Confederacy—Florida, Tennessee, Arkansas, and Texas—had adopted statutes establishing the poll tax, designed, of course, to disenfranchise blacks.

The disenfranchisement of the black man occurred because the states themselves persisted in their efforts to control suffrage, and were successful. Diffusionist principles are of course central in American political theory, but Lincoln had demonstrated that in one crucial respect states could not be allowed autonomy: They could not be allowed to decide whether or not to permit slavery.

But diffusionist principles in respect to equality reigned in the Supreme Court, notably in the *Civil Rights Cases*, decided in 1883,[4] and *Plessy* v. *Ferguson*, decided in 1896.[5] In the *Civil Rights Cases*, the Court, denying that Congress had constitutional warrant to supersede state authority in matters of racial discrimination, gutted the Civil Rights Act of 1875 of its most important sections. And in *Plessy* v. *Ferguson*, the Court interpreted the equal protection clause of the Fourteenth Amendment in such a way as to lend justification—in the doctrine of "separate but equal"—to the fast-arriving institution of Jim Crow.

COUNTING BY RACE

In *Reese*, the *Civil Rights Cases*, and *Plessy*, therefore, the Court blunted the force of the idea of moral equality as it had been reified in three postwar measures—the Fifteenth Amendment, the Civil Rights Act of 1875, and the Fourteenth Amendment. Particularly in the *Civil Rights Cases* and in *Plessy* v. *Ferguson* did the Court encourage and lay the legal foundations for the institution of segregation. But not for this reason alone do the two verdicts merit examination; for both decisions lacked one vote of being unanimous—Justice John Harlan's. In Harlan's dissents one will find significant advancements on the idea of moral equality that Lincoln had recovered and developed and that had been reflected in law during Reconstruction. These advancements were to influence the thinking of twentieth-century advocates of moral equality at a time when these sentiments were to find widespread popular and legislative approval.

The *Civil Rights Cases* were so called because the Court agreed to review together five suits that involved the same complaint brought under the same statute, the Civil Rights Act of 1875. The complaint was that Negroes had been denied, because of their race, admission to public places. Justice Joseph P. Bradley, who wrote the decision of the Court, described the purpose of the law as: "to declare that, in the enjoyment of the accommodations and privileges of inns, public conveyances, theaters, and other places of public amusement, no distinction shall be made between citizens of different race or color, or between those who have and those who have not been slaves."[6] Harlan in his dissent agreed that this was the purpose of the law, and the two men were further agreed that the critical question before the Court involved the statute's constitutionality. "For if," as Bradley wrote in his opinion, "the law is unconstitutional, none of the prosecutions can stand."⁷ The prosecutions did not stand with Bradley. He could find no constitutional warrant for the Civil Rights Act.

Taking up the question of the constitutionality of the Civil Rights Act under the Thirteenth Amendment, Bradley wrote that the "necessary incidents" of slavery were "compulsory service of the slave for the benefit of the master, restraint of his movements except by the master's will, disability to hold property, to make contracts, to have a standing in court, to be a witness against a white person." But denial of the accommodations and enjoyments of an inn to a citizen because of his race is clearly not one of the "necessary incidents" of slavery, said Bradley. "It would be running the slavery argument into the ground," he wrote, "to make it apply to every act of discrimination which a person may see fit to make. . . ."⁸

It is hardly surprising that Bradley's inquiry into whether an act of racial discrimination is a "necessary incident" of slavery should have yielded the result it did. What Bradley should have asked was not whether rejection at the door of an inn and the disability to hold property, for example, are equally manifestations of slavery; but whether the act of enslaving a Negro and that of refusing him a seat at a theater have any essential connection. The abhorrence of slavery, it hardly needs noting, lay not in the so-called "inseparable incidents" of the institution, but in the fact that it denied a man his humanity; it denied a man his existence as a morally autonomous creature. And the wrong that lay in the act of racial discrimination at a hotel or theater consisted, if not to the same degree, of precisely the same kind, in the denial to a man of his due, as a man.

Here Justice Harlan differed with Bradley:

I hold that since slavery . . . was the moving or principal cause of the adoption of [the Thirteenth Amendment], and since that institution rested wholly upon the inferiority, as a race, of those held in bondage, their freedom necessarily involved immunity from, and protection against, all discrimination against them, because of their race, in respect of such civil rights as belong to freedmen of other races.[9]

For Harlan, the act of racial discrimination, like the act of enslaving a man, was based upon the notion that Negroes, as a race, were inferior—an attitude that denies an individual his due as a man. And to free a man, for Harlan, entailed—note his use of the word "necessarily" in the quote above—that he should be free of racial discrimination.

Through Harlan's opinion the connection between freedom from slavery and freedom from racial discrimination is evident. Harlan talked of the "fundamental rights" that "inhere" in "a state of freedom" and of the "civil rights" such as "were fundamental in freedom." "Personal liberty," he wrote, quoting Sir William Blackstone, the English jurist, "consists in the power of locomotion, of changing situation or removing one's person to whatever places one's own inclination may direct, without restraint, unless by due course of law." Slavery denied a man the power of locomotion; clearly, too, did rejection by reason of race at the door of an inn. "What value is this right of locomotion, if it may be clogged by such burdens as Congress intended by the Act of 1875 to remove?" Harlan perceptively noted that these burdens "lie at the very foundation of the institution of slavery as it once existed." "The Thirteenth Amendment," he said, "alone obliterated the race line, so far as all rights fundamental in a state of freedom are concerned."[10] In Harlan's view, Congress very definitely had the power under the Thirteenth Amendment to pass the Civil Rights Act of 1875.

Bradley's majority opinion was an excellent example of the widespread failure of his age to perceive that enslaving a Negro and denying him public accommodations were acts fundamentally related, in that both denied a man his due as a man. His opinion was also typical of his age in another respect—in its restricted understanding of the idea of citizenship contained in the Fourteenth Amendment. Citizenship, for Bradley, was a minimal concept, requiring of the federal government only that it secure and protect personal liberty. Bradley recognized other civil rights, but he left these to be protected in the so-called "ordinary modes"; indeed to ask federal protection of these other rights would have been, for him, to ask for special treatment—not the kind of treatment a "mere citizen" could justifiably require.[11]

For Harlan, however, citizenship

necessarily imports at least equality of civil rights among citizens of every race in the same state. It is fundamental in American citizenship that, in respect of such rights, there shall be no discrimination by the state or its officers, or by individuals or corporations exercising public functions or authority, against any citizen because of his race.[12]

Harlan would not allow civil rights—the rights inhering, as he put it, in "fundamental freedom"—to be left up to the "ordinary modes of protection" in the states.

"Exemption from racial discrimination in respect of civil rights" was a "new constitutional right," wrote Harlan; and as a *constitutional* right, responsibility for its protection lay with Congress. "It has been," he noted, "the established doctrine of this court during all its history . . . that Congress . . . may, by its own legislation, enforce and protect any right derived from or created by the National Constitution."[13] For Harlan, citizenship entailed that blacks enjoy the same rights as whites and that these rights must be protected by the federal government.

The differences between Bradley and Harlan can be most

easily seen, perhaps, by considering remarks Bradley made toward the end of his opinion, together with Harlan's response. "When a man has emerged from slavery," wrote Bradley, ". . . there must be some stage in the progress of his elevation when he takes the rank of a mere citizen, and ceases to be the special favorite of the laws, and when his rights, as a citizen or a man, are to be protected in the ordinary modes by which other men's rights are to be protected."[14] Harlan replied that it was "scarcely just to say that the colored race has been the special favorite of the laws"; that the Civil Rights Act of 1875 was for the benefit of citizens of *every* race and color; and that what the nation, through Congress, had tried to do in respect to Negroes was what it had already done in respect to whites—secure and protect the rights that belong to every man by virtue of his citizenship.[15]

Lincoln had argued that because all men are created equal, no man may be the slave of another. His understanding of the idea of equality may be regarded as commanding other conclusions—such as that every man should be treated equally at law. Harlan's opinion in the *Civil Rights Cases* was bare of reference to the Declaration of Independence and the Lincoln-Douglas debates, but he nevertheless stands with Lincoln in the tradition of the idea of moral equality. Where Lincoln reasoned from the Jeffersonian language of the Declaration, Harlan reasoned from the concept of citizenship. One may question whether it was necessary to invoke this concept of citizenship, arguing that Harlan could have made his points without this legal construct. But in any event, Harlan's essential points were consistent with the idea of moral equality. He recognized that if men were free, they should also be free of racial discrimination in respect to the exercise of their civil rights; he understood that freedom from slavery and exemption from racial discrimination were essentially related in that both slavery and racial discrimination denied a man his due as a man.

Harlan's contribution to the idea of moral equality in its historical development should be apparent. Lincoln understood that not until the individual states ceased to have authority in the matter of personal freedom could slavery be condemned. Harlan contended that not until the individual states ceased to have authority in the matter of civil rights could racial discrimination be condemned. His insight was that civil rights must be of federal concern and have federal protection. "There cannot be in this Republic," he said, "any class of human beings in practical subjection to another class, with power in the latter to dole out to the former just such privileges as they may choose to grant."[16] One lengthy sentence of Harlan's in his dissenting opinion in the *Civil Rights Cases* summarizes his position well:

What I affirm is that no State, nor the officers of any State, nor any corporation or individual wielding power under state authority for the public benefit or the public convenience, can, consistently either with the freedom established by the fundamental law, or with that equality of civil rights which now belongs to every citizen, discriminate against freed men or citizens, in those rights, because of their race, or because they once labored under the disabilities of slavery imposed upon them as a race.[17]

Lincoln's moral idea found in Harlan's dissent the insistence that moral equality have authoritative national expression.

The decision by the Court in the *Civil Rights Cases* met with a significant amount of opinion in favor of equal rights. Hundreds of editorials were written, a number of rallies were held by indignant citizens, and several congressional bills were drafted—all in opposition to the decision. But thirteen years later "a great change had taken place," as C. Vann Woodward has noted, for it was obvious that "the Court [in *Plessy* v. *Ferguson*] had [now] given voice to the dominant mood of the country."[18]

Plessy v. *Ferguson* arose in New Orleans, where members of the Negro community decided to contest a Jim Crow railcar bill passed by the Louisiana legislature in 1890. On June 7, 1892, Homer Adolph Plessy, a black man, bought a ticket in New Orleans for Covington, Louisiana, and boarded the East Louisiana Railroad, taking a seat in the white coach. Refusing to move to the Jim Crow car, Plessy was arrested and charged with violating the law. Plessy's attorneys, Albion Tourgee, a former carpetbagger, and James C. Walker, a native of New Orleans, argued that the railcar law violated Plessy's rights under the Fourteenth Amendment.

Citing numerous decisions in lower federal courts to the effect that accommodations did not have to be identical to be equal, the Louisiana court found the railcar law constitutional. On appeal to the Supreme Court, Tourgee argued that the law violated the spirit and intent of both the Thirteenth and Fourteenth amendments. Segregation was of a piece with slavery, he said, in that it perpetuated distinctions of a "servile character." It had been said that the law was impartial as between the races and that it did afford blacks the "equal protection of the laws," as specified in the Fourteenth Amendment. But Tourgee emphatically disagreed.

The object of such a law is simply to debase and distinguish against the inferior race. Its purpose has been properly interpreted by the general designation of "Jim Crow Car" law. Its object is to separate the Negroes from the whites in public conveyances for the gratification and recognition of the sentiment of white superiority and white supremacy of right and power.[19]

In a decision written by Justice Henry Billings Brown, the Supreme Court rejected Plessy's plea. Brown began his opinion by taking up the constitutional question, first with the Thirteenth Amendment. Like Bradley in the *Civil Rights Cases*, Brown did not inquire into whether there was any generic connection between enslaving a man and segregating him by race; so it was an easy matter for him to conclude that segregation by race was no incident of slavery. The Thirteenth Amendment does not abolish distinctions "founded in the color of the two races"; nor, he said, turning to another possible constitutional authority, does the Fourteenth. Brown rejected the notion that laws requiring the segregation of people by race implied the "inferiority of either race to the other." In an effort to support his position, he merely pointed to existing custom. "The most common instance of this [segregation] is connected with the establishment of separate schools for white and colored children."[20]

Brown thought the question before the Court could be reduced to that of whether the statute in question was "reasonable." And "reasonableness," in his view, must be considered in light of "established usages, customs, and traditions of the people, and with a view to the promotion of their comfort and the preservation of the public peace and good order."[21] By this point, given the established customs in Louisiana, it was foregone that Brown would conclude that the statute was reasonable.

Brown's closing remarks are notable. The fundamental error in the *Plessy* case, he wrote, consisted "in the assumption that the enforced separation of the two races stamps the colored race with a badge of inferiority." Brown said that if this were so, it was only by reason of the construction the colored race wished to put upon the act of separation.[22] He thus understood the "badge of inferiority" as a psychological fact about Negroes, not as an objective description of their situation, when discriminated against. Here again, Brown failed to comprehend that discrimination because of race fails to give a man his due as a man, no matter how that man may feel about it.

Brown also said in closing that the *Plessy* argument "also assumes that social prejudices may be overcome by legislation, and that equal rights cannot be secured to the Negro except by an enforced commingling of the two races."[23] But Plessy's contention was not that social prejudice could be overcome by legislation, nor that a man's rights could not be secured other than by "an enforced commingling of the two races." Plessy's contention was that a man should be allowed his due as a man, to be free to move where he willed on a passenger train.

John Harlan, who had dissented in the *Civil Rights Cases*, dissented here again. He rejected Brown's entire inquiry into the "reasonableness" of the legislation. He rejected, too, Brown's implicit statement that the segregation of the races was benign. The purpose of the Louisiana railcar law, he said, was to exclude "colored people from coaches occupied by or assigned to white persons," not to do the reverse.[24] What was at issue was whether Negroes could be treated in this fashion, not the "reasonableness" of the law. What was at issue was principle. And Harlan's answer was that discrimination against Negroes, or any persons, for that matter, because of their race could not be tolerated under American institutions and ideals.

The Thirteenth and Fourteenth amendments, he said, are

in the Constitution to protect all the "civil rights that pertain to freedom and citizenship." These two amendments, together with the Fifteenth, "obliterated the race line from our systems of governments, national and state, and placed our free institutions upon the broad and sure foundations of the equality of all men before the law." In consequence, "in respect of civil rights, common to all citizens, the Constitution of the United States does not, I think, permit any public authority to know the race of those entitled to be protected in the enjoyment of such rights." The Louisiana railcar law, in Harlan's view, was inconsistent both with the idea of equality and with the notion of personal liberty.[25] Here he quoted the same passage from Blackstone as he had quoted in his dissent in the *Civil Rights Cases*. Summarizing his position, Harlan wrote:

In view of the Constitution, in the eye of the law, there is in this country no superior, dominant, ruling class of citizens. There is no caste here. Our Constitution is color-blind, and neither knows nor tolerates classes among citizens. In respect of civil rights all citizens are equal before the law. The humblest is the peer of the most powerful. The law regards man as man, and takes no account of his surroundings or of his color when his civil rights as guaranteed by the supreme law of the land are involved.[26]

Ideas have consequences, and the ideas that Justices Bradley and Brown endorsed had theirs. By 1896 the only Jim Crow statutes passed by a majority of the southern states concerned railroad transportation. South Carolina had yet to pass such a law, however, but opinion in the state seemed to be favoring one shortly after the verdict in *Plessy*. When, in 1898, such a law was up for a formal vote in the South Carolina legislature, the editor of the *Charleston News and Courier*, firmly against legally enforced railroad segregation, argued against it by constructing this humorous *reductio:*

> If there must be Jim Crow cars on the railroad there should be Jim Crow cars on the street railways. Also on all passenger boats. . . . If there are to be Jim Crow cars, moreover, there should be Jim Crow waiting saloons at all stations, and Jim Crow eating houses. . . . There should be Jim Crow sections of the jury box, and a separate Jim Crow dock and witness stand in every court—and a Jim Crow Bible for colored witnesses to kiss. It would be advisable also to have a Jim Crow section in county auditors' and treasurers' offices for the accommodation of colored taxpayers. The two races are dreadfully mixed in these offices for Christmas. . . . There should be a Jim Crow department for making returns and paying for the privileges and blessings of citizenships. Perhaps, the best plan would be, after all, to take the short cut to the general end . . . by establishing two or three counties at once, and turning them over to our colored citizens for their special and exclusive accommodation.[27]

As the years passed, no doubt it was not amusing to the editor of the *News and Courier* that, as C. Vann Woodward has noted, "apart from the Jim Crow counties and Jim Crow witness stand, all the improbable applications of the principle suggested by the editor in derision had been put into practice—down to and including the Jim Crow Bible."[28]

The spread of Jim Crow in the two decades subsequent to *Plessy* (1896) was remarkable. Streetcars, steamships, and ferries had their Jim Crow sections. White eating houses and bars were off-limits to Negroes. Whites and Negroes had separate drinking fountains, separate entrances to circuses, tent shows, and theaters. White nurses were forbidden to attend Negroes in hospitals, and vice versa; black barbers were forbidden to cut the hair of white women and children. Juries were segregated, as were public parks. In some places Negroes ascended buildings in elevators set aside exclusively for them. Even the phone booths were divided into some for "coloreds," others for whites. There were separate floors for Negroes and whites in mental hospitals, and in homes for the aged, the indigent, the orphaned, the blind, and the deaf and dumb. Whites used textbooks of their own, and so did blacks. In some cases textbooks were required to be stored separately. Even in the prisons there was no escaping Jim Crow: Inmates were segregated and chained only to members of their own race. There were even laws against whites frequenting houses of black prostitution, and vice versa. Much of the spread of Jim Crow was accompanied by law, but much also by custom. Woodward has concluded that there was more Jim Crow in practice than there was Jim Crow in law.[29]

Parallel with the legal development of Jim Crow was the rise of more discrimination against blacks at the voting booth. And, too, there were other developments that by 1910 signified the Negro's second-class status. By that year, the only states not having constitutional provisions or laws against intermarriage between the races were Connecticut, Illinois, Iowa, Kansas, Massachusetts, Minnesota, New Hampshire, New Jersey, New York, Pennsylvania, Vermont, Washington, and Wisconsin.[30] Also, in twelve states—Alabama, Florida, Georgia, Kentucky, Louisiana, Mississippi, North Carolina, South Carolina, Tennessee, Texas, Virginia, and West Virginia—both constitution and statute required the separation of the races in public schools; in two states—Arizona and Indiana—school boards were authorized to establish separate schools; and in Kansas, cities with populations of more than 150,000 were allowed to establish separate schools if those chose to do so.[31]

To put these developments in perspective, one should bear in mind that, in 1910, almost 90 percent of the nation's Negroes lived in the South. Therefore, to note the spread of Jim Crow in the South is to recognize that nearly all Negroes in America were subjected to it; to note the disenfranchisement of the Negro in the South is to recognize that blacks ceased to be a force in the nation's political life; to note the thirteen states all outside the South that did not have either constitutional provisions or laws against intermarriage is to recognize that most black Americans were forbidden to intermarry; and, finally, to note requirements for school segregation throughout the South and elsewhere is to recognize that very few black Americans were not prohibited from attending "separate but equal" schools. Still, one should not assume that the North was very hospitable to the Negro or enthusiastic about the cause of equality. Some northern states, for example, did have laws forbidding intermarriage. These laws were objective indices of the North's attitude toward the Negro, and if there was a difference in the North's attitude as against the South's at the turn of the century, it was one of degree, not kind. Here the debate precipitated by the annexation of the Philippines in 1902 is instructive.

This debate concerned the nature of American foreign policy and national destiny, and one of its major themes was the inequality of man. Southern Democrats were almost unanimous in condemning "imperialism" on grounds that Asiatics, like Negroes, were innately inferior to white people and could not be assimilated to American life. Two decades earlier such a point of view would have elicited angry rejoinders from the North, but in 1902, as historian Christopher Lasch has pointed out, the South's arguments were met by northern silence, even acquiescence.[32] In considering the conditions of citizenship, both parties to the debate—imperialists and anti-imperialists, North and South—were concerned not with a point of principle but with an almost Darwinian point—that is, whether a people had "developed" to the point they could assume the rights and responsibilities incidental to republican government. Rights as fundamental guarantees lost their meaning in the debate over the Philippines, as they were considered by both sides to be entirely relative to time and place; rights now depended, in the minds of all, entirely on a people's readiness to enjoy them.[33]

Thus, as Lasch writes, "the retreat from idealism was a national, not a local, phenomenon."[34] This point is made impressively by the conversation Lasch notes between Senator Knute Nelson of Minnesota, once an abolitionist, and Senator Ben Tillman of South Carolina. When Nelson declared that the Filipinos were incapable of self-government, Tillman replied:

I want to call the Senator's attention to the fact . . . that he and others who are now contending for a different policy in Hawaii and the Philippines gave the slaves of the South not only self-government, but they forced on the white men of the South, at the point of bayonet, the rule and domination of those ex-slaves. Why the difference? Why the change? Do you acknowledge that you were wrong in 1868?[35]

The decision in *Plessy* v. *Ferguson* was written by Henry Billings Brown, a graduate of Yale and a native of Michigan. It came at a time when racism, supported by social Darwinism, had insinuated itself into most every part of the nation. Most Americans believed that certain races and cultures were inherently inferior, and this sentiment was manifested in the legal advent of Jim Crow in the South, in the heavy restrictions placed on immigration, and in the popular sentiments regarding foreign policy.[36] In the first decades of this century, it was clear that the Negro, in being identified by color and not by individual right, had been abandoned. It is hardly surprising to recall that Woodrow Wilson, president from 1913 to 1921, introduced in Congress more bills proposing discriminatory legislation against the Negro than had ever been introduced before. Most of these failed to pass, but by executive order and other means Wilson managed to segregate, and in other ways humiliate, Negro federal employees. The era begun with the *Civil Rights Cases* in 1883 and extending into the Wilson administration marked the reign of color, not principle. The idea of moral equality had been frustrated, and the dissents of John Harlan in 1883 and 1896 had proved tiny resistance to a flood tide of racism and its apologists.

Chapter 6

No Distinctions...
No Discriminations
The Victory of Moral Equality

JUSTICE JOHN HARLAN had fought a lonely battle on the Supreme Court, but outside the Court could be found a number of people—blacks in particular—who shared his conviction that matters of race should be irrelevant at law. As the twentieth century progressed, this small minority would grow in size, the arguments of intellectuals and the democratizing experience of two world wars taking effect. By the middle of the century, the executive, judicial, and finally the legislative branches of the federal government had begun to accept, and act in ways consistent with, the idea of moral equality. With the passage of the Civil Rights Act of 1964, the idea of moral equality was decisively and unequivocally federalized; the institution of Jim Crow was finally overthrown. The purpose of this chapter is to tell the story of how the United States came to accept the proposition that color does not matter in any estimate of the worth of an individual—a proposition central to the claim of Allan Bakke and his supporters. This is a story, as Harlan clearly perceived in 1896, that would involve the federal government's assumption of responsibility for the protection of individual rights.

Of all those who spoke during the period of 1865 to 1900, a number of Negroes spoke with the conviction of a certain mind. Many tenaciously held to the theory of human rights expressed in the Declaration of Independence—that all men are created equal, endowed by their Creator with certain inalienable rights—life, liberty, and the pursuit of happiness—and believed that this theory formed the base upon which they could build their claims for political recognition and status.[1] Many blacks believed that the right to vote could be deduced from this theory of human rights. The elective franchise, they believed, was every American's "natural, inalienable right":[2] Freedom and the right to vote were indivisible and individual. Influential blacks like Dr. R.B. Roundanez, editor of the *New Orleans Tribune,* typically would note the contradiction between American ideals and the discriminations commonly experienced by members of their race.[3] Roundanez wrote that all the members of his race wanted was to be given a fair chance—"each unobstructed to find his own level according to his education and means."[4] Over and over Negroes were saying: "We ask but an equal chance before the law, no more, no less." They emphasized that they did not ask for "class legislation," saying "we have had enough of that."[5]

Richard Cain, a black who represented North Carolina in the House, clearly spoke for all men during debate on the Civil Rights Act of 1875. Said Cain:

All we ask is that you, the legislators of the nation, shall pass a law so strong and so powerful that no one shall be able to elude it and destroy our rights under the Constitution and laws of our country. That is all we ask. . . .

We do not want any discrimination to be made. If discriminations are made in regard to schools, then there will be accomplished just what we are fighting against. If you say that the schools in the state of Georgia, for instance, shall be allowed to discriminate against colored people, then you will have discriminations made against us. We do not want any discriminations. I do not ask any legislation for the colored people of this country that is not applied to the white people. All that we ask is equal laws, equal legislation, and equal rights throughout the length and breadth of this land.[6]

Cain's request would go unanswered for the better part of a century, but his vision of a color-blind society would not in subsequent years be without an increasing number of adherents.

Scholars are agreed that the low point for blacks after the Civil War occurred in the first two decades of the twentieth century. Not Cain's vision of equality, but great tension and conflict between the races defined these years. Race hatred was such that in 1908 riots struck Springfield, Illinois—Lincoln's hometown. Upset by the riots, several citizens banded together, hoping to focus attention on the plight of blacks. This group, the embryo from which would spring the National Association for the Advancement of Colored People (NAACP), an institution that would have much to do with the refutation of the belief that color matters, issued, on Lincoln's birthday in 1909, a call for a national conference on "the Negro question." Mary White Ovington, a social worker in New York, gave an account of "Lincoln's birthday call."[7]

The celebration of the centennial of the birth of Lincoln, began the call, "will fail to justify itself if it takes no note of and makes no recognition of the men and women for whom the great Emancipator labored to assure freedom." So his birthday, in addition to being an occasion for rejoicing, should be a time for "taking stock of the nation's progress since 1865." The birthday call proceeded to ask the critical questions: How far has the country lived up to the obligations imposed on it by the Emancipation? How far has the country "gone in assuring to each and every citizen, irrespective of color, the equality of opportunity and equality under the law, which underlie our American institutions and are guaranteed by the Constitution?" The answers, in 1909, were of course depressing. If Lincoln were here today, the birthday call continued, "he would be disheartened and discouraged." Georgia had just disenfranchised the Negro, and the Supreme Court had refused to take up the question of disenfranchisement. Meanwhile, the Court had permitted individual states to "make it a crime for white and colored persons to frequent the same market place at the same time, or appear in an assemblage of citizens convened to consider questions of a public or political nature in which all citizens, without regard to race, are equally interested."[8] Furthermore, judges elected by one part of the community were deciding the fate of others in the community. Black men and women were segregated on trains, paying first-class fares for third-class service. They were segregated, too, in restaurants and places of entertainment. And the states themselves were doing little to educate the Negro "for the best exercise of citizenship." Lawless attacks upon the Negro were widespread, and the North was silent, tacitly approving the violence. Lincoln, to sum up, would have found almost total acquiescence in the proposition that the color of the Negro means that he should be discriminated against; he would have found the states autonomous in their charge of civil rights, with the federal government doing nothing to protect the Negro from racial discrimination. "A house divided against itself cannot stand," the birthday call said, quoting Lincoln's memorable passage. "This government," the call concluded, "cannot exist half-slave and half-free any better today than it could in 1861."[9]

Booker T. Washington (1856–1915) ranks with Martin Luther King, Jr., as one of the great Americans and as one of the great spokesman for black Americans. Washington frequently differed with W. E. B. Dubois, another black leader of his day, but his estimate of what it meant to be black and whether color should matter at law or in societal advancement—an estimate that recalls Richard Cain's dream—was shared by most blacks. In his autobiography, *Up From Slavery,* published in 1901, Washington wrote that, from any point of view:

I had rather be what I am, a member of the Negro race, than be able to claim membership with the most favored of any other race. I have always been made sad when I have heard members of any race claiming rights and privileges, or certain badges of distinction, on the ground simply that they were members of this or that race, regardless of their own individual worth or attainments. I have been made to feel sad for such persons because I am conscious of the fact that mere connection with what is known as a superior race will not permanently carry an individual forward unless he has individual worth, and mere connection with what is regarded as an inferior race will not finally hold an individual back if he possesses intrinsic, individual merit. Every persecuted individual and race should get consolation out of the great human law, which is universal and eternal, that merit, no matter under what skin found, is in the long run, recognized and rewarded. This I have said here, not to call attention to myself as an individual, but to the race to which I am proud to belong.[10]

In 1910, the newly formed NAACP stated its purposes:

COUNTING BY RACE

To promote equality of rights and eradicate caste or race prejudice among the citizens of the United States; to advance the interest of colored citizens; to secure for them impartial suffrage; and to increase their opportunities for securing justice in the courts, education for their children, employment according to their ability, and complete equality before the law.[11]

Between 1915 and 1958 the NAACP's Legal Defense and Educational Fund would argue more than fifty major cases affecting the franchise, residential segregation, restrictive covenants, public education, interstate and local transportation, recreation, and "due process" and "equal protection" controversies. Discussion of a few of these is illustrative of the successes the NAACP enjoyed in its efforts to abolish racial discrimination.

In the two cases stemming from the sensational trials in 1931 in Scottsboro, Alabama, where nine black youths aged thirteen to nineteen had been convicted of rape and sentenced to death, the Supreme Court accepted and affirmed its role as protector of constitutional rights. In *Powell* v. *Alabama* (1932) the Supreme Court ruled that the constitutional right to legal counsel had been denied the accused;[12] and in *Norris* v. *Alabama* (1935) the Court set aside the convictions of the accused because blacks had been excluded from jury service.[13] No Alabama law had prohibited Negroes from serving as jurors, but state practices had nevertheless systematically and arbitrarily excluded them from jury lists. This, the Court said, was a violation of the Equal Protection Clause. No Negro had sat on a jury for the county in question in its entire history, according to testimony in the trial, and yet as many as thirty Negroes were qualified, some of them having been called to jury service in federal cases. Consistent with this ruling, the Court later decided in *Smith* v. *Texas* (1940) that as the Fourteenth Amendment prohibits racial discrimination in the selection of grand juries, a Texas court had wrongly denied Negroes jury service.[14]

Elsewhere there were movements toward the abolition of Jim Crow in transportation and in public accommodations. In *Mitchell* v. *United States* (1941) the Court overturned an Interstate Commerce Commission (ICC) ruling that the small demand for Pullman accommodations by Negroes on an Arkansas railroad justified the train's making only limited space available to them.[15] The Court said that the "comparative volume of traffic cannot justify the denial of a fundamental right of equality of treatment. . . . It is the individual . . . who is entitled to the equal protection of the laws,—not merely a group of individuals, or a body of persons according to their numbers."[16] And in *Henderson* v. *U. S. ICC and Southern Railway* (1950) the Court rendered a similar verdict, basing its decision on a section of law from the ICC Act of 1887, which prohibited railroads in interstate commerce to "subject any particular person . . . to any undue or unreasonable prejudice or disadvantage in any respect whatsoever."[17] Traveling from Washington to Atlanta, a black man named Henderson had been refused service in the dining car, although vacancies existed. The ICC had followed the practice of reserving one table in eleven for Negroes on the grounds that such a reservation was "proportionately fair." The Supreme Court agreed with Henderson's contention that this arrangement violated his civil rights.

The right to be free from unreasonable discriminations belongs . . . to each particular person. Where a dining car is available to passengers holding tickets entitling them to use it, each such passenger is equally entitled to its facilities in accordance with reasonable regulations. . . . Under the rules, only four Negro passengers may be served at one time and then only at one table reserved for Negroes.

Other Negroes who present themselves are compelled to await a vacancy at that table, although there may be many vacancies elsewhere in the diner. . . . We need not multiply instances in which these rules sanction unreasonable discriminations. The curtains, partitions and signs emphasize the artifice of a difference in treatment which serves only to call attention to a racial classification of passengers holding identical tickets and using the same public dining facility.[18]

None of the Reconstruction measures in behalf of equality, one will recall, affected the public schools. Here segregation persisted, and it was unthinkable that the arrangement of sending black students to one school (if indeed they were to be sent to any school) and white students to another should be disrupted. Perhaps it was fitting that, in order for Jim Crow to be dealt a decisive blow, it would have to occur in public education.

In 1938, almost half the states either required or expressly permitted segregation in the public schools, and yet it was clear that separate black schools were not equal, the white ones being far superior. If the notion of separate-but-equal was to be taken seriously, it seemed that blacks could not be said to be enjoying the equal protection of the laws. After all, by the reasoning in *Plessy,* as historian J. R. Pole of Cambridge University has pointed out, society could be regarded as organized into vertical structures according to race and ethnicity, within each of which a racial (or ethnic) group would live unto itself.[19] For each group, so segregated, to be "equally protected," each would have to be considered equal in the sight of government; no group could be superior. Only this way could each group be said to have the equal protection of the laws.

With *Missouri ex rel. Gaines* v. *Canada* in 1938 the Supreme Court began to make a number of decisions that tested the doctrine of separate but equal, with which the idea of moral equality was incompatible, before finally rejecting that doctrine outright in *Brown* v. *Board of Education* in 1954.[20] Here again the NAACP was involved in a manner consistent with the idea of moral equality: The long-range strategy of the organization was to have the Court rule that separate facilities were *inherently* unequal.

In *Gaines,* Lloyd Gaines, a Negro, was refused admission to the School of Law at the University of Missouri. He sued on grounds that this refusal violated his constitutional rights as guaranteed under the equal protection clause of the Fourteenth Amendment. Gaines had been graduated from Lincoln University, which the state maintained expressly for black students. Upon application to the state law school, Gaines was referred to the president of Lincoln University, who advised him of the relevant state law. That law, premised on maintaining separate but equal school facilities, directed the curators of Lincoln to arrange for the legal education of Missouri blacks "at the university of any adjacent state" and to pay "the reasonable tuition fees for such attendance" while a law school for Missouri blacks was being built. Within the constraints of the separate-but-equal doctrine, however, the Supreme Court found the Missouri law unconstitutional: Gaines was denied "equality of legal right" because, while a white student may have a legal education provided for within the state, a black student had to go outside it. Here the Court did not reject the separate-but-equal doctrine, but it maintained that a state must adhere to the principle within its own borders.

Ten years later in *Sipuel* v. *Board of Regents of the University of Oklahoma,* the university took the position that refusal to allow blacks admission to its law school did not constitute a denial of the equal protection of the laws because a law school for blacks was in the process of being organized.[21] The university so argued, of course, in order to maintain its exclusively white law school; and insofar as the university did not have other professional and graduate schools for blacks only, the logic of the university's position seemed to require that whenever a black desired any kind of graduate or professional education, the university would have to quickly organize the requisite school, a *blacks*-only school. The practical absurdities of the university's position were apparent even to its attorney. In conversation with one of the witnesses in the case, he had a burst of insight. "Oh, my God," he exclaimed, "suppose one of them wanted to be a petroleum engineer! Why, we've got the biggest petroleum-cracking laboratory in the country here."[22]

Thurgood Marshall, arguing *Sipuel* for the NAACP, was aware of the absurdities of the university's position, but his concern centered on the racial classification made by the university and also on the question of whether a separate school for blacks could be a truly "equal" school. "Classifications and distinctions based on race or color have no moral or legal validity in our society," he argued in his brief. "Segregation in public education helps to preserve a caste system which is based upon race and color. It is designed and intended to perpetuate the slave tradition. . . . Equality, even if the term be limited to a comparison of physical facilities, is and can never be achieved . . . the terms 'separate' and 'equal' cannot be used conjunctively in a situation of this kind; *there can be no separate equality.*"[23]

The Court's decision in *Sipuel* was simple. Oklahoma, it said in a one-paragraph *per curiam* decision, had to provide

Ada Sipuel with a legal education "in conformity with the equal protection clause of the Fourteenth Amendment and provide it as soon as it does for applicants of any other group."[24] Overnight the state of Oklahoma created a separate law school: A section of the state capitol was roped off with three law teachers assigned to teach Miss Sipuel and "others similarly situated." Marshall took the case back to the Court, but it was unwilling to go further. He had been unable to persuade the Court of his essential points regarding race and equality, but nonetheless it had restricted the compass in which the doctrine of separate-but-equal could be considered authoritative.

By the time of *Sipuel*, with the Supreme Court now more seriously scrutinizing the "equal" side of the separate-but-equal formula, the South had begun to shovel money into elementary and secondary schools for blacks and to talk of creating regional graduate and professional schools for blacks only. To sustain Jim Crow in higher education, the South apparently was willing to incur the very high expense of maintaining more nearly equal but still separate facilities.

In 1950 the Court decided two cases involving professional school education on the same day. One came from Texas, the other Oklahoma. As Chief Justice Vinson said at the outset of his decision in *Sweatt* v. *Painter*,[25] the two cases "present different aspects of this general question: To what extent does the Equal Protection Clause of the Fourteenth Amendment limit the power of the state to distinguish between students of different races in professional and graduate education in a state university?"[26] Heman Marion Sweatt, a black letter carrier, had applied for admission to the most prestigious law school in the state of Texas, the University of Texas Law School at Austin, but was turned down on racial grounds. Sweatt brought suit, and the state's trial court found that the state had denied him the equal protection of the laws. The judge declared that the state would have six months to establish a law school for blacks—thus to fulfill the mandate of "equal protection"—or else Sweatt would have to be matriculated at the law school in Austin. At the end of the six-month period, the lower court decided that the makeshift facilities newly established at Prairie View State Normal and Industrial Colleges for Negroes did provide equality for Sweatt; but Sweatt continued his case to the Court of Civil Appeals. Meanwhile the state appropriated $3 million to create a so-called "first class" Texas State University for Negroes; of this sum, some $100,000 was to go for the creation of a law school. The Court of Appeals ruled against Sweatt, thus setting the stage for his ultimate battle before the Supreme Court.

Meanwhile, in Oklahoma, George McLaurin had unsuccessfully applied to the graduate school in education at the University of Oklahoma. With the backing of the NAACP's Legal Defense Fund, he sued, and his case was channeled through the federal courts, arriving first at a special federal district court. Here it was ruled that "the state is under the constitutional duty to provide the plaintiff with the education he seeks as soon as it does for applicants of any other group."[27] Oklahoma, however, had no graduate school in education for blacks; the mandate now was to provide that education, and Oklahoma did so, for McLaurin, in a curious way. He was matriculated as a graduate student at the University of Oklahoma but, in accordance with the legislature's revisions of the stated laws, he was to be instructed "on a segregated basis" within the university. So he was required, as Chief Justice Vinson later would recount, "to sit apart at a designated desk in an anteroom adjoining the classroom; to sit at a designated desk on the mezzanine floor of the library, but not to use the desks in the regular reading room; and to sit at a designated table and to eat at a different time from the other students in the school cafeteria."[28] Richard Kluger, author of *Simple Justice*, the comprehensive history of the *Brown* case, has commented that thus did Oklahoma provide the "most inventive contribution to legalized bigotry" since its adoption of the 'grandfather clause,' a device whose effect was to disenfranchise blacks and which was ruled unconstitutional in 1915. "The state was punishing George McLaurin," Kluger wrote, "for requiring it to honor his rights as a citizen."[29] McLaurin returned to court to argue against his peculiarly segregated education, but with no success. Later the university slightly altered the segregated conditions of his education, as if the relief due him consisted in marginal changes in his school environment. Officials now allowed McLaurin onto the main floor of the library, although they still restricted him to his own table, and they now let him eat at the same time as whites in the cafeteria, although he was confined to a table reserved for one—George McLaurin.

At this point, the NAACP Legal Defense Fund was still following the strategy of arguing that segregation was illegal because, as practiced, it did not provide true equality for Negroes. The Fund was afraid to press beyond this argument, which necessarily called for empirical inquiries into a particular case to determine whether facilities were in fact "equal." But now, with *Sweatt* and *McLaurin* rising to the Supreme Court, and with Texas apparently about to gird for an all-out defense of segregation, the organization considered a change in tactics.

COUNTING BY RACE

But the NAACP's posture in *Sweatt* could not allow a strategic switch. For, as Kluger has written, "all the Court had to do, really, was rule that *Plessy* meant what it said and that Texas had to provide Heman Sweatt with a truly equal law school or let him into the white one."[30] Marshall, arguing the case for the NAACP, which paid most of the costs, decided to stay within the confines of *Plessy*; but he also managed to satisfy his desire for an all-out attack on the *concept* of segregation. Marshall persuaded Thomas Emerson, a Yale law professor, to draft an *amicus curiae* brief in *Sweatt*, which eventually was signed by 187 law professors. The Committee of Law Teachers Against Segregation in Legal Education argued the case that

laws which give equal protection are those which make no *discrimination* because of race in the sense that they make no *distinction* because of race. As soon as laws make a right or responsibility dependent solely on race, they violate the Fourteenth Amendment. Reasonable classifications may be made, but one basis of classification is completely precluded; for the Equal Protection Clause makes racial classifications unreasonable *per se*.[31]

Mindful of the committee's *amicus* brief and aware that the ultimate position of the NAACP was that segregation was inherently wrong and illegal under the Fourteenth Amendment, Chief Justice Vinson remarked that "broader issues have been urged for our consideration."[32] But his Court, conscious of the times, decided to construe the issues more narrowly: The question in *Sweatt* was whether the separation of the races into two professional schools was constitutionally permissible. Regarding the idea of separate-but-equal carefully, not yet ready to maintain that "separate" meant "unequal," the Court said in *Sweatt* that the facilities of the two law schools had to be truly equal or else the separation of the races was constitutionally intolerable. Vinson inquired into the conditions at the University of Texas Law School and then into those first at the original, and then at the new, law school instituted for Negroes, and found that the conditions were clearly unequal. "We cannot," he wrote, "find substantial equality in the educational opportunities offered white and Negro law students by the State."[33] In consequence, no equal facilities being available, the Court ordered Sweatt admitted to the University of Texas Law School at Austin.

In *McLaurin*, the exact question of equal protection present in *Sweatt* did not arise, obviously, since McLaurin was enrolled at the University of Oklahoma. Avoiding the question of segregation, Chief Justice Vinson merely said that the conditions under which McLaurin was made to go to school visited upon him "inequalities."[34] These, he said, had to end.

Sweatt did not overturn *Plessy*; *Plessy* had been the controlling legal premise. And although *Plessy* was technically irrelevant in *McLaurin*, the Court ruled as if it were considering a case under the separate-but-equal doctrine: The conditions under which McLaurin labored were deemed "inequalities." Still, it seemed clear that the Court soon would have to consider the legality of Jim Crow head-on. And the NAACP Legal Defense Fund, sensing that the moment had finally come to argue the case against segregation, did so in 1954 in *Brown* v. *Board of Education*.[35]

Brown refers to four cases decided as one. From Kansas, South Carolina, Virginia, and Delaware came cases to the Supreme Court that challenged the constitutionality of segregated public schools. The separate schools for Negroes were considered, as the Supreme Court's decision would acknowledge, equal to those for whites; so the question of whether segregation itself was constitutionally permissible was unavoidable. The NAACP argued that the substantive question was whether the exclusion of Negroes *qua* Negroes from public schools contravenes the Constitution. "The question is," said its brief, "whether a nation founded on the proposition that 'all men are created equal' is honoring its commitments to grant 'due process of law' and 'the equal protection of the laws' to all within its borders when it, or one of its constituent states, confers or denies benefits on the basis of color or race."[36] Arguing that distinctions drawn by state authorities violated the Fourteenth Amendment, the brief referred to a line of cases, finishing with *Sweatt* and *McLaurin*.

The Supreme Court, in a unanimous decision by Chief Justice Earl Warren, ruled that "in the field of public education the doctrine of 'separate but equal' has no place. Separate educational facilities are inherently unequal."[37] The importance of the decision was not simply, however, that in public education the doctrine of Jim Crow had no place. *Brown* was widely interpreted as obliterating the color line, not just in schools, but everywhere. And in subsequent *per curiam* decisions, the Court began to condemn Jim Crow wherever it existed. One week after ruling on *Brown* the Court remanded to a federal district court in Kentucky a case in which blacks were denied recreational facilities used by whites; the Court asked for reconsideration in light of *Brown*. In following years, the Court itself decided in *per curiam* decisions that "separate-but-equal" facilities were invalid on public beaches (in Maryland), public golf courses (in Georgia), and on buses (in Alabama).

The color line was finally being officially obliterated, and soon, as we shall see, Congress would join the judicial branch of government in federalizing the proposition that color does not matter at law. But it should be noted that the complete story of the obliteration of the color line cannot be told in reference only to the efforts of the NAACP and the work of the federal government. For even while the Negro was at his nadir in the first two decades of the twentieth century, a number of new ideas were being circulated that, over time, would have consequences favorable to the tradition of moral equality. And, too, America's involvement in the two world wars would have similarly favorable consequences. The new ideas and the experience of the wars may be regarded as factors influencing the society at large, factors that paved the way for the societal acceptance, by the 1950s and 1960s, of the idea of moral equality.

Social Darwinism, giving force to the belief that Negroes were inherently inferior to whites, was the dominant ideology at the turn of the century. There was no shortage of what J. R. Pole has called the "pluralists"—those who believed that man best develops within his own racial or ethnic group, a belief obviously compatible with the separate-but-equal doctrine emerging from *Plessy*. In time, however, racial egalitarians would arise to challenge the pluralists, and their ideas would lend support to the conception of our political institutions that Justice Stephen Johnson Field had offered long ago, namely, that "all men have certain undeniable rights . . . and that in the pursuit of happiness, all avocations, all honors, all positions are alike open to everyone, and that in the protection of these rights all are equal before the law."[38]

In 1894, Franz Boas, a young scholar who had immigrated from Germany, delivered an address that was the first serious scientific challenge to racism by an American academic. In *The Mind of Primitive Man*, published in 1911, Boas set

COUNTING BY RACE

forth his understanding that it was not race but cultural influences and environment that account for the principal differences that divide men. "An unbiased estimate of the anthropological evidence so far brought forward," he wrote:

does not permit us to countenance the belief in a racial inferiority which would unfit an individual of the negro race to take his part in modern civilization. We do not know of any demand made on the human body or mind in modern life that anatomical or ethnological evidence would prove to be beyond the powers of the negro. ... there is every reason to believe that the negro, when given facility and opportunity, will be perfectly able to fulfill the duties of citizenship as well as his white neighbor.[39]

The influence of Boas was such that during the 1920s and 1930s his pupils manned most of the anthropology departments in the universities across the country. The new idea that race did not determine mentality and temperament received such wide acceptance within academic circles generally that, in 1930, as sociologist Gunner Myrdal reported in his study of American race relations, a questionnaire circulated among scholars in the area of racial differences revealed that only 4 percent of the respondents believed "in race superiority and inferiority."[40] In time, as historian Richard Bardolph has commented, the efforts of Boas and others similarly minded began to reach beyond the universities and the scholarly journals, to the "textbooks, and through them to the people whom these agencies instruct—the teachers and editors, writers, lawyers, jurists, religious leaders, and in time even entertainers and makers of movies."[41]

World War I served to heighten the concern of black soldiers for their own situation back home. As enlisted men, Negroes were segregated from whites and frequently insulted. And they were reminded of their status even by the enemy.

The Ninety-Second Division, composed entirely of blacks, was in battle with a German regiment that sought to demoralize them through circulars proclaiming the following message.

What is Democracy? Personal freedom, all citizens enjoying the same rights socially and before the law. Do you enjoy the same rights as the white people do in America, the land of Freedom and Democracy, or are you rather not treated there as second-class citizens? Can you go into a restaurant where white people dine? Can you get a seat in the theater where white people sit?[42]

The pitch was coming. Negroes were invited to come over to the German side, where they would be treated, of course, "as first-class citizens"; however, *no* Negroes deserted. For the most part, American Negroes supported the war to make the world safe for democracy, but in the process they came to feel, as their ancestors in the Revolution felt, that the United States itself should be made safe for democracy and be true to its founding and defining principle—the principle of equality.

World War II had a more galvanizing effect on blacks than did World War I, spurring them to action that produced specific changes in race relations. One instance of this occurred even before the bombing of Pearl Harbor. With the Allied forces battling against the Nazis, holders of a patently antiliberal, racist dogma, it became evident that racism must be unequivocally and everywhere resisted. American plants and factories were booming as the nation's defense industries were supplying the Allied forces, and yet blacks were not among the beneficiaries of this economic boom: Unemployment among blacks was running at extremely high rates. So A. Philip Randolph, president of the Brotherhood of Sleeping Car Porters, decided to organize a "March upon Washing-

ton," scheduled for July 1, 1941. Wrote Randolph in explanation of the planned march:

... American Negroes, involved as we are in the general issues of
the conflict, are confronted not with choice but with the challenge
both to win democracy for ourselves at home and to help win the
war for democracy the world over.

There is no escape from the horns of this dilemma. . . . For if the
war for democracy is not won abroad, the fight cannot be won at
home. If this war cannot be won for the white peoples, it will not
be won for the darker races.

Conversely, if freedom and equality are not vouchsafed the peoples of color, the war for democracy will not be won. . . . That is
why those familiar with the thinking of the American Negro have
sensed his lack of enthusiasm. . . .

What have Negroes to fight for? What's the difference between
Hitler and that "cracker" Talmadge from Georgia? Why has a
man got to be Jim-Crowed to die for democracy? If you haven't got
democracy yourself, how can you carry it to somebody else?

What are the reasons for this state of mind? The answer is: discrimination, segregation, Jim Crow. . . .

Randolph demanded, among other things, "the abrogation of
every law which makes a distinction in treatment between
citizens based on religion, creed, color, or national origin."[43]
President Franklin D. Roosevelt, fearing that the march
would produce ill consequences, conferred with Randolph
and decided to issue an executive order "with teeth in it"
prohibiting discrimination in employment in defense industries and in the government. Accordingly, on June 25, 1941,
Roosevelt issued Executive Order 8-802, which said that
"there shall be no discrimination in the employment of workers in defense industries or Government because of [in now
familiar language] race, creed, color, or national origin."[44]
Clauses prohibiting discrimination were consequently put in
all defense contracts, and a Committee on Fair Employment

Practices was organized to investigate complaints of discrimination.

The executive order by Roosevelt offers a chance to consider the nature of the attitudes held by presidents toward the idea that race is morally irrelevant. Whereas most presidents before Roosevelt had given, at best, lip service to the idea of moral equality, Roosevelt took action and so did Truman. Truman, even more outspoken on civil rights than Roosevelt, attended the annual conference of the NAACP in 1947. Delivering an address from the Lincoln Memorial, he said that the "immediate task is to remove the last remnants of the barriers which stand between millions of our citizens and their birthright" and that "there is no justifiable reason for discrimination because of ancestry, or religion, or race, or color." The national government, he said, "must show the way."[45] Within a year's time Truman would find himself issuing an executive order that indeed would "show the way."

The NAACP, exasperated by the new wave of lynching, race riots, and racial discrimination that occurred right after the war, pleaded with Truman for forthright and effective executive action on behalf of Negroes. Truman acted quickly, his executive order establishing the President's Committee on Civil Rights. The committee investigated the status of civil rights and submitted a report, complete with recommendations, to Truman. That report, *To Secure These Rights*, published in 1947, set the agenda, in effect, for the legislative action on civil rights that would take place in the 1950s and 1960s. It was the most significant statement of equality from a government body or public official since Harlan's dissent in *Plessy* in 1896.

COUNTING BY RACE

The report began by noting that "twice before in American history the nation has found it necessary to review the state of its civil rights." These two times were the fifteen years between 1776 and 1791, when the country was being founded, and the years in the late 1850s and early 1860s, when the "union was temporarily sundered over the question of whether it could exist 'half-slave' and 'half-free.'" Now, said the document, "we have come to the time for a third reexamination of the situation." One reason for this "third reexamination" was ethical: "We have considered the American heritage of freedom at some lengths. We need no further justification for a broad and immediate program than the need to reaffirm our faith in the *traditional American morality*."[46] (Emphasis added.) The document thus correctly comprehended the problem of civil rights as a matter of moral principle. It went on:

The pervasive gap between our aims and what we actually do is creating a kind of moral dry rot which eats away at the emotional and rational bases of democratic beliefs. There are times when the difference between what we preach about civil rights and what we practice is shockingly illustrated by individual outrages. There are times when the whole structure of our ideology is made ridiculous by individual instances. And there are certain continuing, quiet, omnipresent practices which do irreparable damage to our beliefs.[47]

The report cited as examples of "moral erosion" the consequences of the suffrage limitations in the South. Also cited was the wartime segregation of the armed forces. White officers and enlisted men saw Negroes "performing only the most menial functions" in the services. Whites saw Negroes recruited for the common defense "treated as men apart and distinct from themselves." Consequently, "men who might otherwise have maintained the equalitarian morality of their forebears were given reason to look down on their fellow citizens."[48]

In 1954 it was clear that both the judiciary and the executive branch of the federal government had taken action to obliterate the race line, to turn back Jim Crow. What was left was for the federal legislature to act; still needed were laws to secure the idea of moral equality.

It is not surprising that the legislature was the last of the three branches to act. Congress, after all, is the branch of government most intimately related to the people, and in consequence it generally must act more slowly than do the judiciary and the executive office. Yet, by the middle 1950s, it was apparent that the people of the United States, except in scattered pockets of resistance across the South, had undergone a great additudinal shift since the turn of the century.[49] And no doubt the civil rights movement, led by Martin Luther King, Jr., had much to do with this shift and with the consequent passage of four civil rights bills between 1957 and 1965.

Much has been written about the decade from 1954 to 1964 and the emergence of the civil rights movement. But what is most pertinent to observe is the unrelenting attack the movement made against Jim Crow and the idea that Jim Crow, at root, represented: namely, that race makes a difference in the assessment of character or qualification. Here the speech by Martin Luther King, Jr.,—the "I Have a Dream" speech—made during the March on Washington in 1963 and President John F. Kennedy's response to the march are instructive. King said that "we've come to our Nation's capital to cash a check"—the check written by the framers of the Declaration and the authors of the Constitution to the effect that "all men, yes, black men as well as white men, should be guaranteed the inalienable rights of life, liberty, and the pursuit of happiness." "I still have a dream," King said.

It is a dream deeply rooted in the American dream. I have a dream that one day this nation will rise up and live out the true meaning of its creed: 'We hold these truths to be self-evident, that all men are created equal'.... I have a dream that my four little children will one day live in a nation where they will not be judged by the color of their skin but by the content of their character.[50]

In response, Kennedy said:

Efforts to secure equal treatment and equal opportunity for all without *regard* to race, color, creed, or nationality are neither novel nor difficult to understand. What is different today is the intensified and widespread public awareness of the need to move forward in achieving these objectives—which are older than this Nation.... The executive branch of the Federal Government will continue its efforts to obtain increased employment and to eliminate discrimination in employment practices.[51] [Emphasis added.]

In his "Birmingham" letter, King wrote that "all segregation statutes are unjust because segregation distorts the soul and damages the personality.... Segregation is not only politically, economically, and sociologically unsound, but it is morally wrong and sinful."[52]

On June 11, 1963, Kennedy expressed his views on the problems of civil rights. The occasion was the defiance of the state of Alabama, which had denied blacks admission to the University of Alabama. Kennedy appealed to the tradition of moral equality by noting that the nation was founded on the "principle that all men are created equal," and invoked Lincolnian language by saying that the "rights of every one are diminished when the rights of one man are threatened." In a great statement fully consistent with the idea of moral equality, Kennedy said:

It ought to be possible ... for every American to enjoy the privileges of being American without regard to his race or his color. In short, every American ought to have the right to be treated as he would wish to be treated, as one would wish his children to be treated.[53]

This, though, was not the case, so America was "confronted primarily with a moral issue." "We preach freedom," Kennedy said, "and we mean it," but here in America Negroes are "second-class citizens." Kennedy proposed that in one week he would ask Congress to act—"to make a commitment it has not fully made in this century *to the proposition that race has no place in American life or law.*" (Emphasis added.) "The federal judiciary has upheld that proposition," Kennedy noted, and so had the executive branch, but it was left to Congress to act.

I am, therefore, asking the Congress to enact legislation giving all Americans the right to be served in the facilities which are open to the public, hotels, restaurants, theaters, retail stores, and similar establishments.[54]

Civil rights legislation had been passed in 1957 and again in 1960 primarily to secure the right to vote, but with the Civil Rights Act of 1964, a great milestone was reached. The idea animating the legislation was, as Kennedy said in his speech, that "equality of treatment which we would want ourselves; to give a chance for every child to be educated to the limits of his talents." While eschewing the notion that "every child has an equal talent or an equal ability or an equal motivation," Kennedy endorsed the notion that each child "should have the equal right to develop [his] talent and ability and motivation, to make something of [himself]." "We have a right to expect that the Negro community will be responsible, will uphold the law, but they have a right to expect that the law will be fair, that the Constitution will be color blind," Kennedy said, echoing Justice Harlan.[55]

113

COUNTING BY RACE

As University of Texas law professor Lino Graglia has pointed out, the Civil Rights Act of 1964 provided that the prohibition announced in *Brown* would become government policy.[56] The act was concerned with the right to vote, with access to places of public accommodation, with the desegregation of public facilities, and public education, with the expansion of the powers of the Commission on Civil Rights, with nondiscrimination in federally assisted programs, and with equal employment opportunity. Nathan Glazer has noted that throughout the legislation were placed the "sonorous phrases" of the nondiscrimination principle: "no discrimination or segregation 'on the ground of race, color, religion, or national origin' (Titles II and VI), 'on account of . . . race, color, religion, or national origin' (Title III), 'by reason of race, color, religion, or national origin' (Title IV), 'because of . . . color, religion, sex, or national origin' (Title VII).[57]

After passage of the Civil Rights Act of 1964 came two more important pieces of legislation: the Voting Rights Act of 1965 and the Immigration Act of 1965. The former, in conjunction with previous legislation on voting rights, virtually secured the right of suffrage for blacks. And the latter, as Glazer has pointed out, "marked the disappearance from Federal law of crucial distinctions on the basis of race and national origin."[58] One will recall that *Plessy* v. *Ferguson,* which encouraged the institution of Jim Crow by giving it legal sanction, was followed by tighter restrictions on immigration; so it was fitting that the Civil Rights Act of 1964, the final blow to Jim Crow, was followed by a liberalizing immigration act.

With the Declaration of Independence, the idea of moral equality appeared in its first form, in the proposition that because all men are created equal, no man can be the slave of

another. Lincoln contended for this proposition in his debates
with Stephen A. Douglas, and yet Lincoln went further: He
argued that the principle of equality lies at the very foundation of self-government. Neither Douglas's principle of popular sovereignty nor the sovereignty of the states, nor any diffusionist principle, could take precedence over the principle
of equality, according to Lincoln. The Thirteenth Amendment withdrew from the states their authority in regard to
slavery; it effectively federalized Lincoln's argument that
"there can be no moral right in connection with one man's
making a slave." The Fourteenth Amendment affirmed that
blacks were citizens, and Justice Harlan, arguing from the
concept of citizenship (as well as from the Thirteenth
Amendment) contended, in effect, that there can be no moral
right in connection with one man's discriminating against another on account of race. Harlan, developing Lincoln's
thought, recognized that not until the individual states ceased
to have sovereignty in the matter of civil rights could racial
discrimination finally be condemned, could a man be ensured
that he would be given his due, in every respect, as a man.

By the close of the nineteenth century, the need to federal-
ize the corollaries drawn from the proposition that no man
should be the slave of another was evident. As the twentieth
century grew past middle age precisely this federalizing occurred, attended by the ultimate conversion of the people of
the United States to the idea that color is irrelevant in the
consideration of a man's worth. Because these two things
happened, one may speak of the tradition of moral equality,
dating from the Declaration of Independence, as the American tradition. And it was this tradition that Allan Bakke
clearly affirmed in his suit against the University of California.

Chapter 7

Special Measures
Are Necessary
The Rise of Numerical Equality

IN *Sweatt* v. *Painter,* decided in 1950, 187 of the nation's
most distinguished law professors filed an *amicus curiae* brief
in which they argued the position Justice Harlan had maintained in dissent in *Plessy* v. *Ferguson,* namely, that the Constitution is color-blind. "Laws which give equal protection
are those which make no *discrimination* because of race in
the sense that they make no *distinction* because of race," said
the brief. "As soon as laws make a right or responsibility dependent solely on race, they violate the Fourteenth Amendment. Reasonable classifications may be made, but one basis
of classification is completely precluded; for the Equal Protection Clause makes racial classifications unreasonable *per
se.*"[1] Twenty-seven years later, in *The Regents of the University of California* v. *Bakke,* the nation's legal teaching fra-
ternity contradicted the position taken in *Sweatt. Amicus*
briefs filed by the Society of American Law Teachers and by
the American Association of Law Schools supported the contention that classification based on race is *not* unreasonable

per se under the Equal Protection Clause. The striking contrast in these two positions suggests that more than simply the Constitution decides matters of constitutional law, for obviously the Constitution, in particular the Equal Protection Clause of the Fourteenth Amendment, did not change during this span of years.

What did occur, however, primarily among leaders of minority groups and among the nation's elites, was a dramatic change in perspective regarding the nature and meaning of equality. The 187 law professors who had filed the *amicus* brief in *Sweatt* called themselves the Committee of Law Teachers Against Segregation; their concern—the concern of the NAACP in *Brown*—was the color line: Erase that and segregation would be gone. Racial discrimination likewise concerned the civil rights movement and its allies during the balance of the 1950s. But in the early 1960s, even as Americans were culminating a long and historic drive to have accepted into law and life the idea of moral equality, new attitudes concerning race and integration and the American dream were faintly perceptible. And, by the late 1960s, these attitudes could be clearly brought into focus.

The opposite of segregation is desegregation, so naturally and quite rightly the leaders of the civil rights movement had wished from its beginning to see American society desegregated, with the races intermingling or integrating. And many Americans proved sympathetic with this idea. The early and middle 1960s witnessed a number of actions taken to ensure the possibilities of this kind of integration, to ensure the possibilities of equal employment and equal opportunity: Antidiscrimination notices were posted at places of business and in newspapers; recruiting nets were cast into previously neglected areas. Even so, one could hear, at this time, the suggestions that integration defined as the intermingling of the races was inadequate, that merely ensuring the possibilities of equal employment and equal opportunity were not enough. A different idea of integration began to arise—that requiring racial balance or racial representation in every area of American life. Toward the end of the 1960s this became the dominant view of integration held by not only many black leaders but also many leaders of a number of other minority groups, most notably Chicanos, American Indians, and Asian-Americans. And with this new idea of integration came a new idea of equal opportunity—that requiring equal results, as defined by the advances not of individuals but of the racial and ethnic groups to which they belong.

For integration as racial balance to occur, for equal opportunity defined as equal results to be realized, public officials and indeed members of the private sector began to be called upon to depart, in effect, from the proposition central to the idea of moral equality, namely, that race is a moral irrelevance; they now were called upon to note the race (generically speaking) of members of minority groups, not, to be sure, for the purpose of discriminating against them, but in order to help them, to give them a "special boost" or "preferential treatment" in the competition for society's rewards and benefits. When justification for this action was asked for, it lay, for most supporters of this extra help for blacks, in the oppression that race had endured for more than three centuries, in slavery and segregation; now was the time, many argued, to compensate for the historic wrongs against the group. Other minority groups had similar, if less oppressive, histories to adduce as justification for the special treatment due them. And the measure for whether satisfactory compensation was being made a particular group began to be conceived as numerical: Comparisons began to be drawn between the percentage of blacks and other minorities in a given occupation and their percentage relative to the total population; terms such as "underrepresentation" and "underutilization" began to appear.

These, then, were the new attitudes clearly observable in the late 1960s, and they amounted to nothing less than a new expression of the idea of equality: the idea of numerical equality. By the end of the 1960s this idea of equality had become, if only implicitly, government policy. It had also become, again if only implicitly, the policy in the admissions departments of many of the nation's universities and professional schools. And, too, it had become the implicit policy in the boardrooms of many American foundations, large and small.

In the *Bakke* case, the new idea of numerical equality was laid on the table for all to see for the first time; the idea necessarily came to be explicitly defended. And that is why, in the *amicus* briefs by the Society of American Law Teachers and the Association of American Law Schools filed in *Bakke*, a case is made on constitutional grounds for the proposition central to the idea of numerical equality—namely, that an individual's race is a relevant consideration in the allocation of benefits and rewards and in the achievement of opportunity. It is remarkable enough that in such a short span of time the elites in American society should have so changed their minds on such fundamental matters as race and equality; it is yet more remarkable that this should have happened when one considers that the nation only recently had accepted the idea of moral equality. What is needed to understand this reversal of opinion is an account of the origins and development of the new idea of numerical equality that emerged in the 1960s, an idea unthinkable at the time of *Sweatt* but that had become almost passé by the time of *Bakke*. Interestingly, this account begins in 1954 with *Brown* v. *Board of Education*.[2]

This case was widely understood as obliterating the color line in public education and as, more generally, condemning the proposition central to segregation—that the color of a man's skin is relevant to a consideration of his worth. Yet it is clear that despite this understanding of the case, the Court in *Brown* did not explain just why segregation is wrong, thereby losing a historic opportunity to do so. The pertinent distinction is between the Court's decision and the justification for its decision; as we shall see, the justification involved the Court's failure to center its argument in the very principle that the decision was everywhere interpreted as affirming—that distinctions based on race are invidious and unconstitutional.

As discussed in chapter 6, the separate-but-equal doctrine emerged in 1896 in *Plessy* v. *Ferguson*. When seriously applied to education the doctrine meant that the segregation of students by race into different schools was constitutionally permissible so long as the separate schools could be regarded as "equal." In a series of decisions affecting higher education, beginning with *Gaines* v. *Canada* in 1938, the Court asked whether separate schools for blacks were in fact "equal" to those established schools that whites exclusively attended. It had become apparent by the late 1940s that the Court might receive a case in which the black and white schools were "equal," and this is what happened in *Brown*. Delivering the unanimous opinion of the Court, Chief Justice Earl Warren noted that the lower courts had found the black and white schools in question to have been "equalized" or in the process of being "equalized, with respect to buildings, curricula, qualifications and salaries of teachers, and other 'tangible' factors."[3] The question of the equality of the schools ceasing to matter, Warren thus had before him only the matter of segregation. Here was a great opportunity to cite the Declaration of Independence or Lincoln or Harlan; here was a great opportunity to affirm that the concept of segregation was incompatible with the idea of moral equality, that segregation by race denies a man his due as a moral agent.[4] But, as it happened, Warren did not quite say this, though he has been widely thought to have done so.[5]

Finished with the question of the equality of the schools, Warren said that the Court must decide *Brown* by considering "the *effect* of segregation itself on public education" (emphasis added). The effect of segregation on minority children, he said, was "a feeling of inferiority as to their status in the community"—a feeling "that may affect their hearts and minds in a way unlikely ever to be undone." The lower court in Kansas had said as much when it found that "a sense of inferiority," the product of segregation, had affected the motivation of black schoolchildren to learn, thus retarding their educational and mental development and depriving them of some of the benefits available in a racially integrated school system. Furthermore, the lower court in the Delaware case had also said as much when it found that segregation results in the availability of inferior educational opportunities for black schoolchildren.[6]

By this point it was clear that Warren was indeed considering the "effect" of segregation, not the concept itself, and that in considering that effect, his inquiry was necessarily concerned with the psychological and educational condition of black schoolchildren. "Whatever may have been the extent of psychological knowledge at the time of *Plessy* v. *Ferguson*," said Warren, in reference to the decision by Justice Brown and conceivably in an effort to make *Brown* appear consistent with the previous cases, "is amply supported by modern authority." Here came famous footnote 11, in which Warren cited, as his modern authorities, six reference works in psychology.[7] With this Warren was done. "We conclude," he wrote, "that in the field of public education the doctrine of 'separate but equal' has no place. Separate educational facilities are inherently unequal."[8] And they are, Warren added, unconstitutional, because they violate the equal protection clause of the Fourteenth Amendment.

Brown has been justly hailed as a great decision. It was a decision, as we have seen, consistent with the idea of moral equality. And unquestionably the purpose of the Supreme Court in *Brown* was to reject, for the first time, the proposition central to Jim Crow—that the color of a man's skin is morally important. For in subsequent *per curiam* decisions the Court, having erased the color line in public education, proceeded to do so elsewhere—in such areas as public beaches and bathhouses (*Mayor of Baltimore* v. *Dawson*); municipal golf courses (*Holmes* v. *City of Atlanta*); and buses (*Gayle* v. *Browder*). Lower courts, taking their cue from the Supreme Court, proceeded on the same course, citing *Brown* as justification. Those seeking to find a rationale broader than the one given in *Brown*, a rationale that could explain the obliteration of the color line in all public facilities, did so by reference to the color-blind principle.[9] So it was that although the intention of the decision in *Brown* was broad, the language was limited. It is one of the ironies in the story of equality in American history that the Declaration of Independence contained far broader language—indeed it contained the very idea of moral equality—and yet it had a purpose much more limited than that of *Brown*—of asserting the rights of Americans as Englishmen.

Brown, as important as it is to the story of the idea of moral equality, is also important to the story of the idea of numerical equality.[10] By failing to center its justification in the idea of moral equality, the Court retained a flexibility that enabled it to move from the position of *Brown,* whereby no student may be assigned to a school because of race, to the position of *Green* v. *County School Board of New Kent County,* fourteen years later, whereby students may indeed be assigned to school solely because of race. In thus certifying the relevance of race in public policy, the Court provided judicial support for the racial and ethnic consciousness that, as we shall later see, then was arising in many quarters of American life. Also, although *Brown* correctly can be regarded as causing the downfall of the institution of segregation, it cannot be regarded as decisively countering the idea that individuals should be thought of as members of certain racial groups. At best the Court hedged, at worst it reinforced, the long-standing habit of thinking of blacks as members of a group and not as individuals. This last point requires explanation.

In 1954, when the Court rendered its verdict in *Brown,* it found the question of relief to the plaintiffs sufficiently difficult to require further argument the following year. But in 1955 the Court could come to no conclusion on the question of relief and remanded the issue, with very little guidance, to the district courts. Of course, *Brown* affected not just the school districts in question but school districts all across the country, and obviously an order for immediate implementation of *Brown* throughout the country would have been counterproductive. As Alexander Bickel has discussed, a decision of such magnitude and representing such a radical departure from two hundred years of practice would need the cooperation of the other two political branches and some large measure of support from local authorities; time, clearly, was needed.[11] Yet it is possible to distinguish the actual plaintiffs in *Brown* from the affected class of schoolchildren the country over; and in doing so one finds that the Court did virtually nothing for the actual plaintiffs. This relative inaction suggests that the Court did not fully regard them as individuals; it suggests that the Court viewed them as individuals submerged within their racial group and perhaps of secondary importance to the group itself.

Professor Louis Lusky has commented that one of the subtler manifestations of regarding black individuals as members of a racial group is "that Negroes (unlike whites) possess rights as a race rather than as individuals, so that a particular Negro can rightly be delayed in the enjoyment of his established rights if progress is being made in improving the legal status of Negroes generally." It is hard, says Lusky:

to avoid the conclusion that this premise infects the so-called deliberate speed formula . . . The Court had determined to deal with the problem as involving the rights of the Negro race rather than the rights of individuals. Citing the traditional power of courts of equity to shape remedies so as to reconcile public and private needs, the Court applied that power in a way that is believed to be unprecedented. It left open the possibility that the plaintiffs themselves would be denied any relief from the legal wrong they were found to have suffered, if only steps were taken to protect other Negroes—at some later date—from similar harm.[12]

The argument has force that had the Court operated from the premise of moral equality, it would have immediately given each plaintiff his due as a person—it would have ordered that none of the school assignments of the plaintiffs be based on race. It would have done this as surely as it would have said the dual system of schools was unconstitutional, without having to assess the "effects" of segregation. And yet what the successful plaintiff in *Brown* actually got from the Supreme Court, as Lusky has said, was "no more than a promise that, some time in the indefinite future, other people would be given the rights which the Court said he had."[13]

In neither 1954 nor 1955 in its actions regarding the plaintiffs in *Brown* did the Supreme Court do what could be interpreted as asserting that individuals should be thought as individuals. Certainly there were decisions after *Brown,* both by the Supreme Court and lower courts, to the effect that individuals should be thought of as individuals. But this does not diminish the point that neither *Brown* nor *Brown* on remand denied that individuals should be considered solely by reference to their membership in a racial group. And by 1964, the end of the decade following *Brown,* there would be apparent an increasing tendency to think in terms of racial and ethnic groups, a tendency not yet observable in many judicial decisions but clearly apparent in the culture at large, in the assertions of black and other minority leaders.

One must be careful to note that this tendency appeared at the end of the decade following *Brown,* for the evidence is abundant that for a while the nation acted in ways consistent with the prohibition of *Brown,* consistent with the idea of moral equality. Spurred by the decision in *Brown,* the civil rights movement took a more activist turn in battling against those—mainly in the South—who insisted on maintaining walls of racial segregation. Such acts of courage as that of Mrs. Rosa Parks, when she resisted efforts to force her to the back of a public bus one evening in 1955, were performed in outrage at the fact of racial discrimination; so were the sit-ins, first accomplished in 1960 in Greensboro, North Carolina, at the downtown Woolworth's. Furthermore, as for the public schools, it became clear by 1962 that one of the evasive tactics employed in the southern states—the use of pupil placement plans that, while purporting to assign students by nonracial means, actually assigned them by race—could not stand. And in 1963, in *Goss* v. *Board of Education of Knoxville, Tennessee*, the Supreme Court, reiterating that *Brown* had held racial classifications to be invalid, ruled that a transfer plan based upon race was no less unconstitutional than the use of race in original school assignments. Finally, in this decade, there were numerous efforts—not based on race—to help bring blacks into the so-called mainstream of American life. The phrase "affirmative action," which, in a general sense, means the taking of steps to ensure that past practices of racial discrimination have no future, discriminatory effects, appeared first in the counsels of the Eisenhower administration and then in an executive order issued by President Kennedy in 1961.[14] The specific ways affirmative action might be taken in accordance with the Kennedy order were understood as race-neutral. Old-boy networks would be dispensed with and employment searches would be conducted everywhere, to find the best person qualified, regardless of race. Training in certain skills would be offered, and employment tests would be scrutinized to rid them of any bias against minorities. Transfer, layoff, and demotion practices would be cleansed of any racial discrimination. While all of this came at the government's behest, outside of government private institutions voluntarily began to reshape their policies by taking racially neutral affirmative action steps.

But in the early 1960s there were signs of the change in attitude that would be dramatically evident by the end of that decade. School boards did not assign pupils by race to their schools and yet, while such a policy seemed to satisfy the prohibition in *Brown,* it ceased to satisfy a number of black leaders. G. W. Foster, a journalist writing in the April 20, 1963, issue of *Saturday Review,* reported a shift in the strategies of black leaders in the North as they decided to make an issue of *de facto* school segregation.[15] In Philadelphia, for example, he noted that the position of the school board was, consistent with *Brown,* that no student would be assigned to a school because of his race. But an attorney representing a group of blacks who were taking judicial action against the board argued that this policy was "not enough." "The board," he said, "cannot be color-blind. It is the affirmative responsibility of the board to work toward integration. Every choice which may arise in making decisions about school matters must be made in such a way as to accomplish results leading to the integration goal."[16]

By the term *integration* something other than desegregation was obviously meant. Harvard professor Oscar Handlin, looking back from the perspective of 1966, observed that black leaders, increasingly since 1961, had become concerned with an integration defined in terms of "racial balance"—in the racial representation of blacks in every sector of life.[17]

The idea of achieving a racial balance emerged in other areas besides the public schools. Many had believed that with the barriers to full participation in American life removed, blacks would quickly climb the socioeconomic ladder by virtue of their own qualifications and abilities; an integration defined in terms of racial balance would result of its own accord. Yet when it became apparent that this was not happening very quickly, a number of black leaders sought to redefine their goals in terms of the number of blacks actually employed.

The concern for racial balance or representation, whether

in the context of public schools or employment, entailed a focus on the group by reference to race. And, in the area of employment, it entailed a redefinition of the idea of equal opportunity, the conditions for which had previously been thought to have been satisfied when employers followed the nondiscrimination principle of *Brown* and took racially neutral affirmative-action steps. The new definition of equal opportunity involved the idea of moral compensation. In 1964 Whitney Young, then executive director of the National Urban League, wrote that "our basic definition of equal opportunity must include recognition of the need for special efforts to overcome serious disabilities resulting from historic handicaps."[18] Author Charles Silberman, two years earlier, had expanded on the historical origins of those "serious disabilities" and pointed out where the consequent responsibilities lie. The present problems of blacks, he said, are rooted in slavery and the Negro's "systematic exclusion from American society since slavery ended a century ago. . . . These are sins for which all Americans are in some measure guilty and for which all Americans owe some act of atonement."[19]

The idea of moral compensation was not altogether new. It had appeared in 1865 as partial justification for the creation of the Freedmen's Bureau, an agency which, though short-lived, assisted blacks as they left slavery behind and undertook their new pilgrimage as American citizens.[20] Slavery was the admitted evil for which the freedmen were said to deserve this special treatment, but now, a century later, black leaders and others could—and did—point not only to slavery as the justification for moral compensation, but also to the treatment of blacks since slavery, to the promises of equality made during Reconstruction and their subsequent frustration, to the many decades in which the color line had been unfailingly and reprehensibly drawn.

The atonement Silberman had in mind entailed more than an end to discrimination against blacks and the use of race-neutral methods of hiring. It entailed nothing less than the hiring of blacks, and in substantial numbers. "As soon as we agree that special measures are necessary to overcome the heritage of past discrimination," wrote Silberman, "the question of numbers of *how many* Negroes are to be hired in what job categories inevitably arises. Not to use numbers as a yardstick for measuring performance is, in effect, to revert to 'tokenism.' "[21] In retrospect it is apparent that Silberman and not, say, Whitney Young, augured the future. Young, like Silberman, asserted the necessity of compensating blacks for the previous injustices visited upon their race, but the degree of preferential treatment he advocated—"if a business has never hired Negroes in its offices or plants and two equally qualified people apply [one white, presumably, and one black], it should hire the Negro"[22]—would not prove sufficient to satisfy black leaders or the government or white elites as the decade progressed. Silberman's thinking, rather, would prove to be a model for the future not only in the context of employment but also for university and professional school admissions. And while, in 1964, he did not talk of "quotas" or "goals" or "targets," his advocacy of numbers was congruent with each of these devices, which would be used widely by the early 1970s in both the private and public sectors as the idea of numerical equality, faintly apparent in the early 1960s, now became clearly visible and increasingly influential.

The voting rights legislation having been passed by Congress, President Lyndon B. Johnson gave, in 1965, his famous commencement speech at Howard University. Here Johnson said it was not enough to give blacks freedom and "legal equity" and "equality as a right"; rather, it was now compelling that blacks have "equality as a fact" and "equality as a result." Paul Seabury, professor of political science at the University of California at Berkeley, has remarked that President Johnson was probably not mindful of the implications of his words and of the contradiction they could pose for the Civil Rights Act of 1964.[23] That legislation had specified in Title VII* that no employer would be required to hire on the basis of race in order to correct some racial imbalance in the work force—a stipulation that would seem to bar efforts to achieve an equality of "fact" or "result." The following conversation during debate on the legislation between Senator Hubert Humphrey and Senator George Smathers may be regarded as certifying the intent of Congress on this matter.

Mr. Humphrey: [T] he Senator from Florida is so convincing that when he speaks, as he does, with the ring of sincerity in his voice and heart, and says that an employee should be hired on the basis of ability—
Mr. Smathers: Correct.
Mr. Humphrey: And that an employer should not be denied the right to hire on the basis of ability and should not take into consideration race—how right the Senator is . . .
But the trouble is that these idealistic pleadings are not followed by some sinful mortals. There are some who do not hire solely on the basis of ability. Doors are closed; positions are closed; unions are closed to people of color. That situation does not help America
. . .
I know that the Senator from Florida desires to help American industry and enterprise. We ought to adopt the Smathers doctrine, which is contained in Title VII. I never realized that I would hear

*Title VII, section 703 (j) says: "Nothing contained in this title shall be interpreted to require any employer . . . to grant preferential treatment to any individual or to any group because of the race, color, religion, sex, or national origin of such individual or group on account of an imbalance which may exist with respect to the total number or percentage of persons of any race, color, religion, sex, or national origin employed by any employer."

such an appropriate description of the philosophy behind Title VII as I have heard today.

Mr. Smathers: Mr. President, the Senator from Minnesota has expressed my doctrine completely.[24]

In 1965 President Johnson issued, pursuant to the Civil Rights Act of 1964, Executive Order 11246. In 1967, in Executive Order 11375, he amended the previous order to include "sex" as one of the prohibited reasons for treatment. Together, the two orders provided:

> The contractor will not discriminate against any employee or applicant for employment because of race, color, religion, sex, or national origin. The contractor will take affirmative action to ensure that applicants are employed, and that employees are treated during employment, without regard to their race, color, religion, sex, or national origin.

With this President Johnson seemed clearly to position himself in the "description of philosophy behind Title VII" Humphrey had referred to, but as the 1960s wore on, as the authority for enforcement of Johnson's executive orders passed to the Department of Labor, a concern for the very equality of "fact" and "result" that the President perhaps unwittingly had spoken of at Howard became evident.

In 1967, the Department of Labor issued regulations pursuant to Johnson's executive orders. "An affirmative-action program," said the regulations,

> is a set of specific and result-oriented procedures to which a contractor commits himself to apply every good faith effort. The objective of these procedures plus such efforts is equal employment opportunity. Procedures without effort to make them work are meaningless; and effort, undirected at specific and meaningful procedures, is inadequate. An acceptable affirmative-action program must include an analysis of areas within which the contractor is deficient in the utilization of minority groups and women, and fur-

ther, goals and timetables to which the contractors good faith efforts must be directed to correct the deficiencies and thus, to increase materially the utilization of minorities and women, at all levels and in all segments of his work force where deficiencies exist.[25]

This directive would prove to mark a change in government policy, for if the government would continue to pay lip service to the idea of moral equality, it would implicitly operate from the premise of numerical equality. The moral concern of Title VII and Executive Order 11246 would now be enforced through sociological method. One now would have to analyze a work force in order to correct "deficiencies" and to improve "utilization." Too, the concern would be for minority groups, not blacks only, and here lies a story.

By the late 1950s, as Orlando Patterson, Harvard professor of sociology, has pointed out, ethnicity had become "if not a dirty word, something to be shunned publicly by all except politicians (who were expected to be gross), a minor national vice to be indulged behind ghetto walls and discreetly defined neighborhoods." But in the early 1960s, as black leaders began to press for racial balance and representation—a goal necessitating that attention be paid to the group and to the color of the group—the politics of ethnicity began, as Patterson has said, to be "relegitimized."[26] Leaders of Chicanos, Asian-Americans, and American Indians stepped forward to press their claims in racial and ethnic terms. And, as Nathan Glazer has pointed out, as these groups "came onto the horizon of public attention, still others which had not been known previously for their self-consciousness or organization in raising forceful demands and drawing attention to their situation entered the process."[27] Leaders of the various minority groups, following the example of their black counterparts, began to stress the disparities in employment, education, and other areas of life that existed between their particular group and the general population; and, too, they began to stress the patterns of discrimination and oppression their group had endured. Adducing histories of discrimination, and making political and economic claims in sociological language—on the basis of the group—became the order of the day. It is not surprising that in 1969 the U. S. Census, which had never before recorded ethnic origins, began to do so.

In 1969, the Department of Labor in its enforcement efforts of Johnson's executive orders instituted the Philadelphia Plan, by which construction contractors in that city were required to hire minorities in accordance with numerical goals. This was, as Laurence Silberman, then serving in the Labor Department, has described it, the department's "maiden voyage" in its efforts to expand employment opportunities for minorities. The department had made sure that there had been a history of specific discrimination against blacks, fearing that otherwise the plan would not stand up in court. The plan was legally challenged, but it survived, and soon the department began spreading "construction plans across the country like Johnny Appleseed." Manufacturers who "underutilized" minorities were to fashion numerical goals for minority hiring and to adopt timetables in which to meet them. Gradually, though, the department moved away from certain characteristics of the Philadelphia Plan. The department ceased to square affirmative-action plans on specific findings of discrimination against specified minority groups; the presumption, rather, was that the opportunities for all minorities today had been narrowed because of "200 years of American history."[28]

In testimony before Congress in 1971, Silberman said:

We and the compliance agencies put pressure on contractors to come up with commitments even though those contractors are not guilty of any discrimination, but because we think they are required under the Executive order to go beyond, to provide affirmative action. Since they are not guilty of discrimination, it is not exactly the kind of situation where you can go to an enforcement posture, but rather you say to that contractor, you have to make an extra effort beyond what the civil rights laws are in this country and go beyond that in order to get a Government contract.[29]

In consequence, employers who were justified in saying that the statistical imbalances in their work forces were not caused by discriminatory practices were nevertheless required either to devise an affirmative-action plan or face the sanction proceedings for noncompliance with government regulations. Because the sanctions for noncompliance are extremely harsh and litigation against the government very expensive, the usual course, the practical course, was the adoption of an affirmative-action plan. "We have so much clout over government contractors," Silberman said in his 1971 testimony, "that very few of them are willing to or want to fight that through litigation. They usually come into compliance."[30]

The way government contractors began to come into compliance was not merely by hiring *more* minority members but by hiring them in *proportion* to their representation in a given labor market. The Philadelphia Plan had as its object merely getting *more* blacks into the skilled construction trades because there had been very few. But most affirmative-action plans thereafter, according to Silberman, eventually were directed "towards proportionate minority representation."[31] As a result, firms contracting with the government began to count by race in their employment decisions in such a way that race and ethnicity necessarily became a decisive factor in hiring; race and ethnicity, serving the idea of numerical equality, began to override individual merit and ability.

Meanwhile, the same phenomenon began to occur in academe, in the area of faculty, administrative, and staff hiring. The Department of Health, Education, and Welfare (HEW), charged with enforcement of the labor department's regulations adopted pursuant to Johnson's executive orders, began, in 1971, to press those universities and colleges contracting with the federal government to adopt affirmative-action plans. As with those plans adopted by industries contracting with the government, the ones in academe were not triggered by findings of specific racial and ethnic discrimination. And like the ones in industry, the ones in academe adopted "goals" that resulted from considerations of "underutilization" and "deficiency." By the middle 1970s a university was required to determine the "available pools" of labor qualified for each job, from janitor and secretary to provost and professor; some of these labor pools would be local in nature (those for janitor and electrician, for example), some national (those for faculty positions). A university then would compare, by job category, the number of minorities in its work forces with their estimated "availability" according to the labor pool analyses. If, for example, Chicanos had earned, say, 4.5 percent of the doctorates in mathematics but a university had a mathematics faculty of which only 2 percent were Chicanos, then the university was "underutilizing" Chicanos and thus had a "deficiency." Accordingly, it would become necessary to adopt numerical goals to correct the deficiency; it would become necessary, in other words, to operate in accordance with the idea of numerical equality. In 1974, the Office of Civil Rights within HEW concluded an agreement with the University of California at Berkeley that was considered the model for all university affirmative-action programs; accordingly, a hundred faculty positions would be filled with women and members of minorities over the next thirty years. Because of the pressure to hire blacks and other minorities, many universities ceased to be coy about their needs. A prospective appointee for a sociology position at a university in Florida received a reply that included: "All unfilled positions in the University must be filled by blacks or females. Since I have no information regarding your racial identification, it will only be possible to consider you for a position in the event you are black."[32]

So it was, then, that by the middle 1970s, the idea of numerical equality, premised on generalized discrimination against minority groups but requiring no specific findings of discrimination against minority individuals and using as the measure for adequate affirmative action numerical and statistical goals, came to be, through the bureaucratic implementation of executive orders, government policy. We have described what occurred as a result of actions taken by the Departments of Labor and HEW. But by no means was the new government policy of numerical equality observable merely in these two bureaucracies. The Equal Employment Opportunity Commission (EEOC), created by the Civil Rights Act of 1964, and the Department of Justice both began to act, by the end of the 1960s, in ways consistent with the idea of numerical equality. And so did the federal courts, including the Supreme Court, most notably in the requirement, which can be seen in its 1968 decision in *Green* v. *County School Board of New Kent County,* that school assignments be made on the basis of race.[33] The works of the EEOC, the Department of Justice, and the Supreme Court, particularly in the area of busing, are rich mines for additional examples of the government's implicit policy by which equality is to be comprehended in numerical terms. We have adduced the history of the bureaucratic implementation of

Johnson's executive orders because it well illustrates the gradual change in the idea of affirmative action and the meaning of equality that occurred since, and even as, the Civil Rights Act of 1964 was passed.

The change that occurred in government policy was paralleled in the private sector, to some degree in the hiring decisions of private employers, but mainly in the actions of admissions committees of universities, colleges, and professional schools. Just as desegregation of the schools did not result in their widespread integration and just as the elimination of the discriminatory barriers to employment did not result in any great ascension of blacks and other minorities up the economic and social ladders, the elimination of discriminatory policies did not result in the admission of large numbers of minority applicants to universities. Starting in the late 1960s, universities began voluntarily, often out of a sympathy for the educational state of minorities, to adopt admissions policies weighted in favor of minority applicants. For the most part, explicit quotas such as were used at the University of California at Davis Medical School were not adopted. But the effect of the policies were by and large the same as if quotas had been used: Large numbers of minorities were admitted in spite of their qualifications and because of their race; nonminorities who would have been admitted had conventional admission policies reigned were not admitted. At the undergraduate level the impact of such policies was not so great as at the graduate and professional level: For at the latter, it was clear that opportunity was being more obviously allocated, that it was being decided who would become a lawyer, a doctor, a dentist, and who would not.

In *Bakke* the relatively new idea of numerical equality was on trial. Or, to put the matter another way, in *Bakke* the Supreme Court was asked to ratify the idea of numerical equality. The Court was asked to approve the changes that had occurred in the practice of affirmative action, to approve the use of racial and ethnic quotas, and thus to give government and private organizations a clear signal that now they might move ahead, explicitly, without fear of judicial interference.

Some thirty-five briefs were filed as friends of the court on the side of the University of California. And in these briefs one could find abundant evidence of the influence of the idea of numerical equality. One could read, for example, about the racial discrimination and exclusion from the "mainstream" that has, for the most part, been the experience of blacks.[34] One could read as well about the discrimination and similar exclusion that has been the lot of American Indians, Puerto Ricans in America, Mexican-Americans, and Asian-Americans.[35] One could study, even in statistical charts and displays, the disparities in terms of professional, educational, and economic achievement between these ethnic and racial groups and the general population.[36] One could read, too, about the necessity to maintain the admissions policies now so widespread in professional schools, because otherwise minorities would become even more "underrepresented."[37] One could read, furthermore, of the need to permit states or agents of the state "discretion" and "autonomy" in their efforts to bring minorities into the mainstream.[38] And common to all the briefs filed in *Bakke* on the side of the University of California was an adherence to the proposition central to the idea of numerical equality, the proposition the Committee of Law Teachers Against Segregation had sought to contradict just twenty-seven years earlier—namely, that the Equal Protection Clause of the Constitution permits, if it does not require, racial classifications.[39]

Chapter 8

Create in Him a Habit of Dependence

The Case Against Numerical Equality

BY the middle 1970s it was apparent that those who operated from the premise of numerical equality, whether in regard to university and professional school admissions, faculty and staff hiring in higher education, employment generally, housing, or the assignment of pupils or teachers in the public schools, fell into two groups. On the one hand, there were those who in counting by race thought they were working to bring about a day when race, except in untroubling instances*, finally would be irrelevant, when Americans would no longer have to consider each other on the basis of skin color and ancestry but could regard each other instead on the

---

*By "untroubling instances" we mean the obvious ones: those, for example, in which a doctor might examine a black patient for signs of sickle cell anemia, a disease most commonly found among blacks; in which an anthropologist might statistically analyze, by race, a given population; in which a journalist might count by race in certain neighborhoods of his city in order to assess school busing or to ascertain housing patterns; in which a social psychologist like Kenneth Clark might study the effects of school segregation on black or Asian-American schoolchildren; or in which an economist, as Thomas Sowell has done in *Race and Economics*, might study the differences race makes in economic transactions.

basis of ability and merit. For this group, numerical equality was a means to an end—the end of moral equality; accordingly, the current age was viewed as "transitional," one in which, as educator McGeorge Bundy said in an influential article on *Bakke* in the *Atlantic Monthly*, it is necessary to take race into account so that finally we may get beyond racism.[1] How long this transitional age might be, how long the United States might have to endure this "benign" period of race-consciousness, was unclear, estimates ranging from a few years to generations.[2] In any event, it was implicit in the position of those who regarded numerical equality as a means to the end of moral equality, who thought of the present as a "transitional society," that the idea of moral equality was a *worthy* ideal.

On the other hand, there was another group, undoubtedly smaller in number, which regarded numerical equality as an end in itself.* For this group, color-consciousness would have to be a permanent feature of American society; ensuring racial representation and balance would have to be a perpetual concern. Justice John Harlan, accordingly, was simply wrong when he said that no public official should take note of a man's race: The Constitution must not be "color-blind." For this group, the United States was not in any "transitional age"; rather, the nation had embarked on an altogether

---

*The distinction between those who regarded numerical equality as a means to the end of moral equality and those who considered numerical equality as an end in itself is literary. The purpose of this distinction is to confront the argument for numerical equality in what may be regarded as its strongest form—i.e., numerical equality as an end—and in its weakest form—i.e., numerical equality as a means—as well as any position in between.

As a matter of fact, those who believed in and spoke the language of numerical and proportional representation of minorities in the various walks of life did not always or even often identify themselves as supporters of either numerical equality as a means to moral equality or numerical equality as an end in itself. Of those who did identify themselves, an overwhelming majority thought American society was in transition, that it must now attend to race so that a superior age, in which race would not matter, would result.

new course, and the old path of moral equality was best forgotten.

In the *Bakke* case the two positions regarding numerical equality were evident in the legal briefs and in the popular opinion and literature supporting the University of California. So the merits of moral equality, on the one hand, and of numerical equality, whether as a means to moral equality or as an end in itself, on the other, were the gravamen of the case. The proponents of both views of numerical equality advanced more or less the same set of particular arguments in order to justify the Davis admission plan—arguments such as that the participation of men and women drawn from all racial and ethnic segments of society would improve medical education and the profession. But these particular arguments play different roles in the cases the two groups presented. They play the central role in the case presented by those regarding numerical equality as the means to moral equality, but only a supporting role in the case presented by those regarding numerical equality as an end in itself. Those viewing numerical equality as an end in itself, as the blueprint for the organizing of American society, argue fundamentally that color-consciousness ought to be a *permanent* characteristic of our polity, that we ought to guarantee racial representation and ethnic balance, *always*. The idea of numerical equality as an end in itself thus presents a most demanding challenge to the tradition of moral equality, and it ought to be considered first before one undertakes a detailed consideration of the particular arguments advanced to justify the admissions policy of counting by race.*

*Some of these arguments have, *mutatis mutandis,* been employed in other contexts—such as hiring, promotion policies, etc. But we consider the arguments *only* in relation to graduate and professional school admissions. While the historic debate between moral equality and numerical equality applies in these other contexts, we do not consider them here. It should be noted that principles, by themselves, do not decide specific cases. See also pp. 197–210, "*Weber* and After."

COUNTING BY RACE

The tradition of moral equality, which strained for acceptance into American society for two hundred years and which, as we have seen, finally did gain acceptance in the decade starting with *Brown* and culminating with the Civil Rights Act of 1964, holds that in the distribution of awards and benefits color is an irrelevance; that the claims of men, white and black, should be determined on the same basis; that, as Justice Stephen Johnson Field said long ago, "the theory upon which our political institutions rests is that all men have certain undeniable rights . . . and that in the pursuit of happiness all avocations, all honors, all positions are alike open to everyone, and that in the protection of these rights, all are equal before the law." Numerical equality, conceived as an end in itself, denies that tradition. Seeking ethnic balance and representation, it must hold that color shall determine the distribution of awards and benefits; that the claims of men should be determined on the basis of race; that, in contradiction of Justice Field, avocations, honors, and positions shall be more open to *some* than others on the basis of race, that before the law *some* shall be more equal than others. Numerical equality argues against Daniel Clark, who said that the law makes no distinction for or against any man and that every man is left to acquire "that position in society to which his abilities and behavior entitle him." Numerical equality says instead that abilities and behavior may be less important in the apportionment of awards than race. It says, against John Harlan, that the law shall indeed take account of color when individual rights are involved; and, against Richard Cain, that there should be legislation and policies that apply to blacks but do not also apply to whites. It says, against the NAACP, that democracy can and should draw the color line; and, against Martin Luther King, Jr., that we ought to have a nation where men will be judged by the color of their skin and not the content of their character. And of course numerical equality stands against the ideal expressed in the Civil Rights Act of 1964, that there shall be no discrimination on the ground of race. Those who hold to numerical equality believe, against James Otis, that "short hair like wool instead of Christian hair [will] help the argument."

Numerical equality thus challenges what can fairly be regarded as the traditional concept of equality, a concept that has been preeminent since the time of the Declaration of Independence in defining the promise of American institutions. Finally enshrined in the Civil Rights Acts of the 1950s and 1960s, this traditional concept—moral equality—holds that race is a moral irrelevance. While this ideal has been consistently denied in practice through most of American history, it is today, according to all the opinion polls, accepted by the majority of American people. An overwhelming number of Americans reject the notion that race should be a relevant consideration in the worth of an individual.[3] There is then, clearly, an argument for moral equality that is found in our history and traditions. But what is to be said to those who challenge history and tradition as sufficient ground for accepting the idea of moral equality? For, indeed, one can hear the proponents of numerical equality say that tradition and history are not self-validating, that lip-service or even adherence to a concept is not evidence of its worthiness. The argument from "history," after all, was adduced to justify slavery.

How do the proponents of numerical equality, putting aside the history and tradition of moral equality, argue for the superiority of distributing the honors and awards of society on the basis of race? They assume that in the absence of slavery and discrimination in American history blacks and other minorities would "naturally" be represented today in the various walks of life in something like the statistical patterns they now recommend.[4] They offer the vision of a society in which resources, rewards, and benefits are apportioned in accordance with the percentages of blacks, browns, yellows, reds, and whites in that society. They do so by arguing that while individual worth, merit, conduct, behavior, and character are important, these considerations are ultimately less important than membership in a group as defined by race or ethnicity; in such special admissions programs as the one at Davis, therefore, race must be the decisive consideration.

In subordinating merit, conduct, and character to race, moral considerations are subordinated to statistical ones, equality is denied its moral basis, and, as a moral idea, equality is thereby denied. The extreme proponents of numerical equality challenge, therefore, more than the traditional understanding of equality; they challenge the very basis upon which moral distinctions rest. And in doing so they are reduced to a series of "self-evident" sociological assertions, assertions teeming with numbers and statistics suggesting how society should be carved up.[5]

Although the extreme proponents of numerical equality are confident in saying how things today would be in the absence of historical discrimination, the fact is that no one can say, with any confidence, that, in the absence of slavery, a certain percentage of blacks would today be doctors or lawyers or members of any other occupational group.[6] No one can specify just how, had history been otherwise, things today would be different. One cannot remove from American history the institution of slavery and show neatly how this alteration would have issued in an altered present.*

The proponents of moral equality have a tradition to which they may appeal, and this is not an inconsiderable virtue. Principles and ideas foreign to a people hold less promise for efficacy than those with which they are familiar. But further, the tradition and idea of moral equality, which Lincoln regarded as the sheet anchor of republican government, is not just familiar. It is not morally neutral. The idea of moral equality—the "cosmopolitan idea," as Orlando Patterson has described it—is superior as a founding and operating principle of government to one based in caste, class, or racial distinction.[7] It presents itself not just as the tradition of a people but as the founding principle of self-government that honors men and pays tribute to their dignity and autonomy as individuals. The idea of moral equality is thus superior to the idea of numerical equality, not simply because it belongs, as a historical phenomenon, to a free people but because, as we have seen, it has been taken throughout our history to be *worthy* of a free people's allegiance.

Most advocates of numerical equality see it as a means; that is, they see the placement of individuals who belong to certain racial or ethnic groups in jobs, positions of influence and responsibility, and the professions as a necessary means

---

*A society organized so that the percentage of minorities in each profession approximates closely the percentage of minorities relative to the total population is, as a practical matter, impossible to achieve, unless one is prepared to have a large number of teenagers wielding scalpels and arguing before juries. Every "underrepresented" group, as Thomas Sowell has pointed out, has a lower than average age; it is mainly composed of children or inexperienced young adults. See Sowell, "Are Quotas Good for Blacks," *Commentary* 65, no. 6 (June 1978):39–40; and Sowell, "Ethnicity in a Changing America," *Daedelus* 107, no. 1 (Winter, 1978):213–237.

to the achievement of a society of true moral equality. They believe race-conscious measures must be undertaken for the interim in order to equalize the position of some disadvantaged minorities vis-à-vis whites; once this is done, but only when this is done and only by the means of numerical equality, will the end of moral equality be achieved.

This position was evident in the *Bakke* case in the supplemental brief based on Title VI of the Civil Rights Act of 1964 by the University of California. The university argued that an increase in the number of minority students in the class at Davis was sought for four main reasons: "(1) to improve medical education and the medical profession through the participation of men and women drawn from all segments of society; (2) to reduce the separation of blacks, Chicanos, Asians, and American Indians from the mainstream of American life by drawing them into higher education and the professions; (3) to demonstrate to boys and girls in still-isolated minority groups that the historic barriers to their entering the medical profession raised by racial discrimination have now been eliminated; and (4) to improve medical care in the minority communities now so seriously underserved."[8] At Davis, of course, the administration instituted a special admissions policy under which sixteen seats in each class of one hundred were set aside to be filled by minority applicants, to ensure that a substantial increase in minority students would occur. In this the Davis Medical School was exceptional, for only about a dozen institutions in all of higher education—including undergraduate, graduate, and professional schools—operated in this way, on what may fairly be called a "quota" system.[9] Yet if they differed from Davis in this particular, they nonetheless agreed—and most schools are still agreed—that it is necessary to take race *by itself* into account in individual admissions decisions. And, moreover, they were and most still are agreed that it is necessary to consider race in enough individual instances so that a substantial number of minority applicants is admitted; that is, Davis and most professional schools have operated and still do operate today from the premise of numerical equality. Finally, they were and most still are agreed that the reasons for taking race by itself into account so that a large number of minority applicants are admitted—in shorthand, "counting by race"—are essentially, *mutatis mutandis,* the reasons that were given by the University of California in its supplemental brief in the *Bakke* case.

These reasons were central to the university's claim that numerical equality is necessary to bringing about an age in which race is no longer a consideration in admissions decisions. One by one these reasons must be considered, but first it is essential to see that those who supported numerical equality as a means appealed fundamentally to American history—to the episodes and events canvassed in this book. Numerical equality thus depends on a recognition of the persistence of the consequences of slavery and racial discrimination—consequences that serve to recall America's failure to realize the promises of the Declaration of Independence. And of course here there can be no quibbling with the record; the notion that the wrongs of the past must be righted has undeniable moral appeal. As we have seen, the meaning of the idea of equality, as first stated in the Declaration of Independence, as further articulated and placed in the center of the American political creed by Lincoln, as enunciated in the plain language of the Fourteenth Amendment, as relied upon by Justice Harlan in his dissenting opinion in *Plessy* v. *Ferguson,* as appealed to by Richard Cain before Congress in

1875, and as embodied in the civil rights acts of the late 1950s and early 1960s, has not been paralleled by adherence in practice. If, down through the years, few Americans have denied the meaning of the Declaration, many have denied its truth both in word and deed; for many, their intentions in regard to equality have been far more equivocal than their words, and, in some cases, equality has meant little more than a promise, little more than words accompanied by acts of cruelty and brutality, prejudice and condescension.

It is clear as well that despite progress toward the realization of the promise of equality, this progress has not been steady. History does not suggest that the triumph of an idea is inevitable; steps may go forward, steps may go backward. However small, the steps taken in the years after the Civil War culminating in the Civil Rights Act of 1875 were definitely steps forward for the idea of moral equality. But by 1913—ironically, the fiftieth jubilee of the Emancipation Proclamation—so many steps backward had been taken that blacks were almost back to square one, in terms of equality; by 1913 blacks had reached their lowest point in the United States since slavery. Clearly, the history for blacks in America has moved, but not always onward and upward. The plans and schemes of men can effect progress or regress, and they can produce results quite different from, even contrary to, their authors' intentions.

It is, therefore, not enough to ratify a scheme that professes to work toward the realization of the idea of moral equality simply because it is well intentioned or even because it is new. And it is in this light that the claims of numerical equality as a means to the realization of moral equality must be considered. No matter what invocations of the past are summoned, any policy that speaks to the question of whether some Americans are less equal than others, and seeks to improve the conditions of equality for those who are reckoned less equal, must be considered on its own terms for what it will do both to those who are living and those yet to be born.

For many, of course, it is unimaginable that, in the final quarter of the twentieth century, efforts that unquestionably intend the realization of the promise of equality and that are defended as the only sound means of achieving moral equality as a fact should produce a retrogression in race relations and do damage to the idea of moral equality. But professional school admissions policies—including both the one at issue in the *Bakke* case and all those that believe in "counting by race"—in putting race by itself in some "balance" so that it might tip in favor of a number of applicants in need of "special" help—all such admissions policies based on race will do precisely that.

Admissions by race call for different standards for admission for different racial groups. Where admissions by race is the policy, minority applicants are evaluated by standards lower than those by which all other students are evaluated. Once it was axiomatic that wherever different standards are found for blacks and other minorities, there also is racism.[10] Defenders of admissions by race insist that their motives are benign, and indeed they are. But despite these motives, admissions by race deny the heart of the principle of equality— moral equality. To count by race, to use the means of numerical equality to achieve the end of moral equality, is counterproductive, for to count by race is to deny the end by virtue of the means. The means of race counting will not, cannot, issue in an end where race does not matter.

Moral equality is a condition of mutual respect among men. It insists, as Jefferson believed, on the dignity of all men, their capacity for moral autonomy and responsibility. Respect and moral equality, however, are denied when the color line is drawn, when distinctions of birth are made, when legislation applies unequally to whites and blacks; respect and moral equality are denied when the claims of men are determined on unequal bases, when men are treated as if they were not men, as if they had no dignity, as if they were not moral equals, as if they were only half or three-fifths men. Respect and moral equality are denied, in other words, when men are treated as blacks (and many others) have been treated during such a large part of American history. This denial has often entailed severe dependence, as can most clearly be seen, perhaps, under slavery. In *The Black Family in Slavery and Freedom, 1750–1925,* Herbert Gutman produces these thoughts of a Louisiana cotton planter on how to train a slave: "What is essentially necessary for his happiness you must provide for him Yourself and by that means create in him a habit of perfect dependence on you—Allow it once to be understood by a negro that he is able to provide for himself and you that moment give him an undeniable claim on you for a portion of his time to make for this provision."[11] Respect and moral equality may be denied not only by harsh measures such as slavery but also such seemingly benign ones as special admissions policies that count by race. To be sure, the consequent dependence is not so severe as that induced by slavery. It may be regarded as a benign insult, but it is an insult nonetheless, one that results in dependence. "There can be no moral equality where there is a dependency relationship among men," says Orlando Patterson. "There will always be a dependency relationship where the victim strives for equality by vainly seeking the assistance of his victimizer. In situations like these we can expect sympathy, even magnanimity from men, but never—and it is unfair to expect otherwise—the genuine respect which one equal feels for another."[12]

In the *Bakke* case, then, the Supreme Court was not only asked, in effect, to ratify a policy that denied respect and moral equality to America's minorities. It was also asked to ratify a policy that would make minorities dependent upon others for their achievements, thus making difficult, if not impossible, any future bids for moral equality.*

We come, then, to the particular arguments advanced by the University of California in defense of the special admissions plan at Davis. And these arguments, on inspection, will be seen to have produced results incompatible with, and antithetical to, the idea of moral equality.

There is, to begin with, the argument that medical education and the medical profession will be improved by the participation of men and women drawn from all segments of society. Diversity, like integration, is in general a desirable social goal. But in what way is color by itself a contribution to diversity? Surely the argument depends on something other than aesthetics, for color by itself is in no way a contribution to medical education or the medical profession. Diversity of experience, of point of view, and of sympathies can be achieved only by a consideration of the individual, not his racial category.

And what is it that the minority student or the minority

*The Davis medical school set aside several seats in each new class that were to be filled, at the discretion of the dean of admissions, with applicants who were the sons and daughters of wealthy and influential California politicians. Under pressure during the debate on *Bakke*, this policy was discontinued. But so long as it operated, *this* policy, like the one that favored applicants because of their race, denied respect and moral equality to the students benefited. Thus did these students become dependent upon others for their achievements in an appropriate way. See the *Los Angeles Times*, July 5, 1977, and July 18, 1977.

151

doctor is supposed to contribute? It is inappropriate for admissions committees or anyone else to treat people simply as bearers of some imagined racial or ethnic perspective—to treat them, in other words, as categories. Someone doesn't have a "black" perspective or "black" point of view just because he is black. True academic diversity is a laudable goal, but it is not achieved by looking to what Ben Martin, a professor of politics at the University of Missouri at Kansas City, has described as the "personal qualities crude enough to be obvious to sense perception."[13]

Ironically, efforts justified in terms of promoting diversity within a student body have resulted in patterns of behavior hardly suggesting diversity. Surely one sign of having achieved true diversity would be the intermingling—the integration—of most if not all of those admitted by race with those not. But at Davis, during its special admissions era, this integration did not occur. Those admitted by virtue of their race were asked to come to a special three-week session before the start of school. There they met the faculty, learned their way around campus, and in general became acclimated. There, too, they established their friendships. Once school began, they started segregating themselves from the rest of the students. The specially admitted would eat together, study together, sit in class together, and do things socially together.[14] One is reminded, in all this behavior, of George McLaurin, who in 1950 was ordered admitted to the University of Oklahoma graduate school. It was his experience, being black and the only black, to sit apart from whites in class, dine alone at his own table in the school cafeteria, study alone at his own desk in the library, and spend his free time alone. The behavior of students at Davis suggests a regression.

When all is said and done about "diversity" in the context of professional schools, this aim is surely frustrated if the students providing "diversity" are not themselves as qualified to do class work as their "nondiverse" classmates. Whatever value diversity may have, a diverse student body must be an able one. In training future professionals, their academic qualifications and abilities must be considered. Much of the talk about "diversity" has proceeded on the assumption that there is a large pool of "highly qualified" minority applicants to professional schools. But, as we have seen, the scores of those students specially admitted at the Davis Medical School were not, on average, 5 or 10, not 15 or 20, percentiles below those regularly admitted, but rather 55 percentiles below in one year, 60 in the next. The facts at Davis are more typical than those at a Harvard or a Yale, and yet even such prestigious institutions are reluctant to make public the scores of those who have been admitted by virtue of their race. Rather, there have been misleading statements to the effect that quantitative indicators are not good predictors of academic performance and that the difference in quantitative scores do not bear out in differences in individual performance.[15] Yet intelligence matters, and tests are one measure of intelligence. It does matter how proficiently one can read, analyze, count, and understand a formula; it does matter what the meaning of words and the significance of facts are. All these abilities the tests currently used are designed to reveal. And, although there may not be much academic difference between two students, one of whom scores in the ninetieth percentile and the other who scores in the eighty-fifth, it is ludicrous to think there is not a great deal of difference between one who scores in the eightieth and one who scores in the thirtieth.[16] Despite monumental and continuing efforts to show that the Medical

COUNTING BY RACE

College Admissions Test and the Law School Admissions Test are culturally and racially biased against minorities, this allegation has not and does not seem able to be proved.[17]

It would be irrational for professional schools to decree at once that tests do not matter at all, but at least it would be somewhat more consistent with the arguments put forward in favor of "diversity" in professional school admissions. If scores do not matter for blacks, then by fairness, they should not matter for whites. If in serving the goal of diversity, the scores of minority applicants are waived so that their contribution to "diversity" may be scrutinized, then so in fairness should the scores of white applicants be waived. Then Polish-Americans, Sephardic Jews, Irish Catholics, and WASPs could all have their applications considered not on the merits of individual abilities but on the merits of their contributions to diversity—on the merits, to speak bluntly, of their race.

The second argument in favor of admissions by race is that by drawing more members of minority groups into higher education and the professions, their separation from the mainstream of American life will be reduced. No one, of course, seeks the separation of blacks and other minorities from the "mainstream" of American life; no one seeks to deny minorities the opportunity for higher education and a professional career. The issue is how to do this, how minorities might enter the mainstream; in particular, the issue is whether counting by race is a sound and efficient means for their entry.

What must be asked initially is, what is meant by the "mainstream"? According to supporters of admissions by race, the mainstream is materially defined, in terms of prestigious titles and high-paying jobs and influential positions. Admissions by race do place minorities in professional schools, but mere admission is of course no guarantee that any student will be academically successful and finally graduated. Because the goal is the mainstream, the logic of the argument requires that minority students be kept in school, promoted, and graduated; and because the first step toward the mainstream is admissions by race, there is no difficulty in taking the successive steps, if need be, also by race. So there is, at times, as everyone knows, grading, promotion, and graduation by race—as necessary, in order that minorities might "get ahead in America."[18]

But what are the consequences of this first step—counting by race to admit minority applicants to professional schools? For one, the message suggested to many is that blacks and other minorities are losers because in order to be something—in order to be wealthy or well-known or influential—they have to be given something from those already in the mainstream.[19] Second, because the minority student himself knows that he has been admitted by virtue of his race, not his grade-point average or his aptitude-test scores, the message is indelible to him that it is his skin that has made the difference; he is aware that his success as a person with a particular skin, not his success as a person, period, is what matters most to the institution that has ostensibly acted in his interest.[20] Third, because professional schools are interested in certain students because of the color of their skin or their ancestry, they invariably wind up admitting either the wrong students or, as in many cases, too many minority students. Thomas Sowell has called this "mismatching." Good minority students are "mismatched" with excellent institutions, while fair minority students are "mismatched" with good and very good institutions; and poor minority students, who shouldn't be in these schools at all, are mismatched with a range of institutions from mediocre to good.[21] Thus, as a condition of entering the mainstream, many of the specially admitted find themselves in educational contexts where the academic standards are too severe for them; it is no wonder that some of these students come to think of themselves as failures.[22] The picture that emerges is of the professional schools, on the one hand, pursuing the goal of numerical equality in devotion to the idea of helping minorities "get ahead," and, on the other hand, of many of the minority students, who in absolute terms are not unqualified for higher or professional school education, experiencing doubts about their abilities.

Many excellent minority students, of course, have no concern about any "mismatching"; but they do have a concern of a different sort. They have been admitted not by virtue of their race, but they nevertheless may have to live the rest of their lives trying to prove to others that indeed they were not admitted by race to a professional school; that they were not graded and promoted and graduated by virtue of their race; and that they do not now practice medicine or law because of their race.

The presence of admissions policies whereby certain persons are admitted by virtue of their race resurrects the claim of the racial bigot. The hardened bigot is probably a lost cause, but the softening one, who possibly is not, takes note of the different admissions criteria used for minority applicants. He is invited once more to believe his earlier judgment, that black and brown are synonymous with incompetence or worse. He is invited to join his hardened cousin in saying, "I told you so." In this way counting by race is a prescription for disharmony among the races. It focuses on race in such a way that it draws attention to racial differences, and, though not intending to do so, exacerbates them in some minds. And it is obvious that drawing attention to race, as these programs do, hardly draws us closer to the realization of a color-blind society.

Those who advocate counting by race often unwittingly deliver an insult to those whom they intend to serve. Counting by race is not the only means for getting minorities into the mainstream. The civil rights legislation of the 1960s has provided minorities a real chance and a real opportunity, despite a popular notion that any achievement on the part of minorities must be credited to the beneficence of government.[23] The facts suggest otherwise.[24] Studies indicate that once the historic barriers of racial discrimination to achievement for minorities were removed, minorities were able on their own to make very substantial achievements, educationally and economically.[25] The notion that blacks and other minorities "just don't have it," and must be given "something in order to be something" not only violates the assumption of moral equality by which democratic society is ordered and by which other minorities have advanced; also, it simply isn't true. What minorities need is further time to take advantage of those equal opportunities recently promulgated by law. Counting by race is thus an invitation to distort not only the abilities of minorities but also the real and substantial achievements they have recorded during the past decade, as well as their real and substantial achievements in the future.

The third argument for admissions by race is that it is needed to "demonstrate" to children in still-isolated minority groups that the historic barriers raised by racial discrimination to their entering the professions have now been eliminated. This argument assumes two things: First, that the proof for the elimination of the historic barriers of racism is the presence of special admissions policies that count by race; and second, that one way, if not the only way, to teach minority children that the historic barriers have been overcome is by pointing to the policies and the graduates of special admissions. But the proof that the historic barriers have been overcome is that, in fact, they no longer exist. The last of the racially discriminatory policies in university admissions fell in 1971;[26] thus were all admissions policies brought in line with the spirit of *Brown* v. *Board* and with the mandates of the civil rights legislation of the 1960s. Surely children of all races can be taught that the historic barriers have been destroyed.

For many, the great virtue of the policy of admissions by race lies in a putative correlation between numbers and motivation. The more minority professionals there are, goes the reasoning, the more encouraged will be minority youngsters to become professionals. Now, it is true that admissions by race increases the minority enrollment in professional schools. As many as 50 percent of minority students, according to reliable estimates, would not be enrolled were it not for admissions by race.[27] To translate: Nine percent of all the freshmen in medical schools in 1977 were minorities, but without admissions by race, roughly 4.5 percent would have been enrolled; and 8 percent of all the freshmen in law schools in 1977 were minorities, but without admissions by race roughly 4 percent would have been enrolled. We are talking, then, about the difference 4.5 percent makes in the one case, and 4 percent in the other. But can it be plausibly maintained that this difference has a significant effect on the motivation of minority schoolchildren? What is the critical number of minorities in the professions sufficient to motivate substantial numbers of minority children to become professionals? Is it 6 percent of an entering class, 7, 8, 10, or even

20? And does the number differ as among minority groups? Do blacks need a greater number and Chicanos a lesser one? And do the numbers vary as among the professions? Do blacks need only twice as many doctors as "role models" as they now have but, say, three times as many lawyers? And do Chicanos, by contrast, need three times as many doctors as "role models" as they now have but only twice as many lawyers? No one has yet demonstrated the correlation between the marginal numerical increase in the prestige professions brought about by admissions by race and the motivation on the part of minority children to become professionals.

There is the question, moreover, of whether minority children only respond to so-called role models of their own skin color or ethnic background. The assumption that this is so excludes from the attention and admiration of minority children the accomplishments and worthy lives of many whites— doctors and lawyers among them, but also explorers, philosophers, presidents, and prophets. No black has ever been president or vice-president of the United States. Should we therefore instruct black children not to aspire to be president or vice-president? Should we think exclusively in terms of blood and restrict our role models to those of the same caste and hue? Should we, in other words, require that black and minority schoolchildren grow up to occupy only the same positions in society that blacks and minorities now hold? And as for white children, should they be denied the examples of Martin Luther King, Jr., or Ralph Bunche or Henry Aaron? Should they, too, be taught that they must choose their heroes by attending to the crudest fact—to what is apparent only to the senses—to race?[28] Should the hopes of children be restricted to vertical columns of aspiration on the model of Jim Crow?

COUNTING BY RACE

Clearly, no. To reject this notion of "model by ethnicity" is not to be unduly quixotic, for in fact children do not distinguish their models on the basis of race. Black children do not say they wish to become "black" doctors or "black" baseball players; they wish to become doctors, baseball players, whatever—period. To be sure, black children (as well as white) may begin to identify what they wish to become in terms of race if adults and teachers insist on drawing attention to race; in this as in so much else the children of one generation will follow those of the last.

In this discussion of role models, one too easily forgets they are persons known for their exemplary character and achievements. A person such as Booker T. Washington is an example to others not because he fits a category like race but because he transcended such a category; he was preeminently an individual, a person who, though discriminated against because of his race, rose above that treatment, by relying on qualities other than the color of his skin. Washington, one will recall, rejected the notion that rights and privileges and "badges of distinction" should be grounded in the fact of anyone's race.

Consider then the kind of "role models" that admission by race produces: not persons who achieved the same standard and competed on equal terms with whites and all others and succeeded but persons who were, because of low scores and low abilities, the beneficiaries of affirmative admissions largesse. Leaving aside the comparison between the beneficiaries of special admissions and Booker T. Washington, who competed on a good deal less than equal terms, would not the minority parent rather point his child towards someone who achieved the same standard and competed on equal terms with whites and succeeded?

160

The criterion for a role model should and should always be excellence. Like a hero, he is known for his acts, for what he has done; not for what he is given, for what he is called. Does admissions by race in fact encourage and motivate minority children, by virtue of their own abilities, to become professionals? Or does it breed in them a new consciousness of, and indeed a reliance on, their color?

It is contemptible that admissions by race effectively reward minorities for low achievement, of course. But it is more contemptible that they institutionalize low expectations for minority applicants. This is so because the consequence of low expectation is low achievement, and now we are witnessing something like a chain reaction. Low expectations at the professional schools have led to low expectations at the undergraduate institutions, which have led to low expectations in the high schools, and so on. Consequently, students—all the way down the line—have learned that they can get by with minimal efforts.[29]

Admissions by race ensure low expectations; admissions by race cannot easily coexist with high expectations and its consequence, superior effort. To institutionalize low expectations is not to encourage motivation but to dampen it. It is to tell the minority student that less is expected of him and indeed that he is inferior to those others of whom more is expected. This, of course, resurrects the doctrine of black inferiority— and the legacy of slavery. It encourages the black student to give up in the face of adversity, to think that he is a loser or that he just cannot make it,[30] and that, if he can make it, it is only through the charity or the payoffs he can extort from the white man. This is not good teaching. And it is not true, for blacks manifestly do have the capabilities for success. In his study of black high schools that have produced a remarkably high proportion of the country's black leaders, Thomas Sowell found them to be places where blacks have been held to the same standard if not higher ones than whites in white schools.[31] In such an environment aspiration takes root and achievement results. Admissions by race encourages just the opposite.

The fourth reason given by Davis in behalf of its special admissions program was to improve medical care in the minority communities now so seriously "underserved."[32] This argument should not be taken very seriously. There is no reason, as Justice Stanley Mosk said in his opinion for the California Supreme Court, to suppose that any one race is less selfish or more altruistic than another.[33] Altruism and unselfishness, after all, are *individual* characteristics. With the opportunities available it is naive to believe that blacks or other minorities will automatically return, or return for very long, to their communities to practice medicine or law. Moreover, it is hard to see why they should be encouraged or coerced by presumption to return to serve the underserved communities if indeed another purported aim of admissions by race is to channel minorities into the mainstream, which is manifestly not located in America's ghettoes. It would be a terrible precedent and burden to place upon minority students the responsibility of taking their careers only in those directions that their mentors see as fit and appropriate to them. Not only ought the minority professional be free to practice law on Wall Street or medicine at the Mayo Clinic, he should *feel* free to do so. Davis's argument places the burden of proof upon him—to explain why indeed he should be inclined not to serve the underserved community—should he wish to work elsewhere.[34]

From the point of view of the minority doctor or lawyer, then, this argument is worthless; and from the point of view of the underserved community it is worthless, too. Suppose that all special admittees "return" to the underserved communities from which some of them ostensibly came. Would it be the best service for those communities to have practicing in their midst "special admissions" doctors who are less competent than others? And why should they have "special admissions" doctors while "regular admissions" doctors practice elsewhere? If it is excellent medical care to all the poor of this country that is desired by such institutions as the Davis Medical School, then there is a way to reach that end. This way is simpler, more efficient, and fairer. It could be reasonably asked of *all* graduates of law, medical, dental, health care, and social service schools—schools that rely more on the tax dollar than on any other means of support—that they spend one year working in an underserved community within ten years after graduation.

Those who defend counting by race and numerical equality as the means to a color-blind society appeal to a principle of compensation that such a procedure will help those who have been hurt, that it will give to those from whom much has been taken. But the programs themselves do not honor this principle. First, most of those who have been most seriously hurt—blacks, Chinese, Jews, American Indians—are dead. As Sowell has pointed out, the past is a great, unchangeable fact, and nothing can undo past sufferings and injustices. "Being honest and honorable with the people living in our own time," writes Sowell, "is more than enough moral challenge."[35] Second, the programs are wrong because they help some individuals who have not suffered but fail to help others who have. The moral appeal of the programs depends upon acting in accordance with the principle of giving more than an equal chance to someone who has suffered; it depends upon the idea of compensation. But such programs work by falsely assuming that in the final decades of the twentieth century, victimization, suffering, and deprivation are group, not individual, characteristics. As a result, the remedial principle is denied in two ways. One, the programs fail to distinguish the relevant differences among minority applicants themselves, for some have suffered, others have not. And, two, the programs fail to benefit poor, disadvantaged white applicants who have suffered as much as, or more than, minority applicants. As University of Michigan psychologist Joseph Adelson has pointed out, this leads to the absurd and anomalous and indeed factual situation in which the wealthy daughter of a black ambassador was accepted for admission and the poor daughter of a white farmworker was rejected under the dictates of a plan that justified itself in the language of moral compensation but acted in terms only of race.[36] Taking into account individual circumstances, including racial discrimination, is appropriate, but overlooking individual circumstances and exclusively concentrating on race is not. The Davis program did not focus on the highly motivated victims of hardship who deserved a chance to study medicine; the program rather focused on skin color. The program, as Harvard law professor Alan Dershowitz has said in this regard, asked the wrong question.[37]

A school may consider an individual's race as a factor in an admissions decision. Certainly, when a professional school has racially discriminated against identifiable applicants, it will be necessary to take their race into account in order to give them redress. Taking race into account in this way, it will be noted, is to take race into account in *individual* circumstances. The reason race is taken into account is not the gross presumption that all blacks, say, or all American Indians deserve by virtue of their race the compensation of admissions to a professional school; the reason is not that color of skin is meritorious in itself. Rather, the reason is the specific determination that this black or that American Indian has been discriminated against by a professional school and is therefore deserving to have his injury redressed by that school.

Taking race into account in this way is to "ask the right question." There is another way race may be taken into account that likewise asks a right question. A professional school considering the qualifications of its applicants may, in the consideration of an applicant's character, legitimately regard efforts that an individual has made to overcome individual hardships including poverty, unfortunate family circumstances, and racial discrimination. A school with no record of racial discrimination against its applicants may nonetheless determine whether the racial discrimination an applicant has overcome should count towards his admission. Here the critical factor is not race per se but how a specific applicant has handled the racial discrimination he says he has suffered. This kind of consideration in an admissions policy does not "count by race" but rather assesses *individual* circumstances.

The failure to consider the individual circumstances of applicants and the concern to focus only on race not only blurs any distinction between the relative claims for moral compensation between blacks and whites, it also eliminates recognition of the achievements of individual blacks and minority group members. Special admissions—"counting by race"—is wrong because it demeans exemplary achievement and makes a casualty of the minority student who is accepted through regular admissions. In the years Bakke was rejected at Davis, twenty-four minority applicants were accepted in the regular admissions process.[38] Compare the minority student who was specially admitted with the minority student regularly admitted. Whereas the former needed the help of special admissions, the latter did not. Whereas the former became dependent upon special admissions for his professional career, the latter did not. Whereas the former may be a number in a purely statistical equality, the latter may also be that but he is something far different and far preferable: the equal, in any terms, of anyone in his class.

In these two ways, special admissions—"counting by race"—distort reality by treating people as categories. They distort both the ideal of moral desert and individual merit.* Such distortion is only one of several ways in which special admissions programs are blueprints for deceit and an invitation to duplicity. First, the existence of special admissions invites lying about the qualifications of minority applicants and admittees; university spokesmen feel compelled to speak of pools of very highly "qualified" students containing large numbers of students with excellent qualifications among all minority groups.[39] Second, the fact of these programs invites lying about the performance of minority students admitted under special admissions; again, there are statements to the effect that minority students are doing fine, but little hard data is offered as evidence. Indeed, if there were such data,

---

* Treating people as categories is an offense not only to morality but also to sociology. "American ethnic groups," as Thomas Sowell has written, "differ in . . . many demographic, geographic, and other respects. . . . For example, American ethnic groups differ substantially in median age—by more than a decade, in some cases" (Sowell, "Ethnicity in a Changing America," *Daedalus* 107, no. 1 [Winter 1978]: 213). Because of the differences among groups, "the very concept of ethnic minorities," says Sowell, "is misleading . . . and attempts to generalize about minority problems, or to compare one ethnic group to some national average, are still more misleading" (Ibid., p. 232).

Not only do ethnic groups differ from each other, but there are significant differences within each group. "Black people in the U.S.," says Sowell, "are usually referred to as a more or less homogeneous group—by sociologists, newsmen, government officials, even their own leaders. But the history of black Americans is really the history of *three* distinct groups, whose descendants have very different incomes and occupations, and even fertility rates, in the 20th century." (Sowell, "Ethnicity: Three Black Histories," *Wilson Quarterly* 3, no. 1 [Winter 1979]: 96).

would it not be well known? Would it not have been a critical piece of evidence in every *amicus* brief supporting the University of California? It is obvious that those who defend special admissions would present data to refute the claims of their critics—if they had such data. Third, no one has been candid about the scholastic differences between minority students admitted and minority students graduated and certified in their respective professions.[40] Again, if the evidence showed that such programs were truly effective and that the number of fully qualified professionals was growing, then such facts would be given much publicity by the defenders of special admissions. Fourth, a sort of sequestering or segregation of special admittees from regular admittees has occurred in some cases, and special admittees' own recognition of the facts of their admission tends to encourage what one commentator has called "ethnic thumb-sucking." Many black students, for example, seem compelled to pose as authentic ghetto blacks, fearing that if their middle-class origins were discovered, they would face embarrassment. Here is another example of deceit, for the popular notion is that the most grievously underprivileged, those most deserving, are the ones being helped by such programs as count by race.[41] In order to get the most highly qualified minority applicants, those most in need of help in any form are rejected in favor of those who have already achieved some measure of economic sufficiency—students who, for the most part, were they not admitted to professional schools, would probably find their way into the mainstream in other ways. Fifth, there is deceit—between the claim that special admissions programs are a morally commendable and sound means of achieving racial equality and the claim that critics of such programs need not worry because they are only temporary. Those who defend "counting by race" assume a kind of aggressive moral posture which they almost invariably follow with assurances that special admissions programs will wither away and the nation's universities will return to "normal"—that is, a standard of merit.[42] Sixth, special admissions have created an atmosphere in which public utterance and pronouncement about such programs and their value is simply not to be taken, and is not taken, seriously. Anyone in a university with such a program can observe the difference between the dean's public expression that things are going smoothly and his private admission that things are not so good. But under pressure from the government and others, the university must simply accede to the demands of such programs despite their deleterious consequences.

Counting by race is of a piece with the sociologically approved ethnic revival and legitimizes, as Orlando Patterson has said, "atavistic sentiments." This technique, to use Patterson's words, "awakens and lends respectability to the most primordial of group identities—race."[43] It also leads, not only to nativism, but to nativistic absurdities and to the unconscionable rejections of individual talents. For example, an applicant to the University of Colorado Law School having the surname of DeLeo was first considered by an admissions committee as a minority applicant because it was assumed he was of Hispanic origin. When the committee learned he was of Italian origin, it dropped him from further consideration.[44] In Los Angeles teachers are assigned to schools on the basis of their race and ethnicity. But many teachers, happy where they are, happy in mixed environments, have been assigning themselves new skin colors and new ancestries in an effort to avoid reassignment. As a result, the Los Angeles Board of Education has set up "ethnic review committees." A consultant to the board, who helped develop these committees, has said: "We don't feel that people ought to be able to switch their identities in order to prevent certain things from happening to them." Consistent with this attitude, the review committees have been set up so that the odds are weighted against a person receiving a new identity: Of the five members on a committee, two must be from the race or ethnic background that the person requesting the change wishes to change from and three must be from the race or ethnic background that that person wishes to change to.[45] Not moral equality but such a tyranny of numbers is the end the means of numerical equality produces.

This may seem an absurd example of counting by race; certainly it is an extreme one. But it is not inconsistent with the logic of numerical equality and dictates of numerical equality as a means. Far from bringing closer that society where race, color, skin, and ethnicity—the crudest indices of a person—are morally irrelevant, numerical equality brings attention to race, attention to numbers, and attention to differences. In this way it does not bury but rather resurrects the invidious distinctions by race that marked slavery, Reconstruction, and the era of Jim Crow. Quite simply, numerical equality is an unworthy means for a people dedicated to the proposition that all men are created equal.

Moral equality is at the heart of the phenomenon called Bakke. Certain "benevolent" and certain well-intentioned proponents of special admissions at universities, in businesses, in press rooms, in government, and in courtrooms, along with a large bureaucracy in the federal government, backed by a number of elected and nonelected public servants, have invited in the name of equality both white and black Americans to reject moral equality as a governing principle of American political institutions, at a time when that principle finally has reached its finest and firmest articulation, and to place in its stead the goal of numerical equality and "counting by race." To this date, the majority of American people have rejected the notion that race should be such a measure. Most Americans of all skin colors and ethnic backgrounds still believe in the idea of moral equality, as enunciated by Lincoln, that the claims of each man should be determined on the same basis as the claims of any other man, regardless of color.

Numerical equality, conceived as a means to the end of moral equality, does not further that end, as we have seen. And conceived as an end in itself, it ought to be rejected, not merely because it is not our tradition, but also, and primarily, because it does not merit our acceptance; it is inferior. It is obvious that programs such as the one at Davis do patent harm to those situated as Allan Bakke, by barring them from the opportunity to compete for *all* places in a professional school.* But they also do harm to those who would ostensibly benefit from having the advantage of being "counted by race."

---

*William Van Alstyne, a professor of law at Duke University Law School, has written that the effect of such admissions policies as practiced at Davis is to "displace certain persons from positions and from opportunities they would otherwise have filled but for which they are now rendered ineligible." Their ineligibility arises, finds Van Alstyne, from the fact that they are (1) white and (2) "not sufficiently better qualified than all other whites as to be safely beyond the exclusionary effect" of the admissions policies at issue. These "marginal" students, says Van Alstyne, usually come from the lower socioeconomic classes. (Van Alstyne, "A Preliminary Report on the Bakke Case," *AAUP Bulletin* 64, no. 4 [December 1978]: 295–96).

It may well be that the whites "displaced" by admissions programs that "count by race" have mainly working class backgrounds; this was the case with both Bakke and Marco Defunis. If admissions that "count by race" are viewed as a way to "repay" a historic debt to blacks and other minority groups, then not only does "repaying" that debt deny moral equality to those receiving the payment, but the class of those shouldering the burden of "repayment" is made up mainly of the offspring of working class whites. As Van Alstyne notes, those more affluent and more able to "repay" the debt—the (mostly white) administrators and faculty members at the schools that "count by race"—pay nothing. (Ibid., p. 296.)

Chapter 9

Affirmed in Part, Reversed in Part

Bakke: The Decisions

Supreme Court Gives
Qualified Approval
To Affirmative Action

But It Rejects Rigid Quotas
Used by Medical School
To Determine Admissions

The Decision Everyone Won

By Carol H. Falk
And Urban C. Lehner
Staff Reporters of *The Wall Street Journal*

WASHINGTON—The Supreme Court's long-awaited decision in the Bakke case leaves intact the bulk of affirmative-action programs that give special consideration to minorities and women.

The Court voted five to four yesterday to affirm a lower-court decision ordering the University of California Medical School at Davis to admit Allan Bakke. Mr. Bakke is a 38-year-old white man who twice was rejected by Davis, although the university itself rated him better qualified than some of the 16 minority-group members admitted through a special program.

Most significantly, however, a five-member court majority voted to overturn the lower court's ruling that race can't ever be a factor in admissions decisions. The four other Justices didn't disagree but said it wasn't necessary to decide that broad question at this time.

/ The ruling means that universities may continue affirmative-action programs, so long as they consider candidates on an individual basis and don't set aside a rigid number of places for which whites can't compete. Davis got into trouble because it reserved 16 out of the 100 places in each entering medical-school class for minorities; most schools are more subtle about giving special consideration to minorities.[1] /

More than fifty friends of the court—an all-time record—filed briefs with the United States Supreme Court in *Bakke*. And during the months before the case was argued before the Court (on October 14, 1977) and during the months afterward, as the Court was deciding the case, every news magazine, major newspaper, and television network devoted extra time and resources to reporting and analyzing the nuances of the case. It was no surprise, then, that when the Court finally decided the case—on June 28, two days before the end of its 1977–1978 term[2]—reactions to the decision came quickly from every quarter of American life. This was the "public opinion," as Lincoln might say, and it is in the public's understanding of what *Bakke* means, in how the American people live according to their understanding of this historic decision regarding the meaning of equality, that the case has its ultimate significance. No discussion of *Bakke* can be complete without taking note, at some length, of the many and various responses to the Court's decision and of the traditions of thinking about equality they represented.

First of all, there were those who were altogether dismayed, believing that the Supreme Court had impeded, if not halted, minority progress by invalidating explicit racial quotas. "Bakke—We Lost" blurted the headline in New York City's *Amsterdam News*. Peter Cohn, co-counsel for the regional office of the NAACP in Washington, D.C., said: "I think this is a very sad day in the United States. The *Bakke* decision represents a step back in time." Tyrone Brooks, national field director for the Southern Christian Leadership Conference, said: "I'm very disappointed . . . [The ruling] means that the incentive to carry out affirmative action will be killed." Tom Wicker of the *New York Times* commented: "The validity and potential of affirmative-action programs may have been seriously, if not fatally, undermined." Jose Medina of La Raza, a Chicano political group, said *Bakke* was a very disappointing decision because in it the Court declared that "the Fourteenth Amendment is no longer for the protection of identifiable minorities but an amendment for the protection of the rights of society as a whole." The Reverend Jesse Jackson called the decision a "devastating blow to our civil-rights struggle" and urged "massive street demonstrations" to "educate Americans as to our displeasure." University of Pennsylvania law professor Ralph Smith said that the Court's judgment could be used to attack affirmative action and that was something "a society that purports to cherish domestic tranquility ought to avoid." Congressman Ron Dellums of Michigan regarded *Bakke* as a "racist decision by the Nixon court"; he called on "all people of good will" to denounce it. Professor Kenneth Tollett of Howard University said the decision was "a hammer in the solar plexus." Justice Thurgood Marshall, referring in his dissenting opinion to the Reconstruction era, said that since then we have come "full circle" with *Bakke*. Former Georgia Congressman Julian Bond thought the decision worse even than did Marshall: "It has reinforced," he said, "the 200-year-old racial and sexual quota system."

Many people, however, found good in the decision because, although the Court invalidated the racial quota at Davis, it nevertheless invited universities to count by race. These responses to the decision fell roughly into three groups. One group was made up of various spokesmen who, unlike Jesse Jackson, saw the decision as benefiting minority groups. For example, Vernon Jordan, president of the National Urban League, interpreted the decision as a "green light to go forward with acceptable affirmative-action programs." Arthur Fleming, chairman of the United States Civil Rights Commission, was "heartened by the way the Supreme Court gave unequivocal support to affirmative action." Attorney General Griffin Bell, who noted that President Jimmy Carter was "pleased by the decision," called it a "great victory for affirmative action," and said that "the whole country ought to be pleased." Al Perez, associate counsel for the Mexican American Legal Defense and Educational Fund, commented: "The decision was a minority victory. The Davis admissions system is not constructed like most other systems. Most other programs would meet the constitutional standard that the *Bakke* decision imposes." Joseph Rauh of the American Civil Liberties Union said: "The important thing . . . is that the racists who wanted to turn back the clock on minority progress have received a stunning blow. The Supreme Court's decision that race is a proper factor in admissions decisions is the legal concrete on which further affirmative-action progress can be made. The Supreme Court struck a blow for remedying past wrongs and providing a more equal society." And Gene Boyer of the National Organization for Women said: "Employers and universities who choose to interpret *Bakke* as a license to remain male and pale are in for a rude awakening."

The second group was made up of those attempting to put the decision in perspective—mostly legal scholars and journalists. Sympathetic both to the old tradition of moral equality and the more recent one of numerical equality, this group considered the decision positive. A. E. Howard of the Virginia Law School labeled the decision a "Solomonic compromise"; Lawrence Tribe of the Harvard Law School called it an "act of statecraft"; Charles Alan Wright of the University of Texas Law School said it was a "very civilized ruling"; and Benno Schmidt of the Columbia Law School commented that it was "just about right." The *Washington Post* echoed Howard's praise of the decision as a "sound compromise" in which "everybody won," and which therefore had a "soothing effect." The *New York Times,* in an uncharacteristic endorsement of the Bible, also compared the decision to Solomon's judicial pronouncement and urged its readers to dedicate themselves to the "higher law" in which, the *Times* said, the decision was grounded. Roscoe Drummond of the *Christian Science Monitor* commented: "The decision was precise, constructive, and compassionate."

The third group was made up of those people whose job it is to administer or supervise affirmative-action programs— programs that count explicitly by race; these were people in government and in the institutions of higher learning most directly affected by the *Bakke* decision. Many saw the decision as having little practical effect on what they do, and of this they were glad. Eleanor Holmes Norton of the Equal Employment Opportunity Commission said: "My reading of the decision is that we are not compelled to do anything differently from the way we've done things in the past, and we are not going to." Jack Peltason, president of the American Council on Education, said: "It left the options open. The overwhelming number of affirmative-action programs now in place will meet the standards outlined by the Court." Dr. John Cooper, president of the Association of American Medical Colleges, said: "[The decision] should stimulate efforts to increase the admissions of underrepresented minorities." Clark Kerr, chairman of the Carnegie Council on Policy Studies in Higher Education, commented: "The Supreme Court has supported a continuation of affirmative-action programs in higher education and diversity in college and university student bodies. This is good for higher education and the nation and allows efforts to increase social justice." John Kemeny, president of Dartmouth College, remarked: "Absolutely no way will our [admissions] program be affected." David Saxon, president of the University of California, the petitioner in the case who lost, nevertheless said that *Bakke* was a "great victory for the university." "Any ruling," he continued, "that introduces restriction on the use of race is going to make it more difficult, but not very much more difficult." Many who saw in the Court's decision an invitation to proceed as before quoted approvingly from Justice Harry Blackmun's opinion: "In order to get beyond racism, we must first take account of race."[3]

Amid all these reactions were a few voices speaking in praise of that part of the decision that ruled out racial quotas. Arnold Forster, general counsel of the Anti-Defamation League of B'nai B'rith, said: "We view the Court's decision as a significant victory in the effort to halt the use of quotas and their equivalent in admissions to colleges and graduate schools." The *Wall Street Journal* pointed to the "clear core" of the *Bakke* decision—that "the Court majority ruled unmistakably that California's Davis Medical School was wrong in using a racially-based quota system." The Court thereby "limited the extent to which those seeking equality of results can sweep aside the basic rules of a liberal society."

Those taking this position, however, were not free of worry. Forster also said: "In our view, it would, as a practical matter, seem difficult to allow race to be used as one factor in admissions without that factor eventually becoming the determining factor." And the *Wall Street Journal* was quick to point out the Court's decision left room for "discretionary mischief."

Such concerns and worries dominated the reactions of a few commentators who were gloomy but not in the way Jackson, Dellums, and Tollett were gloomy. These were people who seemed to be concerned that damage had been done to the idea of moral equality. Thus Professor John Kaplan of the Stanford Law School said: "In a sense the *Bakke* people have lost. There are five votes on the Supreme Court saying that while you can't have quotas you can manipulate admissions standards to get a desired level of minorities." Alan Dershowitz of the Harvard Law School, who, on hearing reports of the decision, characterized it as "an act of judicial statesmanship," later wondered whether the Court's decision might not foster programs where "more turns on race alone than it did at Davis." "The *Bakke* decision," he remarked, "reflects the ultimate triumph of ambiguity and discretion over clarity and candor." Robert Bork of the Yale Law School called the law in the decision "unstable." "It doesn't tell us how race counts . . . ," he said. "We're told that we can count race somewhat, but not too much. That's going to be difficult to apply." Sociologist David Riesman worried that what "we are facing now is full employment for lawyers, as the rising sense of entitlement among groups and individuals takes hold with more bitterness at all levels," and psychologist Joseph Adelson noted that "the ambiguity of the decision is an incentive to duplicity." Said Adelson: "It appears that the atmosphere of evasion and hypocrisy at the university is likely to continue." George F. Will, writing in *Newsweek,* said that with *Bakke* the Court now "may not seriously impede the bureaucratic drive to transform the core concept of American justice from 'equal opportunity for individuals' to 'statistical parity for government-approved groups.'" Retired United States Senator Sam Ervin said, simply: "The decision sounds like intellectual clap-trap to me. I think the only rational decision is that you can't discriminate against anybody on account of his race."

The *Bakke* decision was, in fact, two decisions—two 5 to 4 decisions. On the one hand, the Supreme Court invalidated the special admissions program at the University of California Medical School at Davis whereby sixteen seats in each entering class (out of one hundred) were reserved for minority students, and ordered Allan Bakke, a white man, who, the Court said, had been discriminated against by virtue of the Davis program, admitted to the school. On the other hand, the Supreme Court reversed that part of the California Supreme Court decision maintaining that any consideration of race in the admissions process at Davis is constitutionally impermissible.

Justice Lewis Powell occupied the interesting position of being the only justice in the two 5 to 4 majorities. He joined with Justice John Paul Stevens, who wrote for Justices William Rehnquist and Potter Stewart, and Chief Justice Warren Burger, in declaring the admissions program at Davis invalid and ordering Bakke admitted. For these four, Title VI of the Civil Rights Act of 1964, which represents the culmination of the historic drive to have accepted into law the idea of moral equality, was the ground for the decision. Stevens, arguing in his opinion from the plain language of Title VI, noted that the House Report understood Title VI to stand for "the general principle that *no person* ... be excluded from participation on the ground of race, color or national origin under any program or activity receiving Federal financial assistance." Stevens took this to be the "broad view of Title VI"—a view reinforced, he said, by the statute's legislative history. The statute, he said, expressed "Congress' belief that, in the long struggle to eliminate social prejudice and the effects of prejudice, the principle of *individual* equality, without regard to race or religion, was one on which there could be a 'meeting of the minds' among all races and a common national purpose." Title VI, according to Stevens, means that it is not permissible "to say 'yes' to one person but to say 'no' to another person, only because of the color of his skin." In violation of Title VI, Stevens believed, the Davis Medical School said "no" to Allan Bakke because he was white.[4]

For Justice Powell, however, the ground for declaring the Davis admissions program invalid and Bakke admitted was not Title VI but the Fourteenth Amendment. So the legal justification of *this* decision was mixed, with four justices deciding on statutory ground, one on constitutional ground.

As for the other majority, which allowed race to be a constitutionally valid factor in an admissions policy, it was made up of Justices Powell, William Brennan, Thurgood Marshall, Byron White and Blackmun. Brennan wrote an opinion in which he was joined by Blackmun, Marshall, and White, each of whom added individual opinions.

In his opinion, Brennan recognized that "the assertion of human equality is closely associated with the proposition that differences in color or creed, birth or status, are neither significant nor relevant to the way in which persons should be treated." But, he said, such factors need not be "constitutionally an irrelevance," and, indeed, color-blindness has never been "adopted by this Court as the proper meaning of the equal protection clause." The race-conscious admissions procedures at Davis, he wrote, are "reasonable" and do not stigmatize any group or individual; they do not "establish" an exclusive preserve for minority students apart from and exclusive of whites. Furthermore, he said, the purpose of the program at Davis is the laudable and constitutionally permissible one of overcoming the effects of segregation. Thus the program works toward the positive goal and ideal of "bringing the races together." It "does not simply advance less qualified applicants"; rather it "compensates applicants whom it is uncontested are fully qualified to study medicine."[5]

In their individual opinions, Justices Marshall and Blackmun emphasized certain points of the Brennan opinion. Marshall stressed the necessity to overcome the effects of segregation. He was concerned to recount the history of the Negro and the idea of equality. He described the brutality of slavery, the denigration of the Negro through the three-fifths provision of the Constitution, the nature of Jim Crow, and the history of "separate but equal." He pointed to the doctrine of equality as enunciated in the preamble to the Declaration of Independence and finally manifested in the striking down of the Jim Crow laws in the era of *Brown* and the school desegregation cases. It is because of the legacy of unequal treatment, he argued, that "we now must permit the institutions of this society to give consideration to race in making decisions about who will hold the positions of influence, affluence and prestige in America." Such a "race-conscious remedy," he wrote, is necessary to achieve the end of a "fully-integrated society, one in which color of a person's skin will not determine the opportunities available to him or her."[6]

Blackmun, in his opinion, said that he accepted the proposition that the rights guaranteed by the Fourteenth Amendment are personal rights, but he also said that that amendment has not "broken away from its mooring and its original intended purposes." He emphasized that the need to help blacks is still apparent, especially in professions such as law and medicine. Noting that until the early 1970s minorities counted as fewer than 2 percent of the physicians, attorneys, and medical and law students, Blackmun said that "if ways are not found to remedy that situation, the country can never achieve its professed goal of a society that is not race-conscious." In his view, a society that is not race-conscious is one in which "persons are regarded as persons." And the only way to achieve this sort of society, according to Blackmun, is to take race into account. "In order to get beyond racism," he wrote, "we must first take account of race. There is no other way. . . . In order to treat persons equally, we must treat them differently."[7]

Justices Brennan, Blackmun, Marshall, and White rejected the view of the four Justices who held that Title VI proscribes such use of race as was made at Davis. And Brennan, Blackmun, Marshall, and White were agreed that the Fourteenth Amendment permits race to be the *decisive* consideration in a university admissions program. Powell, however, held in his opinion that race may be only *a* consideration in an admissions program, so the five together were agreed only to the extent Powell articulated.

It should now be evident where *Regents of the University of California* v. *Bakke* stood in terms of the historic confrontation between the idea of moral equality and the idea of numerical equality. One of the Court's 5 to 4 decisions—that which spoke the language of Title VI—reflected the tradition of moral equality. The other decision—that which spoke of the necessity to take account of race—reflected the tradition of numerical equality. As for the justices themselves, four—Stevens, Rehnquist, Stewart, and Burger—stood unequivocally in the tradition of moral equality, while another four—Brennan, Blackmun, Marshall, and White—stood unequivocally in the tradition of numerical equality. The remaining justice—Powell—stood with a leg in each tradition. And it is the Powell opinion, providing majorities for both of the decisions in *Bakke* and defining the limits of the decision that permits race to be used as a factor in an admissions program, that obviously requires detailed explication and analysis.

Justice Powell began his opinion with a discussion of Title VI. He found that it incorporates and relies on constitutional standards, and so he turned to a consideration of the Equal Protection Clause of the Fourteenth Amendment. He said: "Its language is explicit: 'No State shall . . . deny to any person within its jurisdiction the equal protection of the laws.' " Of this he said: "the guarantee of equal protection cannot mean one thing when applied to one individual and something else when applied to a person of another color."* During the past thirty years, he pointed out, the Supreme Court

---

* Powell of course does not believe that equal protection is violated when a specifiable individual who has been discriminated against because of his race by a company or a university is given special consideration in order to make him "whole." (See our discussion on page 164–65.) Wrote Powell: "The court of appeals have fashioned various types of racial preferences as remedies for constitutional or statu-

has been called on to assure "to all persons 'the protection of equal laws.' " He then offered the Court's teaching: "Over the years, this Court consistently repudiated 'distinctions' between citizens solely because of their 'ancestry' as being 'odious to a free people whose institutions are founded upon the doctrine of equality.' " Justice Powell therefore rejected the University of California's request that the Court "adopt for the first time a more restrictive view . . . and hold that discrimination . . . cannot be suspect if its purpose can be characterized as 'benign.' " "The clock of our liberties . . . cannot be turned back to 1868," he wrote, and "it is far too late to argue that the guarantee of equal protection to *all persons* permits the recognition of special wards entitled to a degree of protection greater than that accorded others."[8] He quoted from Alexander M. Bickel's posthumous work, *The Morality of Consent:*

The lesson of the great decisions of the Supreme Court and the lesson of contemporary history have been the same at least for a generation: discrimination on the basis of race is illegal, immoral, and unconstitutional, inherently wrong, and destructive of democratic society. . . . [9]

Powell went on to say that what some would characterize as a "white majority" is itself a collection of minorities most of which can lay claim "to a history of prior discrimination at the hands of the state and private individuals." "There is no principled basis," he concluded, "for deciding which groups would merit 'heightened judicial solicitude' and which would not."[10]

At this point, Powell added a footnote: "As I am in agree-

---

tory violations resulting in identified, race-based injuries to individuals held entitled to the preference" (*Regents of the University of California* v. *Bakke,* 98 S. Ct. 2733 [1978], 2754).

ment with the view that race may be taken into account as a factor in an admissions program, I agree ... that the portion of the judgment that would proscribe all consideration of race must be reversed."[11] These words are startling. It has been said that decisions of the Supreme Court often resemble the movement of a vast ocean liner imperceptibly changing course. But here the ocean liner steered by Justice Powell turned 180 degrees.

Powell accomplished this sweeping turn with the idea of "diversity" in higher education. He finds the goal of attaining a diverse student body a matter of academic freedom and a compelling and constitutionally protected end. By selecting a "diverse student body," Justice Powell wrote, a university may create an atmosphere of "speculation, expression, and creation."[12]

Powell thus ratified the University of California's argument that diversity is a goal of paramount importance in the fulfillment of its mission. He warned, however, that this end does not justify any means: "Although a university may have wide discretion in making the sensitive judgments as to who should be admitted, constitutional limitations protecting individual rights may not be disregarded." While "it may be assumed that the reservation of a specified number of seats in each class for individuals" from preferred ethnic groups would contribute to the "attainment of considerable ethnic diversity," such an approach "misconceives the nature of the state interest that would justify consideration of race or ethnic background." The state's interest is not "in simple ethnic diversity" but in a "diversity that ... encompasses a far broader array of qualifications and characteristics." Racial and ethnic origin is but a "single" element among these. It is, however, an "important element," and it "may be deemed a 'plus' in a particular applicant's file."[13]

How is race to be a "single though important element"? To begin with, a university must adhere to a policy of individual comparison as opposed to a method that results in a systematic exclusion of certain groups. In such an individualized, case-by-case process, "the file," as Justice Powell explained, "of a particular black applicant may be examined for his potential contribution to diversity without the factor of race being decisive when compared, for example, with that of an applicant identified as an Italian American if the latter is thought to exhibit qualities more likely to promote beneficial educational pluralism." Race, then, "is simply one element— to be weighed fairly against other elements—in the selection process." But how is one to know when such a procedure is actually being followed? "A court would not assume that a university, professing to employ a facially nondiscriminatory admissions policy, would operate it as a cover for the functional equivalent of a quota system. In short, good faith would be presumed in the absence of a showing to the contrary."[14]

Justice Powell pointed to the Harvard College admissions program as "an illuminating example" of such good faith and a sensitive appreciation of the role of diversity. The Harvard program considers race as a factor in some admissions decisions and, in its own description, found in an appendix to the Powell opinion, says that the race of an applicant may "tip the balance in his favor just as geographic origin or a life spent on a farm may tip the balance in other candidates' cases." Harvard also says that such a tipping of the balance occurs only among those thousands of applicants who are "admissible academically." Powell approvingly cited the flexibility of this program, noting that it does not insulate "the individual from comparison with all other candidates for the available seats."[15]

Powell concluded by finding another difference between the Davis admissions program and that of Harvard College. "Petitioner's program will be viewed as inherently unfair by the public generally, as well as by applicants for admission at the state university." He quotes Justice Felix Frankfurter in "another connection": "Justice must satisfy the appearance of justice."[16] It is the Harvard program, in Justice Powell's view, that satisfies the appearance of justice.

This, then, is the Powell opinion, and it will remain the judgment of the Court until another decision is rendered. And that later decision will treat the Powell opinion as its point of departure. This would be enough to justify a detailed examination of the Powell opinion, but one should also bear in mind that the Powell opinion is not for the eyes of judges and justices alone, for it is the point of departure for public reaction to *Bakke*. And, because of the rise of the idea of numerical equality within the very recent past, there have been ambiguous signals in the public domain as to what the idea of equality should today mean. *Bakke* involves higher education, but the issues transcend the field of education. In recent years universities have been a focal point for the debate on the meaning of equality, but the debate in the universities has clearly reflected a larger one in society at large concerning the significance of race in the allocation of benefits and opportunities. The Supreme Court's notion, as comprehended in the Powell opinion of how a medical or professional school class should be organized, reveals a vision of how society at large should be organized and how American citizens should treat their fellow citizens as "equals."

Analysis of the Powell opinion usefully may begin with his point concerning Justice Felix Frankfurter. In *Offut* v. *United States*, Frankfurter did say that justice must satisfy the appearance of justice; but he also said it was but one "ingredient" among others.[17] And among those others, the most important, of course, is that justice *be done*. It is not enough, then, that an admissions process *appear* fairer than another; it must *be* fair. But this is not the case with Harvard's program.

For that program, while it may satisfy the appearance of justice, is not just. It is not concerned with individuals as individuals, but rather with individuals in the aggregate as defined by race and ethnicity, a categorization this nation has been trying to overcome for more than two hundred years. Moreover, it concentrates on numbers. In trying, says Harvard, to provide:

> a truly heterogenous environment that reflects the rich diversity of the United States, [diversity] cannot be provided without some attention to numbers ... 10 or 20 black students could not begin to bring to their classmates and to each other the variety of points of view, backgrounds, and experiences of blacks in the United States. Their small numbers might also create a sense of isolation among the black students themselves and thus make it more difficult for them to develop and achieve their potential. Consequently, when making its decisions, the Committee on Admissions is aware that there is some relationship between numbers and achieving the benefits to be derived from a diverse student body, and between numbers and providing a reasonable environment for those students admitted.[18]

In other words, numbers matter at Harvard.

Confronted with the question of whether the reservation of sixteen slots for minority applicants at the Davis Medical School amounts to a "quota or goal," Justice Powell, early on in his opinion, said: "This semantic distinction is beside the point: The special-admissions program is undeniably a classification based on race and ethnic background."[19] So it may be said of Harvard College, that whether or not its "numbers" amount to "quotas," "goals," "targets," numerical equivalents, or what-not, the semantic issue is beside the point. For there is a special-admissions program at Harvard College nonetheless. For the past five years, as has been reported in the *Washington Post*, the number of minority students in the entering freshman classes at Harvard College has varied "only a hair."[20] Can this be mere coincidence? Justice Blackmun was right to be skeptical. "I am not convinced, as Mr. Justice Powell seems to be," Blackmun wrote in his opinion, "that the difference between the Davis program and the one employed by Harvard is very profound or constitutionally significant. The line between the two is a thin and indistinct one."[21]

Allan Bakke, one should remember, applied for admission to a professional, not an undergraduate, school. Had Justice Powell wanted to hold up a more exact model, he could have chosen one of Harvard's professional schools. And what would he have found there? Well, Harvard, of course, is Harvard, and the likelihood is that minority applicants to its professional schools are better qualified academically than minority applicants to the schools at most other universities. Still, even Harvard must choose from the available pool of applicants, and, as many of those who filed *amicus* briefs in *Bakke*— on *both* sides—agreed, within that pool, there simply is no "balance" or "equilibrium" between black and white applicants.

Thus, the Association of American Medical Colleges, which supported the University of California and opposed Bakke, said in its brief that the academic qualifications of minority applicants to medical schools "pale in comparison with the much higher academic qualifications of the very large and highly competitive pool of white applicants."[22] The Association of American Law Schools (AALS) said in its brief that "the ineradicable fact" is that as a group, minority applicants to law schools "achieve dramatically lower LSAT [Law School Admissions Test] scores and GPA [grade-point average] than whites." The AALS brief produced the relevant figures: "20% of the white and unidentified applicants, but only 1% of blacks and 4% of Chicanos received both an LSAT score of 600 or above and a GPA of 3.25 or higher. . . . If the combined LSAT/GPA levels are set at 500 and 2.75 respectively, 60% of the white and unidentified candidates would be included but only 11% of the blacks and 23% of the Chicanos." Such disparities, said the AALS brief, exist at all LSAT and GPA levels.[23]

At Harvard—perhaps—the admissions-test scores of minority students may be among the highest of the entire minority applicant pool. But what about schools of lesser prestige? Here it is instructive to recall the difference in admissions-test scores between Bakke and those students specially admitted to Davis, an institution of average quality, in the two years Bakke unsuccessfully applied. As we have seen, the difference was not 5 or 10, or even 15 or 20 percentiles (out of 100), on the Medical College Admissions Test, but 55 percentiles in 1973 and 60 percentiles in 1974. That is, on the four parts of the test, Bakke averaged in the ninetieth percentile and was rejected; those specially admitted in 1973 averaged in the thirty-fifth percentile, those in 1974 not quite in the thirtieth.

These are unhappy facts, but facts nonetheless. And if not much noted before, they should in the interest of good faith be noted now, not only by jurists but also by the media, which demonstrated scant curiosity in ferreting out the truth regarding the academic performance of minority students. William Raspberry, the syndicated columnist, praising *Bakke*, constructed this interpretation of the decision:

Suppose a black applicant to Harvard Law School, a product of the inner-city slum who attended substandard public schools and graduated from a mediocre black college with scores of 650 on his Law School Admissions Test—can anyone suppose such a person is the mere equal of a white applicant, who having graduated from Groton or Columbia College also scores 650 on his LSAT? The Harvard plan permits admissions screeners to give special weight to the black youngster's special achievement.[24]

Now, who would quarrel with an admissions officer's "tipping" the scales in the black youngster's favor? Who indeed is opposed to this kind of "affirmative action"? Unfortunately, the situation Raspberry constructed, though charming, is extremely rare. For all practical purposes, it is fiction. No rough equality in terms of nonracial factors prevails among white and black applicants such that black applicants in any substantial numbers may be favored and thereby gain admissions through only a slight "tipping" on their behalf. Indeed, it is precisely because there is no such rough equality that supporters of programs such as those at both Davis and Harvard want race itself to be given, not mere "tipping" weight, but very substantial weight in the admissions process.

Justice Powell's recommendation of the Harvard College program may have a "soothing effect," but that program bears no relation to the realities of admission to professional schools, and the process he describes is one which no serious student of the case, on either side, can accept as accurate. "Nothing will have changed if the Harvard way becomes the nation's way," the *New York Times* solemnly and approvingly commented. Nothing, that is, except a hold on reality.

Justice Powell did have a hold on reality and on the truth, but then he lost it. He had the truth—he comprehended the idea of moral equality—when he said that the Fourteenth Amendment itself was framed in universal terms, without reference to color, ethnic origin, or condition of prior servitude; when he said that "over the years this Court consistently repudiated 'distinctions' between citizens solely because of their 'ancestry' as being 'odious to a free people whose institutions are founded on the doctrine of equality'"; and when he said that "the guarantee of equal protection cannot mean one thing when applied to one individual and something else when applied to a person of another color.' "[25]

Like Justice Powell, some of the justices in dissent had a glimpse of the truth, only to lose it; Brennan was right to recognize that the assertion of human equality is closely associated "with the proposition that differences in color or creed, birth or status, are neither significant nor relevant to the way in which such persons are treated."[26] But he failed to see just how closely the assertion of human equality is tied to this proposition; he failed to see that it depends, in fact, upon this assertion. Marshall was correct in desiring a society "in which the color of a person's skin will not determine the opportunities available to him or her,"[27] as was Blackmun in desiring a society in which "persons will be regarded as persons."[28] But both, despite having their eyes on the right goal, stumbled in pursuit of it, endorsing the use of race.

In failing to invite the nation to cease thinking in terms of race, the Supreme Court, contrary to the clear wishes of Justices Brennan, Blackmun, White, and Marshall, did not further the cause of equality. Had the Court held to the truth that human equality depends upon the repudiation of distinctions between citizens solely based on race and ancestry, it would have ruled out not only quotas but race as any kind of "plus" factor in an admissions program.

In so ruling the Court would not have foreclosed an admissions committee from considering *personal* attributes such as one's having overcome poverty, sickness, parental abuse, and, to the point most at issue, racial discrimination. In *individual* cases these can, and should be, taken into account. But what cannot be, and should not be, countenanced is thinking in blood. This is the wrong means to the end that most people desire—a society, as Blackmun put it, in which persons are treated as persons. What Powell, Blackmun, Brennan, Marshall, and White failed to see is the intimate relationship between means and ends. A race-conscious means cannot, as Brennan believes, bring the races together. Rather it is a prescription for the disharmony of the races. Nor is it true, as Blackmun put it, that in order to get beyond racism, we must first take account of race. Rather, in order to get beyond racism, the nation must once and for all stop thinking in terms of race.

One is left with an endorsement of a special admissions program (Harvard's) that will indeed produce much the same result as the invalidated Davis program, together with an encouragement to duplicity.

It is clear, then, that those who thought they "lost" in *Bakke*, that the incentive to carry out affirmative action was "killed," that affirmative action was "seriously, if not fatally, undermined," and that universities could no longer "count by race," were wrong, while those who interpreted the decision as a "green light to go forward" with affirmative action were quite right. Most special admissions programs would meet the constitutional standards that were recommended in *Bakke*; Al Perez was right.

As for those who saw the decision as a "Solomonic compromise," a "very civilized ruling," and an "act of statecraft," the charitable explanation is that they were reading *into* rather than reading the decision; the invitation to count by race is no "compromise." There was in their comments, furthermore, a curious view of the judicial function. To say, as the *Washington Post* did, that the decision contains "something for everyone" and that it will have a "soothing effect" on the nation is to suggest that the task of the Supreme Court is one of domestic diplomacy. But the Supreme Court does not have this function; its job is to assay what is just and right according to the Constitution and the laws of the land. If, in the school-prayer cases, in the reapportionment cases, and in the original school-desegregation cases, the Supreme Court had offered "something for everyone," would it have been praised?

Those who, like Roscoe Drummond, thought that the Court's decision was "precise, constructive, and compassionate," were wrong on all counts. The decision was not legally precise, nor was it constructive in the sense of showing institutions of higher education what they responsibly can do. And, perhaps worst of all, the decision was not compassionate. Thomas Sowell has said that it is the opposite of compassion to mismatch students with institutions that have standards too severe for them; this, as we have seen, is to patronize, to condescend, and to do them harm.

Those government officials such as Eleanor Holmes Norton correctly saw nothing in the decision that would force a change in the way things have been done in the recent past—when race has "counted."* And Jack Peltason, John Cooper, Clark Kerr, and David Saxon were all correct in seeing victory for the universities, and business as usual.† Most universities indeed could say, with Dartmouth's John Kemeny, that "absolutely no way will [our programs] change." The Court echoed what Harvard said, the route for academe is now clear, and good faith will be assumed.

Those like Arnold Forster and the editors of the *Wall Street Journal* were right to applaud the outlawing of an explicit and racially based quota system. And they were right as well to worry about the room the Court left, as the *Journal* said, for "discretionary mischief." Given that only ten or twelve institutions run special admissions policies like Davis's, however, these commentators might well have muted their applause and heightened their anxieties. The two decisions in *Bakke* did not promise to have equivalent impact.

John Kaplan of Stanford seemed to have been exactly right in saying that now "you can manipulate admissions standards to get a desired level of minorities." Robert Bork was right to call the law of the decision "unstable," but perhaps he underestimated how clear it is that race will continue to be given much weight. Alan Dershowitz was right to point to the decision's deficiencies in candor and clarity. David Ries-

---

* Race will continue to "count" in the programs administered by the Department of Health, Education and Welfare. Ten months after the Court decided *Bakke,* the department, having conducted a review of its programs, announced that they would continue largely unchanged. (See "HEW Programs Said Unaffected By Bakke Ruling," *Washington Post,* April 22, 1979.)

† The medical school at the University of California at Davis changed its admissions procedures in form but not in substance. Credit is still given an applicant because of his race, as "minority applicants are now *automatically* given five points toward the total of 15 needed to put them in Group A, which receives first consideration for admission" ("Student Bakke: Tough Going," *Newsweek,* April 30, 1979, p. 18; emphasis added).

man was right in fearing a "rising sense of entitlements among groups and individuals . . . with more bitterness at all levels." (Indeed, shortly after the decision, Ralph Perotta, executive director of the National Italian American Foundation, noting that *Bakke* would allow groups not traditionally thought of as disadvantaged to get protection, urged Joseph Califano at the Department of Health, Education, and Welfare to revise the guidelines for the Civil Rights Act so that they would take into account Powell's view of the significance of "diversity"; Perotta was no doubt mindful of Powell's special mention of Italian-Americans.) Joseph Adelson, arguing that the ambiguity of the decision is an incentive to duplicity, was clearly right. George F. Will was right in his assessment that *Bakke* will not impede the drive to transform the concept of American justice from "equal opportunity" to "statistical parity." Above all, and finally, Sam Ervin was right when he said that the decision "sounds like intellectual clap-trap. . . . I think the only rational decision is that you can't discriminate against anybody on account of his race."

What the Court did in *Bakke* was to rule out explicit racial quotas, but in inviting universities to continue to "count by race" the Court encouraged them to achieve the same results as have been reached in an explicit quota system. Thus, the Court allowed universities to do retail what it proscribed them from doing wholesale. The Court paid some attention to the idea of moral equality, but in the end it wound up honoring the idea of numerical equality. In invalidating quotas but allowing counting by race, the Court made a distinction without a moral difference. This, however, cannot be the final word on *Bakke*.

Principles, like civil liberties—to recall another phrase of Justice Frankfurter's—draw at best only limited strength from constitutional guarantees.[29] Traditions and the honoring of principles must be in the bones of a people. And in honoring principles there are some invitations—even invitations from the nation's highest court—that ought to be refused by a people dedicated by their history, their institutions, and their charter to the proposition that all men are created equal.

Epilogue:
Weber and After

On Wednesday, June 27, 1979, fifty-two weeks to the day after *Bakke* had been decided, the Supreme Court announced in the *Weber* case[1] that the Civil Rights Act of 1964 does not prohibit "all private, voluntary, race-conscious affirmative action plans." The same conflict present in *Bakke*—namely, that between the ideas of numerical equality and moral equality—was also present in *Weber,* with the Kaiser Aluminum & Chemical Corporation and the United Steelworkers of America representing the idea of numerical equality and Brian F. Weber, a white employed by Kaiser at its Gramercy, Louisiana, plant, personifying the idea of moral equality.

But *Weber,* both before and after it was decided by the Supreme Court, received far less attention than did *Bakke* from the press and thus the American public. Why? Newspapers and magazines may have decided to give less space to *Weber* on the journalistic ground that, with *Bakke,* the public had had its fill of "affirmative action," "reverse discrimination," and the like. Yet there seemed to be other, more important reasons at work—reasons like class. It is not too daring to suggest that those in the media so interested in exploring *Bakke* and those in academe so outspoken on the issue in *Bakke* were more concerned with the rites of passage to a professional career than with the particulars of on-the-job training programs for blue-collar workers. Furthermore,

COUNTING BY RACE

there was the belief that *Weber* was less significant than *Bakke* because, as the *Washington Post* said, Weber involved the interpretation of a statute and not, as in *Bakke*, "basic constitutional principles"; implicit in this perception of *Weber* was the notion that determining the meaning of equality is somehow a less important task when federal law, not the Constitution, is at issue. Finally, the belief was widespread that Weber was not terribly important because it concerned so-called "private" and "voluntary" action; implicit in this understanding of *Weber* was the notion that where the issue of equality is at stake, what the Court decides in cases involving "public" or government-regulated action is somehow more important than what it decides in cases relating to "private" action.

Nevertheless, in *Weber* as in *Bakke* the same basic question arose: In the nation's pursuit of equality, what attention to race does, and should, the law permit? The circumstances in which this question was asked in *Weber* were, of course, different from those in *Bakke*. Matters "pertaining to intellectual qualifications," as Carl Cohen, a professor of philosophy at the University of Michigan, pointed out, were "replaced by matters pertaining to seniority." To see these different circumstances in *Weber,* and at the same time to see the analytic parallels between *Weber* and *Bakke,* it will be useful to recount the pertinent facts in the case.

Since its opening in 1958, Kaiser's Gramercy plant had hired its employees without regard to race. Furthermore, the plant had practiced affirmative action by specifically seeking out black craftsmen, going so far as to advertise jobs in periodicals and newspapers published mainly for blacks. In 1974, having hired few black craftsmen with this approach, the Gramercy plant instituted, with the blessing of its partner in

production, the United Steelworkers of America, a new
of affirmative action.[2] Thereby, for every white worker ͜
mitted to an on-the-job craft training program, at least one
black worker had to be admitted until the percentage of minorities in the skilled work force roughly approximated the
percentage of minorities in the work force in the surrounding
area. Those wishing to be selected for the program were
placed on two lists, by race, and individuals were then chosen
from those lists on the basis of seniority.

In all this the idea of numerical equality was at work, and
the similarities with *Bakke* are striking. Though neither Kaiser nor the medical school at Davis had discriminated against
blacks, both believed that blacks were due compensation for
the historic discriminations against that race—discriminations which, both Kaiser and Davis believed, had blocked the
movement of blacks into, in the one case, the skilled trades,
and, in the other, the medical profession. In an effort to provide adequate compensation, both Kaiser and Davis settled
on a numerical approach: Kaiser wanted at least 50 percent
of its skilled trainees to be minorities, and Davis was concerned with having at least 16 percent of each class of 100
made up of minorities. Kaiser's approach was explicitly tied
to the percentage of minorities in the surrounding area—a
difference from Davis's.[3] But, as at Davis, duality was present at Kaiser. Dual admissions programs flourished at both
Kaiser and Davis, with the distinction between the programs
at both arising solely on the basis of race.

And, inevitably, as at Davis, so at Kaiser's Gramercy
plant: the admissions process resulted in discrimination
against an individual on the basis of race. In 1974, the first
year of the Kaiser–USWA affirmative action plan, seven of
the thirteen craft trainees chosen from the production work

force at the Gramercy plant were black, the rest white. Two of those blacks selected for the program had less seniority than one of the whites rejected, Brian Weber. Like Allan Bakke, Brian Weber thought that he had a right to have his claims decided on the same basis as any other man's, and that that basis, for both moral and legal reasons, could not be race. Weber sued, claiming that the Civil Rights Act of 1964 prohibits precisely the kind of "counting by race" that Kaiser had introduced to the operations of its admissions program to the on-the-job training program. Weber's contention was upheld both in Federal District Court and in the Federal Court of Appeals (Fifth Circuit, New Orleans). But before the nation's highest court, Weber's case was rejected.)

Justice William Brennan wrote the opinion of the Court in *Weber*. In attempting to justify the Court's decision that (the Civil Rights Act of 1964 does not prohibit all "voluntary, race-conscious affirmative action programs,) Brennan began by emphasizing the "narrowness of our inquiry." The Kaiser–USWA plan, he wrote, doesn't involve "state action"; so there's no question here, he concluded, of any alleged violation of the Equal Protection Clause of the Fourteenth Amendment. Too, the Kaiser–USWA plan was adopted "voluntarily"; so, he concluded, the act could not touch the plan. "The only question before us," he said, "is the narrow statutory issue of whether Title VII forbids private employers and unions from voluntarily agreeing upon bona fide affirmative action plans that accord racial preference in the manner and for the purpose provided in the Kaiser–USWA plan."

Brennan then proceeded to answer that question by taking up the argument of the respondent, Brian Weber. Brennan noted that Weber's argument depends upon "a literal interpretation" of those parts of Title VII—sections 703(a) and 703(d)—that make it unlawful to discriminate on account of race "in hiring and in the selection of apprentices for training programs." Brennan's use of the word "literal" was critical: he meant it pejoratively. (Weber overlooks, wrote Brennan, the "significance of the fact" that the Kaiser–USWA plan was *voluntarily* adopted by *private* parties. While a "literal" reading of the Civil Rights Act would seem to forbid such action, said Brennan, in effect the "spirit" in which the act was promulgated was such as to sanction what consenting parties may agree to do in private in order to ameliorate the condition of blacks today. The prohibition against racial discrimination found in sections 703(a) and 703(d) must be read, concluded Brennan, "against the background of the legislative history of Title VII and the historical context in which the [entire] Act arose."

Brennan's reading of that background found that the primary concern of Congress in passing the prohibition against racial discrimination in Title VII was, in the words of Senator Hubert Humphrey, "the plight of the Negro in our economy." (The goal of the Civil Rights Act, said Brennan, was thought by Congress unachievable unless blacks were integrated into the "mainstream of America society" by economic means. Brennan quoted President Kennedy, as he was introducing what would become the Civil Rights Act, to the effect that what blacks need are "jobs with a future." "There is little value," wrote Brennan, further quoting Kennedy, "in a Negro's obtaining the right to be admitted to hotels and restaurants if he has no cash in his pocket and no job."

Therefore, concluded Brennan, "we cannot agree with [Brian Weber] that Congress intended to prohibit the private sector from taking effective steps to accomplish the [economic] goal that Congress designed Title VII to achieve." The very words of the law, "intended as a spur or catalyst to cause 'employers to self-examine and to self-evaluate their employment practices and to endeavor to evaluate, so far as possible, the last vestiges of an unfortunate and ignominious page in this country's history,' . . . cannot be interpreted as an absolute prohibition against all private, voluntary, race-conscious affirmative action." It would be "ironic," said Brennan, "if a law triggered by a nation's concern over centuries of racial injustice and intended to improve the lot of those who had 'been excluded from the American dream for so long' . . . constituted the first legislative prohibition of all voluntary, private race-conscious efforts to abolish traditional patterns of racial segregation and hierarchy."

That was the major thrust of Brennan's reply to Weber's argument, but Brennan also adduced in support of the Court's decision "an examination of the language and legislative history" of another part of Title VII, section 703(j). That part of the law says that nothing contained in Title VII "shall be interpreted to require any employer . . . to grant preferential treatment . . . to any group because of the race . . . of such . . . group" on account of a de facto racial imbalance in the employer's work force." Brennan made much of the word "require" in this formulation: "Had Congress meant to prohibit all race-conscious affirmative action," he wrote, "it easily could have written Title VII so that it would not require or *permit* racially preferential integration efforts." (The emphasis is Brennan's.) The "natural inference," as Brennan called it, from the use of the word "require," is that "Congress chose not to forbid all voluntary race-conscious affirmative action."

So Brennan finished his reply to the argument brought on

behalf of Brian Weber, and thus the Supreme Court reversed the decision of the Fifth Circuit Court of Appeals. Justices Marshall, White, Stewart, and Blackmun joined in the opinion of the Court written by Brennan, while Justices Burger and Rehnquist dissented.[4]

Discussion of the Court's opinion and the dissents by Burger and Rehnquist usefully begins with a reading of the actual language of the sections of Title VII at issue, 703(a) and 703(d). The first specifies that "it shall be an unlawful employment practice for an employer—(1) to fail or refuse to hire or to discharge any individual, or otherwise to discriminate against any individual with respect to his compensation, terms, conditions, or privileges of employment, because of such individual's race, color, religion, sex or national origin; or (2) to limit or classify his employees or applicants for employment in any way which would deprive or tend to deprive any individual of employment opportunities or otherwise adversely affect his status as an employee because of such individual's race, color, religion, sex, or national origin." Section 703(d) says: "It shall be an unlawful employment practice for any employer, labor organization, or joint labor-management committee controlling apprenticeship or other training or retraining, including on-the-job training programs, to discriminate against any individual because of his race, color, religion, sex, or national origin in admission to, or employment in, any program established to provide apprenticeship or other training." 703(a) is a general prohibition against racial discrimination; 703(d) specifically proscribes such racial discrimination as Brian Weber suffered.

In his dissent Justice Burger found "extraordinary clarity" in these statutes. "Congress expressly prohibited in 703 (a) and (d) the discrimination against Brian Weber the Court approves now," he wrote. And Justice Rehnquist, likewise finding the statutes in question exceptionally clear, wrote pointedly that "were Congress to act today specifically to prohibit the type of racial discrimination suffered by Weber, it would be hard pressed to draft language better tailored to the task than that found in 703(d). . . . Equally suited to the task would be 703(a) (2)."

Turning to the other section at issue, 703(j), Justice Burger wrote that "it is specious to suggest that 703(j) contains a negative pregnant that permits employers to do what 703(a) and (d) unambiguously and unequivocally forbid employers from doing." And, in his dissent, Justice Rehnquist wrote that the Court totally ignored the wording of 703(j), "which is obviously addressed to those charged with the responsibility of interpreting the law rather than those who are subject to its proscriptions." Section 703(j), wrote Rehnquist, "was enacted to prevent precisely what occurred in this case."

The plain language of the sections of law in question and the plain meaning of the words of those sections of law are indeed on the side of Justices Burger and Rehnquist. And, as it has been a burden of this book to demonstrate, the idea of moral equality—an idea which denies the moral relevance of race—was not finally accepted into law until the passage of this very same Civil Rights Act of 1964. Justice Brennan accurately quoted President Kennedy as to the need for blacks' having good and secure jobs, but he neglected to notice other statements of Kennedy's. Kennedy did not suppose that any job should be got by means that deny the most fundamental principle of American government. It was Kennedy, after all, who said that "it ought to be possible for every American to enjoy the privileges of being American without regard to his race or his color." And it was Kennedy—more in point—

who, in the summer of 1963, said that the law he shortly would propose to Congress (which would become the Civil Rights Act of 1964) would commit the national legislature to the "proposition that race has no place in American life or law."

Justice Brennan unfortunately would make economic gain override the fundamental moral proposition on which the country was founded and which was finally placed into law by the Civil Rights Act itself—the proposition, namely, that all men are created equal. Like Stephen Douglas in his historic debates with Abraham Lincoln, Justice Brennan would give self-interest priority over the higher good of the equality of all men.

The answer to Justice Brennan and the majority in *Weber* lies not only in the history of the idea of moral equality; it lies specifically in the legislative history that saw the need to incorporate the idea of moral equality into law. It is this legislative history of the Civil Rights Act of 1964 that Justice Brennan understood most imperfectly, as Justice Rehnquist painstakingly showed in his dissent.

In the House of Representatives, the bill that eventually became the Civil Rights Act met early on with the objection that an employer "may be forced to hire according to race, to 'racially balance' those who work for him in every job classification or be in violation of Federal law." Representative Emanuel Celler, chairman of the House Judiciary Committee and the congressman responsible for introducing the legislation in the House, said this criticism "seriously misrepresented what the bill would do and grossly distorted its effects." "The bill would do no more," said Celler, "than prevent . . . employers from discriminating against or in favor of workers because of their race, religion, or national origin."

205

COUNTING BY RACE

Supporting Celler's point were others, notably Representatives Joseph George Minish and Charles Goodell. "Under Title VII," said Minish, "employment will be on the basis of merit. This means that no quota system will be set up." Representative Goodell said: "There is no quota involved. It is a matter of an individual's rights having been violated, charges having been brought, investigation carried out, and conciliation having been attempted and the proof in court that there was discrimination and a denial of rights on the basis of race or color." Republican supporters of the bill noted in an interpretative memorandum that "Title VII does not permit the ordering of racial quotas in business or unions and does not permit interference with seniority rights of employees or union members."

In the Senate, in the first phase of debate, Senator Humphrey, whom Rehnquist accurately called "the primary moving force behind [the bill] in the Senate," said that Title VII "does not limit the employer's freedom to hire, fire, promote, or demote for any reasons—or no reasons—so long as his action is not based on race." Later, during formal debate on the bill, Senator Humphrey said that not only does Title VII not require use of racial quotas, it does not permit their use. "The truth," said Humphrey, "is that this title forbids discriminating against anyone on account of race. This is the simple and complete truth about Title VII. . . . Title VII prohibits discrimination. In effect, it says that race, religion, and national origin are not to be used as the basis of hiring and firing. Title VII is designed to encourage hiring on the basis of ability and qualifications, not race or religion." Senator Thomas Kuchel, another supporter of the bill, emphasized that "employers and labor organizations could not discriminate in favor of or against a person because of his race, his religion, or his national origin. In such matters . . . the bill now before us . . . is color-blind."

A few days later the floor captains for the bill, Senators Joseph Clark and Clifford Case, "took pains," wrote Rehnquist, "to refute the opposition's charge that Title VII would result in proportional treatment of minorities. "There is no requirement in Title VII that an employer maintain a racial balance in his work force. On the contrary, any deliberate attempt to maintain a racial balance, whatever such a balance may be, would involve a violation of Title VII because maintaining such a balance would require an employer to hire or to refuse to hire on the basis of race. It must be emphasized that discrimination is prohibited as to any individual." Of particular relevance, wrote Rehnquist, to the *Weber* case was the observation of Clark and Case concerning seniority rights. "As if directing their comments at Brian Weber, the Senators said: 'Title VII would have no effect on established seniority rights. Its effect is prospective and retrospective. Thus, for example, if a business has been discriminating in the past and as a result has an all-white working force, when the title comes into effect the employer's obligation would be simply to fill future vacancies on a nondiscriminatory basis. He would not be obliged—or indeed permitted—to fire whites in order to hire Negroes, or to prefer Negroes for future vacancies, or, once Negroes are hired, to give them special seniority rights at the expense of the white workers hired earlier.' "

Rehnquist concluded that "with virtual clairvoyance" the Senate's main proponents of Title VII "anticipated precisely the circumstances of this case and advised their colleagues that the type of minority preference employed by Kaiser would violate Title VII's ban on racial discrimination."

COUNTING BY RACE

When opponents of the bill reiterated their objections that quotas might be required, supporters of the bill reiterated the point that discrimination against both Negroes and whites is prohibited by Title VII. "Some people," said Senator Harrison Williams, "charge that [the bill] favors the Negro, at the expense of the white majority. But how can the language of equality favor one race or one religion over another? Equality can have only one meaning, and that meaning is self-evident to reasonable men. Those who say that equality means favoritism do violence to common sense." And Senator Humphrey remarked: "[Title VII] does not provide that any quota systems may be established to maintain racial balance in employment. In fact, the title would prohibit preferential treatment for any particular group, and any person, whether or not a member of any minority group, would be permitted to file a complaint of discriminatory employment practices."

As for section 703(j), the part in which Justice Brennan found the "negative pregnant" permitting such "counting by race" as is done at Kaiser, Rehnquist showed successfully that the section could hardly have been interpreted as Brennan thought it could be. Section 703(j) was adopted in order to allay the fears of the opposition regarding racial balancing and preferential treatment. Rehnquist wrote: "Not once during the 83 days of debate in the Senate did a speaker, proponent or opponent, suggest that the bill would allow employers voluntarily to prefer racial minorities over white persons. . . . Speakers on both sides of the issue, as the legislative history makes clear, recognized that Title VII would tolerate no voluntary racial preference, whether in favor of blacks or whites." Sections 703(a) and (d), said Rehnquist, are "by their terms directed at entities—e.g., employers, labor unions—whose actions are restricted by Title VII's prohibitions," while 703(j) is specifically directed at "entities—federal agencies and courts—charged with the responsibility of interpreting Title VII's provision." Brennan's failure to understand the history of 703(j) is indicative of his failure to understand the history of Title VII and the Civil Rights Act in general.

In concluding his dissent, Justice Rehnquist took up the argument of the Court's majority—the argument that the spirit in which the Congress passed the Civil Rights Act was a spirit in agreement with the decision rendered in *Weber.* But, said Rehnquist, "close examination of what the Court proffers as the spirit of the Act reveals it as the spirit animating the present majority, not the Eighty-eighth Congress." The spirit of the Act, said Rehnquist, is "equality"—that equality, as Rehnquist correctly perceived, which recognizes the evil inherent in discriminating against blacks and which depends upon an end to "*all* voluntary racial discrimination." (The emphasis is ours.) This equality is the moral equality that was at the founding of the nation and which has guided and instructed its highest aspirations as a republic.

The Court in *Weber* did not merely qualify the tradition of moral equality as it did in *Bakke.* In *Weber* the Court did not have the truth, as it did in *Bakke,* only to lose it. The Court in *Weber* rather was blind to the truth of moral equality, for it openly rejected the tradition of moral equality so well articulated in the Civil Rights Act to which it spuriously appealed.

In *Weber* we see, as we have seen before, that not every step taken is a step forward. With *Weber* the Court approved, for the first time ever, preferential classifications on the basis of race in the absence of any proven constitutional or statutory violations. And the Court did so brazenly, failing to mention the genuine harm done Brian Weber. *Weber* recalls another of the Court's decisions, that handed down in 1883. Just as the Court ruled in the *Civil Rights Cases* so as to allow discriminations on the basis of race that could be called "private" and "voluntary," so also the Court has ruled now in *Weber*.

The fundamental question of what attention to race the law does and should allow arises in *Weber*, just as it did in *Bakke*. And individual rights are important, whether the individual is a doctor or a pipefitter, a lawyer or a janitor. And individual rights should be protected from all racial discriminations, whether they be "private" and "voluntary" or not. *Weber* has unambiguously conferred privilege by the means most deleterious in the history of the country—it has conferred privilege by race. If the *Weber* decision was bad, as we believe it thoroughly to be, what's equally bad is that, given the general acquiesence of the press in the decision, the people—a people dedicated to the proposition that all men are created equal—don't know it.

Notes

Chapter 1

1. Davis strived to admit sixteen minority students through its special admissions program each year. But in 1971 and 1974 the school fell one short of its goal, admitting fifteen.

2. The brief for the University of California says that "in short order the [Davis] faculty realized (as have the faculties of most medical and law schools in this country over the past decade) that existing admissions criteria failed to allow access for any significant number of minority students." Brief for Petitioner, p. 2.

3. Ibid., p. 16. "Color-conscious special-admission programs are not viewed as a permanent fixture of the admissions landscape. The underlying philosophy of programs like the one at Davis is that they will eliminate the need for themselves and then disappear . . . The programs represent a transitional means, a short-term necessity in the process of moving towards a truly free and open multi-racial society." Ibid., pp. 42–43.

4. John Hope Franklin and Isidore Starr, eds., *The Negro in Twentieth Century America* (New York: Vintage Books, 1967), p. 226.

5. Brief for Petitioner, p. 47.

6. The brief in support of the university by the UCLA Black Law Students Association contained a lengthy recitation of the kind of statistical disparities in question, an approach found in most every brief filed in support of the university. "The total population of the United States as of 1970 was 203 million people. Of this total, 22.6 million (11.1 percent) were Blacks, 10.1 million (5 percent) were of Spanish heritage, and 800 thousand (0.4) percent were native Americans. Yet, as of 1972, there were only 5,478 Black doctors in the entire United States, as of 1974 there were only 400 Chicano doctors in the entire United States, and as of 1969 there were only four known full-blooded American Indian doctors in the country. Approximately one of every 560 white Americans becomes a doctor, whereas one of every 3,800 Blacks and one of every 20,000 Chicanos becomes a doctor. In California, Blacks comprise approximately 7.6 percent of the population and Mexican-Americans, 15–18 percent. Yet Blacks currently comprise only 2.2 percent of the employed physicians in California, and Mexican-Americans constitute about one percent of the employed physicians in the State. The magnitude of this deficiency was expressed in a statement issued by the past President of the National Medical Association: 'If every Black physician trained since 1865 were still alive, we would still be more than 12,000 short.' As to the Black population, there is currently an unmet need in this country for 25,000–300,000 more Black doctors." Brief *Amici Curiae* of the UCLA Black Law Students Association and the Los Angeles County Bar Association, pp. 29–30. See also Brief *Amici Curiae* for the Bar Association of San Francisco et al., p. 6; Brief *Amici Curiae* of the Mexican American Legal Defense and Educational Fund et al., pp. 16–32; Brief *Amici Curiae* of the National Council of

Notes

Church of Christ in the United States of America, et al., pp. 10–12; Brief *Amicus Curiae* Cleveland State University Chapter of the Black American Law Students Association, p. 16.

7. See note 17.

8. The American Enterprise Institute, "A Conversation with the Rev. Jesse Jackson: The Quest for Economic and Educational Parity," *AEI Studies* 209 (1978):4.

9. The Record filed with the Supreme Court of the United States in *Bakke* (hereinafter cited as R.), p. 259. The Record contains the opinions, findings of fact, and conclusions of law and judgment of the state trial court in California.

10. R., p. 210.

11. The average GPA of those regularly admitted for the class entering in the fall of 1974 was 3.29, while that of the specially admitted was 2.62. The average GPA in the sciences of the regularly admitted was 3.36, while that of the specially admitted was 2.42. The average percentiles in which the regularly admitted scored on the verbal section of the MCAT was 69, the specially admitted, 34; the average on the quantitative section for the regularly admitted was 67, the specially admitted, 30; the average on the science section for the regularly admitted was 82, the specially admitted, 37; and the average on the general information section for the regularly admitted was 72, the specially admitted, 18. Brief for Respondent, pp. 12–13.

12. Brief for Respondent, p. 13.

13. R., p. 281.

14. Brief for Respondent, p. 56.

15. *Marco DeFunis et al.* v. *Charles Odegaard,* 416 U.S. 312 (1974).

16. Ben Martin, "The Parable of the Talents," *Harpers,* January 1978, p. 22.

17. Brief *Amicus Curiae* for the United States, p. 65.

18. Thomas Sowell, "Affirmative Action Reconsidered: Was It Necessary in Academia?" American Enterprise Institute, *Evaluative Studies* 27 (December 1975): 5–6.

19. McGeorge Bundy, "The Issue Before the Courts: Who Gets Ahead in America," *Atlantic Monthly,* November 1977, p. 54.

20. Ibid. Justice Blackmun, in his dissent in *Bakke,* would echo Bundy's aphorism.

21. Brief *Amicus Curiae* of the American Bar Association, pp. 1–2.

22. Brief for Petitioner, pp. 33–34.

23. A reliable estimate is that minority enrollments would drop by as many as 50 percent in the absence of policies that "count by race." (See "Quotas," a letter to the editor by Malcolm J. Sherman, *Commentary* 66, no. 1 (July 1978): 4. The facts show that minority applicants, as a group, have less impressive academic credentials than those of nonminority applicants. The academic qualifications of minority applicants as a group, says the American Association of Medical Colleges, in a brief supporting the University of California in *Bakke,* "pale in comparison with the much higher academic qualifications of the very large and highly competitive pool of white applicants." Brief *Amicus Curiae* of the Association of American Medical Colleges, pp. 8–9. "In little over a decade the law schools have increased their enrollment of minority students from 700 or 1.3 percent to over 9,500 or 8.1 percent. The regrettable but unalterable fact is that under today's conditions, if indicators of academic potential without regard to race were used by law schools as the sole basis of determining admission, 'few minority students would be admitted to law school.' That is the stark conclusion of an exhaustive study of more than 76,000 applications to law

school for the 1975–76 admission year that was confirmed by a separate survey of 80 percent of all accredited law schools." Brief *Amicus Curiae* of the American Association of Law Schools, pp. 6–7. The AALS also supported the University of California.

24. Brief *Amicus Curiae* of the Equal Employment Council, p. 3.

25. Seymour Martin Lipset and William Schneider said in the spring of 1978 that "every major national study shows that a sizeable majority of Americans are . . . opposed to remedying the effects of past discrimination by giving any special consideration in hiring or school admissions." Seymour Martin Lipset and William Schneider, "The Bakke Case: How Would It Be Decided At the Bar of Public Opinion?" *Public Opinion* 1, no. 1 (March/April, 1978): 40.

26. Some *amici* cited the Civil Rights Act of 1964 as authority for deciding *Bakke*. For them, the legislation had a self-evident meaning by virtue of what they thought was its consistency with either the idea of moral equality or that of numerical equality.

27. Brief *Amicus Curiae* of the Young Americans for Freedom, pp. 5–6.

28. Brief *Amicus Curiae* of the American Federation of Teachers, p. 8.

29. Brief *Amici Curiae* of the Anti-Defamation League of B'nai B'rith et al., p. 13.

30. Brief *Amici Curiae* of the American Civil Liberties Union, p. 6.

31. Brief *Amicus Curiae* of the Asian-American Bar Association of the Greater Bay Area, p. 17.

32. *Harper* v. *Virginia State Board of Elections,* 383 U.S. 663 (1966), 669.

33. Brief *Amici Curiae* of the National Council of Churches of Christ in the United States of America et al., p. 7.

34. Brief *Amicus Curiae* of the American Bar Association, p. 16.

35. J. R. Pole, *The Pursuit of Equality in American History* (Berkeley: University of California Press, 1978).

36. "One hungers," says Glazer, "for a more powerful, systematic, unifying way of ordering these varied materials on equality than we find in Mr. Pole's book." Nathan Glazer, a review of Pole's book, *American Spectator* 11, no. 12 (December 1978).

37. Nathan Glazer, *Affirmative Discrimination: Ethnic Inequalities and Public Policy* (New York: Basic Books, 1975).

Chapter 2

1. J. R. Pole, *The Pursuit of Equality in American History* (Berkeley: University of California Press, 1978), p. 15.

2. Edmund S. Morgan, *American Slavery—American Freedom: The Ordeal of Colonial Virginia* (New York: Norton, 1975), p. 314.

3. Pole, *The Pursuit of Equality in American History,* pp. 51–58. Pole says that as a "self-evident truth" the phrase "all men are created equal" meant that "every member of the human race was . . . held to be provided with his own equipment of moral apprehension; and this statement could be of value only if the truth is universal. It follows that no one could be equipped with the normal moral sense without being accessible to the truth that all men are created equal" (p. 52).

Notes

4. Garry Wills, *Inventing America* (Garden City: Doubleday, 1978), pp. 218–28.

5. Ibid., pp. 211, 225. Jefferson defended blacks against the charge that their "moral sense" was depraved due to an alleged "disposition to theft" (ibid., pp. 223–24); and he defended the proposition that Indians were possessed with moral sense (ibid., pp. 284–92). These defenses indicate how strongly Jefferson believed *all* men were equal in regard to moral sense.

Jefferson held slaves even as he wrote "that all men are created equal." While Jefferson never wavered in opposing slavery in general and further slave importation in particular, he was against individual manumission. (See Wills, pp. 294–98). In *Notes on the State of Virginia,* Jefferson worked out a four-step scheme for a general emancipation. Jefferson, says Wills, thought blacks had "what all men have, the right to self-rule *as a people.* . . . His deportation scheme was meant to assure for blacks the same right Americans were asserting." (Ibid., p. 306.)

6. See Wills, *Inventing America,* and Carl Becker, *The Declaration of Independence: A Study in the History of Political Ideas* (New York: Random House, 1922). Wills argues that Jefferson was influenced primarily by Hutcheson and those of the Scottish school. The Becker thesis, disputed by Wills, is that Jefferson was influenced primarily by Locke.

7. The draft of the Declaration of Independence penned by Jefferson included a diatribe against King George III for his waging "cruel war against human nature itself" by superintending the international slave trade. Congress struck out this passage from the final draft of the Declaration in "complaisance," as Jefferson recorded in his notes, "to South Carolina and Georgia, who had never attempted to restrain the importation of slaves, and who on the contrary still wished to continue it." A. Leon Higginbotham, Jr., "The Roots of Slavery in our Nation's Laws: How Founding Fathers Closed Their Eyes To Black Inequality," *Washington Post,* May 21, 1978, B5. See Wills, *Inventing America,* pp. 72–75 for a discussion of Jefferson's intentions in his charges against George III.

8. Benjamin Quarles, *The Negro in the American Revolution* (Chapel Hill: University of North Carolina Press, 1961), p. 33.

9. Pole, *The Pursuit of Equality in American History,* p. 34.

10. Quarles, *The Negro in the American Revolution,* pp. 33–37.

11. Higginbotham, "The Roots of Slavery in our Nation's Laws," B5.

12. Ibid.

13. Quarles, *The Negro in the American Revolution,* p. 40.

14. Albert P. Blaustein and Robert L. Zangrando, eds., *Civil Rights and the Black American: A Documentary History* (New York: Washington Square Press, 1970), p. 36.

15. Ibid., p. 40.

16. William M. Wiecek, *The Sources of Anti-Slavery Constitutionalism in America, 1760–1848* (Ithaca: Cornell University Press, 1977), pp. 34–36.

17. Ibid., p. 38.

18. Higginbotham, "The Roots of Slavery in Our Nation's Laws," B5.

19. Wiecek, *The Sources of Anti-Slavery Constitutionalism,* p. 41.

20. Quarles, *The Negro in the American Revolution,* p. 36.

21. Ibid.

22. Ibid., pp. 23–24.

23. Wiecek, *The Sources of Anti-Slavery Constitutionalism,* pp. 41–42.

24. Quarles, *The Negro in the American Revolution,* p. 43.

25. Ibid.
26. Higginbotham, "The Roots of Slavery in Our Nation's Laws," B5.
27. Quarles, *The Negro in the American Revolution,* p. 44.
28. Ibid.
29. Higginbotham, "The Roots of Slavery in Our Nation's Laws," B5.
30. Quarles, *The Negro in the American Revolution,* p. 50.
31. Ibid., p. 189.
32. Ibid., p. 190.
33. *Commonwealth* v. *Jennison,* Charge of Chief Justice Cushing, quoted in Blaustein and Zangrando, *Civil Rights and the Black American,* p. 45.
34. Ibid., p. 46.
35. Higginbotham, "The Roots of Slavery in Our Nation's Laws," B5.
36. Wiecek, *The Sources of Anti-Slavery Constitutionalism,* p. 63.
37. Ibid., pp. 63–64.
38. Ibid., p. 64.
39. Higginbotham, "The Roots of Slavery in Our Nation's Laws," B5.
40. Wiecek, *The Sources of Anti-Slavery Constitutionalism,* p. 65.
41. Ibid., pp. 64–65.
42. Ibid., p. 65. One who was not "drawn along" was Gouverneur Morris. His dissent is notable: "The admission of slaves into the Representation when fairly explained comes to this: that the inhabitant of Georgia and S.C. who goes to the Coast of Africa, and in defiance of the most sacred laws of humanity tears away his fellow creatures from their dearest connections & dam(n)s them to the most cruel bondages, shall have more votes in a Govt. instituted for protection of the rights of mankind, than the Citizen of Pa. or N. Jersey who views with a laudable horror, so nefarious a practice. He would add with that Domestic slavery is the most prominent feature in the aristocratic countenance of the proposed Constitution. The vassalage of the poor has ever been the favorite offspring of Aristocracy. And What is the proposed compensation to the Northern States for a sacrifice of every principle of right, of every impulse of humanity. They are to bind themselves to march their militia for the defense of the S. States; for their defense against those very slaves of whom they complain." Max Ferrand, ed., *The Records of the Federal Convention,* paperback ed., vol. 2, (New Haven: Yale University Press, 1966), p. 222.
43. Washington to Benjamin Harrison, Mount Vernon, January 18, 1784, in John C. Fitzpatrick, ed., *The Writings of George Washington from the Original Manuscript Sources, 1745–1799* (Washington, 1931–1944), XXVII, pp. 305–306.

Chapter 3

1. Harry V. Jaffa, *The Crisis of the House Divided: An Interpretation of the Issues in the Lincoln-Douglas Debates,* paperback ed. (Seattle: University of Washington Press, 1973), p. 308.
2. Quoted in Albert P. Blaustein and Robert L. Zangrando, eds., *Civil Rights and the Black American: A Documentary History* (New York: Washington Square Press, 1970), p. 47.
3. Samuel Eliot Morison, *The Oxford History of the American People* (New York: New American Library, 1972), vol. 2, 1789–1877, p. 139.

Notes

4. Jaffa, *The Crisis of the House Divided*, p. 436.

5. Morison, *The Oxford History of the American People*, p. 332.

6. Section 14 of the Kansas-Nebraska Act, quoted in Blaustein and Zangrando, eds., *Civil Rights and the Black American*, p. 144.

7. Ibid.

8. Ibid.

9. Jaffa, *The Crisis of the House Divided*, p. 438.

10. 19 How. (60 U.S.) 393 (1857).

11. Jaffa, *The Crisis of the House Divided*, p. 9.

12. Ibid., p. 33.

13. Ibid., pp. 29–37.

14. Roy P. Basler, ed., *The Collected Works of Abraham Lincoln* (New Brunswick: Rutgers University Press, 1953), vol. 3, p. 220.

15. Jaffa, *The Crisis of the House Divided*, p. 13.

16. Ibid., p. 313.

17. Ibid., pp. 313–14.

18. Thomas Jefferson, *Notes on Virginia, Query 14,* in Saul K. Padover, ed., *Thomas Jefferson on Democracy* (New York: Mentor, 1939), p. 99. See also Jaffa, *The Crisis of the House Divided*, p. 14.

19. Jaffa, *The Crisis of the House Divided*, p. 14.

20. Ibid., p. 325.

21. Ibid., pp. 319–322.

22. Ibid., p. 306.

23. Ibid., pp. 323–327.

24. Ibid., p. 30.

25. Ibid., p. 36.

26. Ibid., p. 375.

27. Ibid., p. 320.

28. Basler, *The Collected Works of Abraham Lincoln*, vol. 3, p. 16.

29. Jaffa, *The Crisis of the House Divided*, pp. 320–21.

30. Ibid., p. 359.

31. Basler, *The Collected Works of Abraham Lincoln*, vol. 2, pp. 499–500.

32. Jaffa, *The Crisis of the House Divided*, pp. 361–62.

33. Ibid., p. 309.

34. Ibid., p. 348.

35. Ibid., pp. 332–33.

36. Ibid., pp. 347–48.

37. Hadley Arkes, *American Spectator* 11, no. 6 (April 1978): 41, in reply to a letter from Rauol Berger concerning Arkes's February 1978 article in the same magazine, "Bakke: The Legal Profession in Crisis."

38. Basler, *The Collected Works of Abraham Lincoln*, p. 29.

39. Jaffa, *The Crisis of the House Divided*, p. 320.

40. Arkes in reply to letter from Berger, *American Spectator,* p. 41.

Chapter 4

1. *Cummings* v. *Missouri*, 4 Wall. 277 (1866), 321–22.

2. For example, see C. Vann Woodward, *The Burden of Southern History* (Ba-

ton Rouge: Louisiana State Press, 1974), pp. 69–88; and C. Vann Woodward, *American Counterpoint* (Boston: Little, Brown, 1971), pp. 163–183.

3. Charles Fairman, *Reconstruction and Reunion 1864–1888,* vol. 6, part 1 of *History of the Supreme Court of the United States* (New York: Macmillan, 1971), p. 1158.

4. Alexander Bickel, *The Morality of Consent* (New Haven: Yale University Press, 1975), p. 40.

5. Quoted in Albert P. Blaustein and Robert L. Zangrando, eds., *Civil Rights and the Black American: A Documentary History* (New York: Washington Square Press, 1970), p. 230.

6. Raoul Berger, *Government by Judiciary: The Transformation of the Fourteenth Amendment* (Cambridge: Harvard University Press, 1977), p. 108, *n.* 35.

7. Alexander Bickel, *Politics and the Warren Court* (New York: Harper and Row, 1965), p. 222.

8. Berger, *Government by Judiciary,* p. 29.

9. The Constitution of the United States, Fourteenth Amendment, Section 1.

10. Charles Fairman, *Reconstruction and Reunion,* pp. 1261, 1265–66, 1269.

11. Ibid., p. 1286.

12. J. R. Pole, *The Pursuit of Equality in American History* (Berkeley: University of California Press, 1978), p. 171.

13. Ibid.

14. Ibid., p. 172.

15. Fairman, *Reconstruction and Reunion,* p. 1300.

16. The Constitution of the United States, Fifteenth Amendment, Section 1.

17. Pole, *The Pursuit of Equality in American History,* p. 173.

18. Woodward, *American Counterpoint,* p. 177.

19. Ibid., p. 178.

20. Ibid., p. 177.

21. Bertram Wyatt-Brown, "The Civil Rights Act of 1875," *Western Political Quarterly* 18, no. 4 (1965): 77.

22. Ibid., pp. 770–74.

23. Quoted in Blaustein and Zangrando, eds., *Civil Rights and the Black American,* p. 241.

24. Woodward, *The Burden of Southern History,* pp. 79–83.

Chapter 5

1. *Slaughter House Cases,* 16 Wall. 36 (1873).

2. Richard Bardolph, ed., *The Civil Rights Record: Black Americans and the Law, 1849–1970* (New York: Thomas Y. Crowell Co., 1970), p. 59.

3. *United States* v. *Reese,* 92 U.S. 214 (1876).

4. *The Civil Rights Cases,* 109 U.S. 3 (1883).

5. *Plessy* v. *Ferguson,* 163 U.S. 537 (1896).

6. 109 U.S. 3, 10.

7. Ibid., 9.

8. Ibid., 22–25.

9. Ibid., 36.

10. Ibid., 39–40.

Notes

11. Ibid., 25.
12. Ibid., 48.
13. Ibid., 50.
14. Ibid., 25.
15. Ibid., 61.
16. Ibid., 62.
17. Ibid., 59.
18. C. Vann Woodward, *American Counterpoint: Slavery and Racism in the North-South Dialogue* (Boston: Little, Brown, and Co., 1971), p. 231. Woodward provides an excellent, concise account of this case and its background in the chapter entitled "The National Decision Against Equality," in *American Counterpoint*, pp. 212–33.
19. Woodward, *American Counterpoint*, p. 225.
20. 163 U.S. 537, 543–44.
21. Ibid., 550–51.
22. Ibid., 551.
23. Ibid.
24. Ibid., 557.
25. Ibid., 554–63.
26. Ibid., 559.
27. C. Vann Woodward, *The Strange Career of Jim Crow* (New York: Oxford University Press, 1974), p. 68.
28. Ibid., pp. 68–69.
29. Ibid., pp. 97–102.
30. Bardolph, ed., *The Civil Rights Record*, p. 130.
31. Ibid., p. 135.
32. Christopher Lasch, "The Anti-Imperialists, the Philippines, and the Inequality of Man," *Journal of Southern History* 24 (1958): 319, 323.
33. Ibid., pp. 323–324.
34. Ibid., p. 320.
35. Ibid., p. 325.
36. Ibid., p. 330.

Chapter 6

1. Elsie M. Lewis, "The Political Mind of the Negro, 1865–1900," in Charles E. Wynes, ed., *The Negro in the South Since 1865* (University: University of Alabama Press, 1965), pp. 23–24.
2. Ibid., p. 24.
3. Ibid., pp. 27–28.
4. Ibid., p. 28.
5. Ibid., p. 34.
6. Richard H. Cain, "Against Segregation in Schools," in Frances S. Freeman, ed., *The Black American Experience* (New York: Bantam Books, 1970), p. 116.
7. Mary White Ovington, "How the NAACP Began," in John Hope Franklin and Isidore Starr, eds., *The Negro in Twentieth Century America* (New York: Vintage Books, 1967), pp. 95–101.

8. Ibid., p. 97.

9. Ibid., p. 98.

10. Booker T. Washington, *Up From Slavery,* quoted in Franklin and Starr, eds., *The Negro in Twentieth Century America,* p. 18.

11. *Freedom to the Free, A Report to the President by the United States Commission on Civil Rights,* quoted in Franklin and Starr, eds., *The Negro in Twentieth Century America,* p. 107.

12. *Powell* v. *Alabama,* 287 U.S. 45 (1932).

13. *Norris* v. *Alabama,* 294 U.S. 587 (1935).

14. *Smith* v. *Texas,* 311 U.S. 127 (1940).

15. *Mitchell* v. *United States,* 313 U.S. 80 (1941).

16. 313 U.S. 80, 97.

17. *Henderson* v. *U.S. ICC and Southern Railway,* 339 U.S. 816 (1950), 818.

18. 339 U.S. 816, 824–25.

19. J. R. Pole, *The Pursuit of Equality in American History* (Berkeley: University of California Press, 1978), pp. 249–50.

20. *Missouri ex rel. Gaines* v. *Canada,* 305 U.S. 337 (1938).

21. *Sipuel* v. *Board of Regents of the University of Oklahoma,* 332 U.S. 631 (1948).

22. Richard Kluger, *Simple Justice* (New York: Vintage Books, 1975), pp. 258–59.

23. Ibid., p. 259.

24. 332 U.S. 631.

25. *Sweatt* v. *Painter,* 339 U.S. 629 (1950).

26. 339 U.S. 629, 631.

27. Kluger, *Simple Justice,* p. 267.

28. *McLaurin* v. *Oklahoma State Regents,* 339 U.S. 637 (1950), 640.

29. Kluger, *Simple Justice,* p. 268.

30. Ibid., p. 275.

31. Ibid., pp. 275–76.

32. 339 U.S. 629, 631.

33. Ibid., 633.

34. 339 U.S. 637, 641.

35. *Brown* v. *Board of Education,* 347 U.S. 483 (1954).

36. NAACP brief, quoted in Albert P. Blaustein and Robert L. Zangrando, *Civil Rights and the Black American: A Documentary History* (New York: Washington Square Press, 1970), p. 421.

37. 347 U.S. 483, 495.

38. *Cummings* v. *Missouri,* 4 Wall. 277 (1866), 321–22.

39. Franz Boas, *The Mind of Primitive Man,* quoted in Richard Bardolph, ed., *The Civil Rights Record: Black Americans and the Law, 1849–1970* (New York: Thomas Y. Crowell, 1970), pp. 176–77.

40. Bardolph, ed., *The Civil Rights Record,* p. 236.

41. Ibid., p. 172.

42. John Hope Franklin, *From Slavery to Freedom: A History of Negro Americans* (New York: Vintage Books, 1969), pp. 464–65.

43. A. Philip Randolph, "Why Should We March?" in Franklin and Starr, eds., *The Negro in Twentieth Century America,* pp. 138–40.

44. Executive Order 8802, June 25, 1941, quoted in Blaustein and Zangrando, eds., *Civil Rights and the Black American,* p. 358.

Notes

45. Harry S Truman, quoted in Bardolph, ed., *The Civil Rights Record*, pp. 242-43.

46. *To Secure These Rights*, quoted in Blaustein and Zangrando, *Civil Rights and the Black American*, pp. 375-76.

47. Ibid., p. 376.

48. Ibid.

49. Bardolph notes in *The Civil Rights Record* that opinion surveys such as that conducted by the *Scientific American* in late 1956 disclosed that "a mere seventh of northerners and two-fifths of southerners still believed that Negroes are inherently less intelligent than whites." (pp. 233-34).

50. Martin Luther King, Jr., "I Have a Dream," quoted in Franklin and Starr, eds., *The Negro in Twentieth Century America*, pp. 144-46.

51. *Public Papers of the President of the United States, John F. Kennedy*, vol. 3, quoted in Franklin and Starr, eds., *The Negro in Twentieth Century America*, pp. 147-48.

52. Martin Luther King, Jr., *Letter from Birmingham City Jail*, quoted in Franklin and Starr, eds., *The Negro in Twentieth Century America*, p. 158.

53. *Public Papers of the President of the United States, John F. Kennedy*, vol. 3, p. 218.

54. Ibid., pp. 219-20.

55. Ibid., p. 221.

56. Lino Graglia, "The Supreme Court's Abuse of Power," *National Review* 30, no. 29 (July 21, 1978): 895.

57. Nathan Glazer, *Affirmative Discrimination: Ethnic Inequality and Public Policy* (New York: Basic Books, 1975), p. 43.

58. Ibid., p. 4.

Chapter 7

1. Richard Kluger, *Simple Justice* (New York: Vintage Books, 1975), pp. 275-276.

2. *Brown* v. *Board of Education*, 347 U.S. 483 (1954).

3. Ibid., 495.

4. The Court had the opportunity in *Brown* to argue from the conditions of American citizenship. The example of Charles Sumner, who argued *Roberts* v. *City of Boston* before the Massachusetts Supreme Court in 1849, is apposite. As counsel for the father of a black schoolchild who claimed that his daughter was being discriminated against on the basis of race by being denied admission to a white Boston school that was closest to her home, Sumner said:

"I begin with the principle, that, according to the spirit of American institutions, and especially of the Constitution of Massachusetts, *all men, without distinction of color or race, are equal before the law....*

"The equality which was declared by our fathers in 1776, and which was made the fundamental law of Massachusetts in 1780, was *equality before the law*. Its object was to efface all political or civil distinctions, and to abolish all institutions founded upon *birth*. 'All men are *created* equal,' says the Declaration of Independence.... These are not vain words. Within the sphere of their influence no persons can be *created,* no person can be *born,* with civil or political privileges not enjoyed equally by all his fellow-citizens, nor can any institution be established recognizing any distinctions of birth. This is the Great Charter of every person who draws his vital breath on this soil, whatever may be his condition, and whoever may be his parents. He may be poor, weak, humble, black—he may be of Caucasian, of Jewish, of Indian, or of Ethiopian race—he may be of French, of German, of English, of Irish extraction—but before the Constitution of Massachusetts all these distinctions disappear. He is not poor, or weak, or humble, or black—nor Caucasian, nor Jew, nor Indian, nor Ethiopian—nor French, nor German, nor English, nor Irish; he is a MAN—the equal of all his fellowmen. He is one of the children of the state, which, like an impartial parent, regards all its offspring with equal care." (Oral Argument for Plaintiff in *Roberts* v. *City of Boston,* quoted in Albert P. Blaustein and Robert L. Zangrando, eds., *Civil Rights and the Black Americans: A Documentary History* (New York: Washington Square Press, 1970), p. 113.

Had the Court in *Brown* argued from the conditions of citizenship, the virtue of such a justification would have been, as constitutional law theorist Edmund Cahn has said, that fundamental rights "would not rise, fall, or change along with the latest fashions of psychological literature" (Cahn, "Jurisprudence," *New York University Law Review* 30, no. 150: 157–58). See note 7.

5. Some have argued that the Court did not mean what by the language of its opinion it appeared to say. As Herbert Wechsler has said, it is "hard to think the judgment really turned upon the facts. Rather, it must have rested on the view that racial segregation is, in principle, a denial of equality" (Wechsler, "Toward Neutral Principles of Constitutional Law," *Harvard Law Review* 73, no. 1 [November, 1959]: 33). See also Lino Graglia, *Disaster by Decree* (Ithaca: Cornell University Press, 1976), pp. 28–29; and Kluger, *Simple Justice,* pp. 706–7.

Despite the text of the decision, the Court may have been resting its decision on the conditions of American citizenship (see note 4). Certainly later courts interpreted *Brown* as a principled decision and even took action against efforts to adduce social science evidence contrary to that adduced in *Brown.* (See *Armstrong* v. *Board of Education,* 333 F.2d 47, 51, 5th Circuit, 1964.) But the point remains that the Court in *Brown* did not articulate the principle in question, and did not make plain that its decision was based on this principle (if it was so based).

6. 347 U.S. 483, 492–94.

7. 347 U.S. 483, 494. The influence of the eminent black psychologist Kenneth B. Clark was evident in Warren's footnote 11. Of the six works referred to in that footnote, the first was to one of Clark's own publications and the remainder were to works that had appeared in a bibliography attached to a paper drafted by Clark and signed by thirty-two social scientists, which concluded that segregation was likely to produce psychological damage in black children. See Hadley Arkes, "The Problem of Kenneth Clark," *Commentary* 58, no. 5, (November 1974): 38.

8. 347 U.S. 483, 495.

9. Terrance Sandalow has remarked that "other principles that would justify [the decisions in the *School Desegregation Cases*] were, no doubt, imaginable, but in the absence of any explanation by the Court, a principle requiring government to be 'color-blind' as urged long ago by the first Justice Harlan, was both plausible and attractive" (Terrance Sandalow, "Racial Preferences in Higher Education: Political Responsibility and the Judicial Role," *University of Chicago Law Review* 42 [1975]: 679–680, n. 84).

Notes

10. Apart from the question of what justification the *Brown* decision merited, there is the question of what decision was possible. There was a desire for unanimity among the members of the Court but, as historians of the Court have pointed out, it was doubtful that a unanimous decision could be based on substantive legal grounds or on the history of the Fourteenth Amendment, because on both there was simply too much disagreement. It has been suggested, plausibly, that it was only in the decree that the justices could join and that it was to this end that Chief Justice Warren worked. See Gerald T. Dunne, *Hugo Black and the Judicial Revolution* (New York: Simon and Schuster, 1977), pp. 318–20. It is likely that although the Court offered a unanimous opinion, the various justices looked in different directions for the decision's justification.

11. Alexander Bickel, *The Least Dangerous Branch* (Indianapolis: Bobbs-Merrill Co., 1962), p. 253.

12. Louis Lusky, "The Stereotype: Hard Core of Racism," *Buffalo Law Review* 13 (1963): 457–58.

13. Louis Lusky, "Racial Discrimination and the Federal Laws: A Problem in Nullification," *Columbia Law Review* 63 (1963): 1172, n. 37.

Lino Graglia, commenting on the Court's refusal to grant the *Brown* plaintiffs individual relief, said: "The most charitable interpretation is that the Court chose to ignore the interests of the individual blacks before it in favor of a supposed interest of racial groups—an approach that, as in *Plessy*, has been a major source of injustice to blacks throughout our history" (Graglia, *Disaster by Decree*, p. 36).

14. Thomas Sowell has traced the origins of the term *affirmative action* to the 1930s. The Wagner Act (1935) specified that employers whose antiunion activities had violated the law should not only "cease and desist" from those activities but also take "affirmative action" to ensure that they did not generate further harm. Thus, as Sowell points out, in the landmark Jones and Laughlin Steel case (1937), the steel company was ordered not only to quit discrimination against union members but also to post notices in conspicuous places and to reinstate unlawfully discharged workers with back pay. See Thomas Sowell, "Affirmative Action Reconsidered: Was it Necessary in Academia?" American Enterprise Institute *Evaluative Studies* 27 (December 1975): 2–3.

15. G. W. Foster, "The North and West Have Problems, Too," quoted in John Hope Franklin and Isidore Starr, eds., *The Negro in Twentieth Century America* (New York: Vintage Books, 1967), pp. 309–20.

16. Ibid., p. 310.

17. Oscar Handlin, "The Goals of Integration," quoted in Franklin and Starr, eds., *The Negro in Twentieth Century America*, pp. 244–45.

18. Whitney M. Young, Jr., *To Be Equal*, quoted in Franklin and Starr, eds., *The Negro in Twentieth Century America*, p. 126.

19. Charles Silberman, "The City and the Negro," quoted in Franklin and Starr, eds., *The Negro in Twentieth Century America*, p. 507.

20. See Brief of Howard University as *Amicus Curiae*, pp. 40–42; and Brief of the NAACP Legal Defense Fund, Inc., as *Amicus Curiae*, pp. 13–42.

21. Charles Silberman, *Crisis in Black and White*, quoted in Franklin and Starr, eds., *The Negro in Twentieth Century America*, p. 434.

22. Young, *To Be Equal*, quoted in Franklin and Starr, eds., *The Negro in Twentieth Century America*, p. 127.

23. Paul Seabury, "A Sure Recipe for Civic Commotion," *The Alternative: An American Spectator* 9, no. 9 (June/July, 1976): 24.

24. Quoted by Paul Seabury, "HEW & the Universities," *Commentary* 53, no. 2 (February 1972): 38–39.

25. Quoted by Seabury, ibid., p. 39.

26. Orlando Patterson, "On Guilt, Relativism, and Black-White Relations," *American Scholar* 43, no. 1 (Winter 1973–74): 129–130.

27. Nathan Glazer, *Affirmative Discrimination: Ethnic Inequality and Public Policy* (New York: Basic Books, 1975), pp. 30–31.

28. Laurence H. Silberman, "The Road to Racial Quotas," *The Wall Street Journal*, August 11, 1977.

29. Brief *Amicus Curiae* of the Equal Employment Advisory Council, p. 13.

30. Ibid., p. 17.

31. Ibid.

32. Statement of Professor Miro M. Todorovich, City University of New York, be ore the Special Subcommittee on Education of the Committee on Education and Labor, September 20, 1974, p. 9.

33. *Green* v. *County School Board of New Kent County*, 391 U.S. 430 (1968). For a discussion of *Green*, see Graglia, *Disaster by Decree*, pp. 67–89.

34. For example: Brief *Amicus Curiae* for the NAACP, p. 21; Brief *Amici Curiae* of the Board of Governors of Rutgers et al., pp. 8–16; Brief *Amicus Curiae* of the National Fund for Minority Engineering Students, pp. 14–26; Brief *Amicus Curiae* of the NAACP Legal Defense and Educational Fund, pp. 54–57.

35. For example: Brief *Amici Curiae* of the UCLA Black Law Students et al., pp. 29–30; Brief *Amicus Curiae* of the Asian-American Bar Association of the Greater Bay, pp. 5–16; Brief *Amici Curiae* of Native American Law Students of the University of California at Davis et al., p. 4; Brief *Amici Curiae* of the Mexican American Legal Defense and Educational Fund et al., pp. 6–16.

36. Brief *Amicus Curiae* of the Law School Admission Council, pp. 16–22; Brief *Amicus Curiae* of the Legal Services Corporation, pp. 14, 17–18; Brief *Amici Curiae* of the Mexican American Legal Defense and Educational Fund et al., pp. 16–28; Brief *Amicus Curiae* of the Asian-American Bar Association of the Greater Bay, pp. 15–16; and Brief *Amici Curiae* of the UCLA Black Law Students et al., pp. 29–30.

37. Brief *Amici Curiae* of Columbia, Harvard University, Stanford University, and the University of Pennsylvania, p. 19; Brief *Amicus Curiae* of the Legal Services Corporation, p. 37; Brief *Amici Curiae* of the Board of Governors of Rutgers et al., pp. 49–50.

38. Brief *Amicus Curiae* of the Lawyers' Committee for Civil Rights Under Law, pp. 13–14; Brief *Amici Curiae* of Columbia University, Harvard University, Stanford University, and the University of Pennsylvania, p. 6, 10, 32; Brief *Amicus Curiae* of the Law School Admissions Council, pp. 16–22; Brief *Amicus Curiae* of the Legal Services Corporation, pp. 33–36; Brief *Amici Curiae* of the Board of Governors of Rutgers et al., p. 41; Brief *Amicus Curiae* of the Fair Employment Practices Commission of the State of California, pp. 18–19.

39. Brief *Amicus Curiae* of the Lawyers' Committee For Civil Rights Under Law, pp. 15–20; Brief *Amicus Curiae* for the NAACP, pp. 22–24; Brief *Amici Curiae* of the Board of Governors of Rutgers et al., pp. 21–26; Brief *Amicus Curiae* of the Fair Employment Practices Commission of the State of California, p. 17; Brief *Amicus Curiae* of the Black American Law Student Association, p. 7; Brief *Amicus Curiae* of the Society of American Law Teachers, pp. 13–16.

Notes

Chapter 8

1. McGeorge Bundy, "The Issue Before the Courts: Who Gets Ahead in America," *The Atlantic Monthly*, November 1977, p. 54. The idea that the country was in such a transition was apparent in many of the briefs supporting the University of California. See, for example, Brief *Amici Curiae* of the Mexican American Legal Defense and Educational Fund et. al., p. 5; Brief *Amici Curiae* of the American Civil Liberties Union, the ACLU of Northern California, the ACLU of Southern California, pp. 2, 10; and Brief *Amici Curiae* for the Bar Association of San Francisco and the Los Angeles County Bar Association, p. 43.

2. Also unclear was the state of affairs necessary before race would cease being a relevant factor in admissions policies. The University of California, for example, disavowed "proportional representation" as the requisite state of affairs (Brief for Petitioner, p. 47). On the other hand, Professor Kenneth Tollett argued that "until . . . oppressed minority groups approach proportional representation . . . preferential or special recruitment programs imperatively should continue apace" (quoted in Brief *Amicus Curiae* of the National Medical Association, Inc. et al., p. 53). See also Brief *Amicus Curiae* of the Black Law Students Union of Yale University Law School, p. 22.

3. "One finds a striking degree of consensus against quotas and special preference, even among groups usually marked by a strong commitment to liberal values—students, faculty members, and self-described liberals." Seymour Martin Lipset and William Schneider, "An Emerging National Consensus," *New Republic* 177, no. 1 (October 15, 1977): 9.

4. Past discrimination is regarded as the critical factor in determining outcomes today. "In order to restore victims of discrimination to the position they would have occupied but for the discrimination, and to make a fair assessment of their achievements and potential, it is proper to credit them with having surmounted obstacles not faced by nonvictims." (Emphasis added.) Brief *Amicus Curiae* for the United States, p. 65.

5. For example: "In 1972, when 12 percent of all Americans were black, only 4,478 or 1.7 percent of the 320,903 active physicians were black. There was one physician for every 649 persons in the general population; but only one black physician for every 4,298 blacks. The ratio of black physicians to black population also worsened between 1942 and 1972, because the increase in the number of black physicians did not keep pace with the increase in the black population." Brief *Amici Curiae* for the National Council of Churches et al., p. 11. See also Brief *Amici Curiae* of the Board of Governors of Rutgers et al., pp. 13–15.; Brief *Amicus Curiae* of the Legal Services Corporation, p. 14; and Brief *Amici Curiae* for Jerome A. Lackner et al., passim.

6. Nor can one say, as the proponents of numerical equality argue by implication, that, as Ben Martin has put it, "modernity would have appeared in any case, even if history had been different, free of the blight of discrimination and injustice." Ben L. Martin, "The Parable of the Talents," *Harper's* 256, no. 1532 (January 1978): 21–22.

7. Orlando Patterson "On Guilt, Relativism, and Black-White Relations," *American Scholar* 43, no. 1 (Winter 1973–1974): 129–32.

8. Supplemental Brief for Petitioner, p. 30.

9. "Only a handful of schools—perhaps only 10 to 12—use systems like the one at Davis," said J. W. Peltason, president of the American Council of Education.

Notes

"Harvard's Admissions Formula: It's All in the Numbers," *Washington Post,* June 30, 1978.

10. For some it is still axiomatic. "Probably the most disturbing manifestation of the persistence of racism is ... that ... blacks are not held to the same standards...." Kenneth B. Clark, "No. No. Race, Not Class Is Still at the Wheel," *New York Times,* March 22, 1978. Sociologist Orlando Patterson, asking what should be the moral stand of the white American in relation to blacks, writes: "The simple answer is that his conception of, and relationship with, blacks should be guided by exactly the *same moral principles* as those that guide his action and attitudes toward his white peers. Anything else ... spells moral and interracial disaster.... Sympathy and compassion [for blacks] should [not] be taken to imply ... *double standards.*" (Emphasis added.) Patterson, "On Guilt, Relativism, and Black-White Relations," p. 125.

11. Herbert Gutman, *The Black Man In Slavery and Freedom, 1750–1925* (New York: Vintage Books, 1977), p. 263. The columnist Michael Novak has observed that "the most glaring burden inflicted upon black culture by three centuries of slavery and discrimination ... is a psychological habit of dependence." Michael Novak, "Blacks and the New Class," *Washington Star,* March 5, 1978.

12. Orlando Patterson, "The Moral Crisis of the Black American," *Public Interest* 32 (Summer 1973): 52.

13. Ben Martin, "The Parable of the Talents," p. 21.

14. Information supplied by Peter Storandt, a former dean of the Davis medical school, in conversation with one of the authors, April 19, 1978. Storandt says that the special admittees at Davis would berate those minority students who had been regularly admitted because the latter had integrated with the rest of the class. Storandt notes that a Filipino, a South American of "very dark skin," and an individual of Lebanese and Argentinian extraction—all regular admittees—were "not with us," in the expression of the special admittees.

15. "Proponents of special admissions, while conceding that most minority students are initially less qualified than whites, argue that many minority students are intrinsically abler than their credentials would suggest, and will ultimately outperform apparently better qualified whites. Grades and test scores, according to this argument, will underpredict subsequent minority performance in the same way that a track coach who relied only on current performance would underestimate the potential of a prospect whose training had been inadequate. But many recent studies have shown that grades and test scores are actually biased in favor of blacks in that blacks with given credentials will, on the average, receive somewhat *lower* subsequent grades than would whites with the same prior grades and scores. This was true at every law school studied in 1972 by William B. Schrader and Barbara Pitcher and in a 1974 study by Schrader (both studies were published by the Law School Admission Council). The same pattern was observed for undergraduate grades at eighteen out of twenty-two colleges in a 1973 survey by Robert Linn." Malcolm J. Sherman of the Russell Sage Foundation in "Quotas," a letter to the editor of *Commentary* 66, no. 1 (July 1978): 4.

16. The impression that there was little difference between the test scores of those specially admitted to Davis and those regularly admitted was widespread. Typical of this misimpression was the letter to the editor of the *Washington Post* (October 2, 1977) by Larry Riedman of Washington, D.C. Riedman characterized the difference in test scores between the specially admitted and the regularly admitted as "modest."

Notes

17. Sowell concludes that there is "some evidence that tests underestimate the mental ability of lower income people in general, as well as blacks in particular," but that "the question of predicting college performance is quite different from the question of innate ability or even of cultural bias. . . . A variety of tests given in a variety of settings indicate that mental tests generally do not underestimate the future performances of lower income people, including blacks, and in fact have a slight tendency to predict a better academic performance than that actually achieved." Sowell, "The Plight of Black Students in the United States," in Sidney W. Mintz, ed., *Slavery, Colonialism, and Racism* (New York: Norton 1974), pp. 182–83.

18. Sowell says that once universities admit "by the numbers," they find it necessary to graduate them "by the numbers." Sowell on "The Advocates," produced for Public Broadcasting, January 26, 1978.

19. Thomas Sowell, *Black Education: Myths and Tragedies* New York: David McKay Co., 1972), p. 292.

20. "The problem is seldom seen for what it is, for it has *not* been approached in terms of the optimum distribution of black students in the light of their preparation and interests, but rather in terms of how Harvard, Berkeley, or Antioch can do its part, maintain its leadership, or fill its quota." Sowell, "The Plight of Black Students in the United States," pp. 179–80.

21. Sowell, "The Plight of Black Students in the United States," pp. 179–83; and Sowell, "Are Quotas Good for Blacks," *Commentary* 65, no. 6 (June 1978): pp. 41–42.

22. Sowell, "Are Quotas Good For Blacks," p. 41. "The possibility of distributing black students in institutions whose normal standards they already meet has been almost totally ignored." Sowell, "The Plight of Black Students in the United States," pp. 180–81.

23. "Those laws, removing as they did constraints on everything from political participation to freedom to have a sandwich in a public place, made it possible for black people to organize energy and enterprise in ways available to the rest of us all along. And I think it is patronizing and wrongheaded to attribute the big changes that occurred after the enactment of those laws to something other than the talent and will of a people only lately liberated. To hear some of the alleged friends of minorities tell it, however, all rank and position and power and progress has had to be . . . well, you know what I mean . . . *given* to them." Meg Greenfield, "How To Resolve the Bakke Case," *Washington Post,* October 19, 1977.

24. "Blacks achieved the economic advances of the 1960s once the worst forms of discrimination were outlawed, and the only additional effect of quotas was to undermine the legitimacy of black achievements by making them look like gifts from the Government." Sowell, "A Black 'Conservative' Dissents," *New York Times Magazine,* August 8, 1976, p. 15.

25. "A newly released RAND study," writes Sowell, " . . . concludes that very little credit should be given to government affirmative action programs for any narrowing of the income gap between white and black workers." Sowell, "Are Quotas Good for Blacks," p. 40.

26. Brief for Petitioner, p. 26.

27. Malcolm J. Sherman, "Quotas," p. 4. See also Brief *Amicus Curiae* for the Association of American Law Schools, pp. 27–28, and Brief *Amicus Curiae* of the Association of American Medical Colleges, pp. 8–9.

28. Arthur Ashe, the tennis player, has raised the question of whether we should expect quotas in professional sports. Ashe, certainly a "role-model," notes that in his

twenty-five years of playing tennis he has signed more autographs for white kids than black kids. But, given the increasing color-consciousness today, "it now appears that when the [white kids] become old enough to economically choose between the Kennedy Center [in Washington, D.C.] or the Capitol Centre, they may opt for the performing arts or stay home. If it ever comes to the point that yesterday's kids avoid the [Washington] Bullets [a professional basketball team that plays in the Capitol Centre] because they're too black, then God help us all." Arthur Ashe, "Are We to Expect Quotas in Pro Sports," *The Greensboro Record* (N.C.), March 22, 1979.

29. Thus the Reverend Jesse Jackson frequently tells high school and college students that low expectations result in low achievements and exhorts them to reach for high academic goals. Jackson, ironically, is a supporter of special admissions schemes that count by race.

30. "Virtually every black child who has grown up in this country over the past 300 years has been told, by word and deed, that he is inferior intellectually." Sowell, *Black Education: Myths and Tragedies,* p. 270.

31. Sowell, "Black Excellence: The Case of Dunbar High School," *Public Interest* 35 (Spring 1974): 3–21.

32. A study released in early 1978 by the Robert Wood Johnson Foundation would seem to be evidence against the assertion that blacks (and minorities) are seriously underserved." In 1976, according to the study, the percentage of blacks seeing a physician was almost equal to that of whites. "Blacks and the Poor Appear to Be Seeing Doctors More Often," *Wall Street Journal,* January 12, 1978.

33. *Bakke* v. *Regents of the University of California,* 18 C. 3rd 34, 56 (1976).

34. "Young blacks resent the assumption of many whites that they will return to black communities to practice their professions. Lynn French [a student at the Virginia Law School] . . . said: 'I'd like to go back home and set up a practice, but I'll argue with anyone who says it's my duty. I should have the option to work anywhere.' " Story by Steven V. Roberts, New York Times News Service, October 24, 1977.

35. Sowell, "Are Quotas Good for Blacks," p. 42. See also Sowell, "The Plight of Black Students in the United States," p. 185.

36. Joseph Adelson, "Living with Quotas," *Commentary* 65, no. 5 (May 1978): 27.

37. Tammy Jacobs, "Professors Support Minority Admissions," *Harvard Law Record* 65, no. 2 (September 30, 1977): 4.

38. Brief for Petitioner, p. 3.

39. In the trial court deposition of Dr. George Lowery of the Davis Medical school, he states that the school "would be hard pressed to admit people to the school if they had MCAT percentiles in science and in verbal which were below 50." It is a matter of record, however, that in neither of the two years in which Bakke applied to Davis did the average science and verbal percentiles of those specially admitted exceed 50. Yet the Brief for Petitioner could speak of "a pool of fully qualified minority applicants for medical schools"—a pool from which, presumably, Davis drew its special admittees. Brief for Petitioner, p. 26. For an example of lying about the *way* in which minorities are admitted (that is, by "counting by race"), see J. W. Foster, "Race and Truth at Harvard," *New Republic* 174, no. 28 (July 17, 1977): 16–20.

40. It is doubtful, furthermore, that institutions candidly inform their minority students of their abilities and prospects. Probably, few institutions are so candid with minority students as was Harvard, in the middle 1950s, with Sowell. In a letter

Notes

of acceptance to Sowell, as he recounts it, Harvard said "they were not convinced that they were doing me a favor by offering me admission and the small amount of aid that they did, for it would be very hard on me, academically and financially." Sowell, *Black Education: Myths and Tragedies*, p. 43.

41. See Adelson, "Living with Quotas," pp. 27–28.

42. "Human nature," said the California Supreme Court in *Bakke*, "suggests a preferred minority will be no more willing than others to relinquish an advantage once it is bestowed (18 C. 3d 34, 62)." So does the evidence suggest. At Boalt Hall, the law school at the University of California at Berkeley, Japanese Americans vigorously protested efforts by the school to drop them from the list of preferred minorities in admissions decisions.

Apart from the moral point about the deceit implicit in saying that at some future date the nation can return to "normal," there is the practical point that preference for certain minorities inevitably causes other minorities to ask for special treatment. Note for example, the reaction of Ralph Perotta, executive director of the National Italian-American Foundation, to the Supreme Court's decision in *Bakke*. "I think that with Bakke, affirmative action will be opened up to lots of other groups that have not been benefited by it before." *Washington Post,* June 30, 1978.

43. Patterson, "On Guilt, Relativism, and Black-White Relations," p. 128.

44. Brief *Amicus Curiae* of Timothy J. Hoy, p. 16.

45. Eliot Marshall, "Race Certification," *New Republic* 177, no. 1 (October 15, 1977): 18–19.

Chapter 9

1. *Wall Street Journal,* June 29, 1978.

2. *Regents of the University of California* v. *Bakke,* 98 S. Ct. 2733 (1978).

3. 98 S. Ct. 2733, 2808.

4. Ibid., 2811–2814.

5. Ibid., 2782–2792.

6. Ibid., 2798–2805.

7. Ibid., 2806–2808.

8. Ibid., 2744–2751.

9. Alexander Bickel, *The Morality of Consent,* quoted in 98 S. Ct. 2733, 2751, *n.* 35.

10. 98 S. Ct. 2733, 2751.

11. Ibid., 2751, *n.* 36.

12. Ibid., 2760.

13. Ibid., 2761–2762.

14. Ibid., 2762–2763.

15. Ibid., 2762–2766.

16. Ibid., 2763, *n.* 53.

17. *Offut* v. *United States,* 348 U.S. 11, 14 (1954).

18. 98 S. Ct., 2733, 2765–2766.

19. Ibid., 2748.

20. "Harvard's Admissions Formula: It's All in the Numbers," *Washington Post,* June 30, 1978.

21. 98 S. Ct., 2733, 2807.
22. Brief of the Association of American Medical Colleges *Amicus Curiae*, pp. 8–9.
23. Brief *Amicus Curiae* for the Association of American Law Schools, pp. 28–29.
24. William Raspberry, *The Greensboro Record*, July 12, 1978.
25. 98 S. Ct. 2733, 2748–2750.
26. Ibid., 2782.
27. Ibid., 2805.
28. Ibid., 2806.
29. *Dennis* v. *United States,* 341 U.S. 494, 5.

Epilogue: *Weber* and After

1. *Weber* is shorthand for three cases decided in one: *United Steelworkers of America, AFL–CIO–CLC* v. *Brian F. Weber* et al.; *Kaiser Aluminum & Chemical Corporation* v. *Brian F. Weber* et al.; and *U.S.* et al. v. *Brian F. Weber* et al.
2. A similar affirmative action program was begun in 1974 at all fifteen of the Kaiser plants, as per a master collective bargaining agreement with the USWA.
3. Obviously there were other differences, too. The Davis medical school instituted its special admissions program in order to, among other things, effect a "diverse" student body and better serve the "underserved" minority communities. The goal at Kaiser was to bring more minorities—blacks—into the economic mainstream of American life.
4. There were four opinions in *Weber:* the opinion of the Court written by Justice Brennan, a concurring opinion by Justice Blackmun, a dissenting opinion by Chief Justice Burger, and a dissenting opinion by Justice Rehnquist in which Justice Burger joined. In his concurring opinion Justice Blackmun argued that it would have been preferable had the Court approved the Kaiser–USWA preferential admissions program by taking the "arguable violation" approach—by saying, that is, that Kaiser sometime in the past may have discriminated against blacks. Blackmun, in other words, would have unarguable violations done to individuals like Brian Weber on the basis of an "arguable violation" by Kaiser Aluminum. Blackmun would have done well to have read Carl Cohen's devastation of the "arguable violation" approach that appeared a month before *Weber* was decided. See Cohen, "Why Racial Preference Is Illegal and Immoral," *Commentary* 67, no. 6 (June 1979): 48.

Suggestions for Further Reading

Chapter 1

McGeorge Bundy, "The Issue Before the Courts: Who Gets Ahead in America," *Atlantic Monthly,* November 1977, pp. 41–54.

The American Enterprise Institute, "A Conversation with the Rev. Jesse Jackson: The Quest for Economic and Educational Parity," *AEI Studies* 209, 1978.

Brief for Petitioner, the Regents of the University of California.

Brief for Respondent, Allan Bakke.

Chapter 2

Leon Higginbotham, *In the Matter of Color* (New York: Oxford University Press, 1978).

J. R. Pole, *The Pursuit of Equality in American History* (Berkeley: University of California Press, 1978), pp. 1–58.

Benjamin Quarles, *The Negro in the American Revolution* (Chapel Hill: University of North Carolina Press, 1961).

William M. Wiecek, *The Sources of Antislavery Constitutionalism in America, 1760–1848* (Ithaca: Cornell University Press, 1977), pp. 15–83.

Garry Wills, *Inventing America: Jefferson's Declaration of Independence* (New York: Doubleday & Company, Inc., 1978).

Chapter 3

Roy P. Basler, ed., *The Collected Works of Abraham Lincoln,* vol. 3, (New Brunswick: Rutgers University Press, 1955).

Harry V. Jaffa, *The Crisis of the House Divided* (Seattle: University of Washington Press, 1959).

Chapter 4

Alexander M. Bickel, "The Original Understanding and the Segregation Decision," *Harvard Law Review* 69, no. 1 (1955).

Albert P. Blaustein and Robert L. Zangrando, eds., *Civil Rights and the Black American: A Documentary History* (New York: Washington Square Press, 1970).

Charles Fairman, *Reconstruction and Reunion 1864–88,* vol. 6, part 1 of *History of the Supreme Court of the United States* (New York: Macmillan, 1971).

C. Vann Woodward, *American Counterpoint: Slavery and Racism in the North—South Dialogue* (Boston: Little, Brown and Co. 1971), pp. 163–83.

Suggestions for Further Reading

Chapter 5

The Civil Rights Cases, 109 U.S. 3 (1883).

Plessy v. *Ferguson,* 163 U.S. 537 (1896).

Richard Bardolph, ed., *The Civil Rights Record: Black Americans and the Law, 1949–1970* (New York: Thomas Y. Crowell Co., 1970).

C. Vann Woodward, *American Counterpoint: Slavery and Racism in the North—South Dialogue* (Boston: Little, Brown and Co., 1971), pp. 212–33.

C. Vann Woodward, *The Strange Career of Jim Crow* (New York: Oxford University Press, 1974), 3rd rev. ed.

Chapter 6

Brown v. *Board of Education,* 347 U.S. 483 (1954).

McLaurin v. *Oklahoma State Regents for Higher Education,* 339 U.S. 637 (1950).

Missouri ex rel Gaines v. *Canada,* 305 U.S. 337 (1938).

Sweatt v. *Painter,* 339 U.S. 629 (1950).

Richard Bardolph, ed., *The Civil Rights Record: Black Americans and the Law, 1949–1970* (New York: Thomas Y. Crowell Co., 1970).

Albert B. Blaustein and Robert L. Zangrando, eds., *Civil Rights and the Black American: A Documentary History* (New York: Washington Square Press, 1970).

John Hope Franklin, *From Slavery to Freedom: A History of Negro Americans* (New York: Vintage Books, 1969).

John Hope Franklin and Isidore Starr, eds., *The Negro In Twentieth Century America* (New York: Vintage Books, 1967).

Nathan Glazer, *Affirmative Discrimination: Ethnic Inequality and Public Policy* (New York: Basic Books, 1975), pp. 1–33, 43–45.

Richard Kluger, *Simple Justice* (New York: Vintage Books, 1975).

Elsie M. Lewis, "The Political Mind of the Negro, 1865–1900," in Charles Wynes, ed., *The Negro in the South Since 1865* (University: University of Alabama Press, 1965), pp. 22–38.

J. R. Pole, *The Pursuit of Equality in American History* (Berkeley: University of California Press, 1978), pp. 214–92.

Chapter 7

Brown v. *Board of Education,* 347 U.S. 483 (1954).

Albert B. Blaustein and Robert L. Zangrando, eds., *Civil Rights and the Black American: A Documentary History* (New York: Washington Square Press, 1970).

John Hope Franklin and Isidore Starr, eds., *The Negro In Twentieth Century America.* (New York: Vintage Books, 1967).

Nathan Glazer, *Affirmative Discrimination: Ethnic Inequality and Public Policy* (New York: Basic Books, 1975).

Orlando Patterson, "On Guilt, Relativism, and Black-White Relations," *American Scholar* 43, no. 1 (Winter 1973–1974): 121–38.

Paul Seabury, "HEW & the Universities," *Commentary* 53, no. 2 (February 1972): 38–43.

Laurence H. Silberman, "The Road to Racial Quotas," *The Wall Street Journal,* August 11, 1977.

Suggestions for Further Reading

Chapter 8

McGeorge Bundy, "The Issue Before the Courts: Who Gets Ahead in America," *Atlantic Monthly*, November 1977, pp. 41–54.

Ben Martin, "The Parables of the Talents," *Harpers*, January 1978, pp. 18–26.

Orlando Patterson, "The Moral Crisis of the Black American," *The Public Interest* 32 (Summer 1973): 40–60.

Orlando Patterson, "On Guilt, Relativism, and Black-White Relations," *American Scholar* 43, no. 1 (Winter 1973–1974): 121–38.

Thomas Sowell, "Are Quotas Good for Blacks," *Commentary* 65, no. 6 (June 1978): 39–43.

Thomas Sowell, *Black Education: Myths and Tragedies* (New York: David McKay Company, Inc., 1972).

Thomas Sowell, "Ethnicity in a Changing America," *Daedalus* 107, no. 1 (Winter 1978): 213–37.

Thomas Sowell, "The Plight of Black Students in the United States," in Sidney W. Mintz, ed., *Slavery, Colonialism, and Racism* (New York: Norton, 1974), pp. 179–96.

Chapter 9

Regents of the University of California v. *Allan Bakke*, 98 S. Ct. 2733 (1978).

Index

Abolitionist movement: Declaration of Independence and, 34; Massachusetts cases in, 35–36; moral equality and, 26, 27; Otis on, 28–29; *Somerset* case and, 29–30; spread of, 31–32, 34

Academic performance, 188–190, 212 n23

Adams, John Quincy, 42

Adams, Samuel, 29

Adelson, Joseph, 164, 178, 195

Admission policies: academic performance as basis for, 188–190; background to changes in, 4–7; Bakke's reaction to, 7–9; correlation between numbers and motivation in, 158; counting by race in, 14; dependency relationships in, 150–151; different standards for different racial groups in, 149; distortions from categorizing people in, 166–169; as example for minority children, 157–162; expectations and, 161–162; of Harvard College, 185–186, 187, 188, 189, 190, 192; improvement of medical care for minorities and, 162–163; individual circumstances of applicants in, 164–166; mainstream argument for minorities in, 154–157; mismatching minority students in, 155–156; notion of compensation in, 13–14; percent of minority students in medical school and, 5–6, 7; by race, 127–128, 149; reverse discrimination in, 14–15; tests in, 153–154; "two-track" system in, 13–14; University of California at Davis, 3–4

Affirmative action: *Bakke* decision and, 192–193; Department of Labor and, 131–132; employment practices and, 11–12; first appearance of, 126, 222 n14; at University of California at Davis, 3–4; *Weber* case on, 15, 197–210

Affirmative Discrimination (Glazer), 22

Alabama, 94, 104, 112

Allan Bakke v. Regents of the University of California, see Bakke case

American Anti-Defamation League, 18

American Bar Association, 13, 19

American Civil Liberties Union, 18

American Federation of Teachers, 17

Amsterdam News, 173

Anthropology, 105–106

Apportionment, under Fourteenth Amendment, 63

Arkes, Hadley, 56, 57

Armed forces, 105–109

Articles of Confederation, 36

Ashe, Arthur, 226 n28

Asian-American Bar Association, 18

Asiatic people, and discrimination, 86–87

Association of American Law Schools (AALS), 116, 119, 189

Association of American Medical Colleges, 13, 188–189

Bakke, Allan Paul, 4, 7–9

Bakke case: affirmative action programs after, 192–193; *amicus curiae* briefs in, 15–20, 138, 188–189; background to, 3–4; Civil Rights Act of 1964 and, 146–147; conflict of ideas of equality in, 10, 16–20, 21; equal protection clause and, 17–19; Fourteenth Amendment and, 16, 17–19, 21; moral equality and, 9–10, 169–170; nondiscrimination principle in, 17–18; numerical equality in, 141; opinions in, 178–192; reaction to,

Index

Index

Harlan, John, 89, 113; citizenship and, 115; in *Civil Rights Cases,* 74–78, 83, 88; in *Plessy* case, 82–83, 88, 116, 147
Harper's Weekly, 68
Harvard College: admission policy of, 185–186, 187, 188, 189, 190, 192, 227 n40; slavery debate at, 27, 30–31
Health, Education, and Welfare Department (HEW), 12, 135–136, 194, 195
Heard, Alexander, 13
Henderson v. U.S. ICC and Southern Railway, 95
Henry, Patrick, 37
Hofstadter, Richard, 55
Holmes v. City of Atlanta, 122
Hopkins, Samuel, 32
Howard, A. E., 175
Howard University, 129, 131
Humphrey, Hubert, 130–131, 201, 206, 208
Hutcheson, Francis, 26

Immigration Act of 1965, 114
Integration, and racial balance, 118, 127–128
Interstate Commerce Commission, 95
Iredell, James, 37
Italian-Americans, 195

Jackson, Jesse, 7, 173, 227 n29
Jaffa, Harry A., 40, 46, 52, 55, 69
Jay, John, 34
Jefferson, Thomas: antislavery arguments and, 32; ideas of equality, 24, 25, 26, 28; as slave-holder, 33, 214 n5
Jennison, Nathaniel, 35
Jennison v. Caldwell, 35
Jim Crow laws, 56; Congressional action against, 111; discrimination in suffrage in, 85–86; in education, 96; moral equality and, 71–88; overthrow of, 89–115; spread of, 83–85; Supreme Court decisions and emergence of, 71–83

Johnson, Lyndon B., 6, 11, 129–130, 131, 133, 135, 137
Jordan, Vernon, 174
Justice Department, 136

Kaiser Aluminum & Chemical Corporation, 15, 197, 198, 199
Kansas, 46–47, 121
Kansas-Nebraska Act, 44–45, 46, 51
Kaplan, John, 177
Kemeny, John, 176, 194
Kennedy, John F., 11, 111, 112–113, 126, 201, 204
Kerr, Clark, 176, 194
King, Martin Luther, Jr., 111–112, 159
Kluger, Richard, 101
Kuchel, Thomas, 206

Labor Department, 131–132, 133
Lasch, Christopher, 86, 87
Law School Admission Test (LSAT), 154, 189
Law schools, 10, 13, 97–100, 102
Lecompton constitution, 46
Legal Defense and Educational Fund (NAACP), 97, 100, 101, 103–105
Lehner, Urban C., 171
Liberator (newspaper), 34
Liberty, and equality, 32
Lincoln, Abraham: celebration of centennial of birth of, 91–93; Douglas debates with, 21, 45–48, 50, 53, 54, 56, 59, 78; Emancipation Proclamation and, 58; Harlan's decisions and, 78, 79; moral equality and, 40–57; 115; state autonomy and, 73
Literacy tests, 72
Locke, John, 26
London Meeting for Sufferings, 28
Los Angeles Board of Education, 168–169
Louisiana, 80, 81
Lowery, Dr. George, 8, 227 n39
Lusky, Louis, 124, 125

Index

Nelson, Knute, 87
Nevins, Allan, 49
New Hampshire, 33
New York Times, 173, 175, 191
Nixon, Richard M., 173
Nondiscrimination principle: in *Bakke* case, 17–18; in *Brown* case, 128
Norris v. Alabama, 94
Northern states: ratification of Fifteenth Amendment in, 67; violent attacks on Negroes and, 92
Northwest Ordinance, 42, 43, 44, 58
Norton, Eleanor Holmes, 175–176, 193
Numerical equality: in admission policy of Davis Medical School, 7–8; affirmative action in executive orders and, 11; arguments against, 139–170; in *Bakke* case, 10, 14, 119–120, 182; *Brown v. Board of Education* and, 120–125; as end in itself, 140–143; government efforts to promote, 11–13; historical discrimination and, 144–145; integration as racial balance and, 118–119; as means to end, 139–140, 145–151; moral compensation and, 118–119, 163–165; traditional concept of equality and, 143–144; *Weber* case and, 197

Office of Civil Rights, 135
Offut v. United States, 186
Oklahoma, 97–98, 99
Otis, James, 28–29, 39
Ovington, Mary White, 91–92

Parks, Rosa, 125
Patterson, Orlando, 132, 145, 150, 168
Pease, Henry, 68
Peltason, Jack, 176, 194
Pennsylvania, 28, 34, 35
Pennsylvania Society for Promoting the Abolition of Slavery and the Relief of Free Negroes Unlawfully Held in Bondage, 34
Perez, Al, 174, 193
Perotta, Ralph, 195, 228, n42

Philadelphia, 31, 127
Philadelphia Plan, 133–135
Philippines, 86–87
Pinckney, Charles Cotesworth, 37
Plessy, Homer Adolph, 80
Plessy v. Ferguson, 73, 74, 80–83, 87, 114, 147; equal protection clauses and, 96; segregation in education cases and, 102, 103, 105; separate-but-equal doctrine in, 120, 121–122
Pluralists, 105
Pole, J. R., 22, 96, 105, 213 n3
Polk, James, 42
Poll tax, 73
Popular sovereignty doctrine, 46, 54
Powell, Lewis, 178, 179, 182–186, 187–188, 190, 191
Powell v. Alabama, 94
President's Committee on Civil Rights, 109–111
Professional schools: compensation policies and, 163–165; *DeFunis* case and, 10; mainstream argument for minorities in, 154–157; minority admission as example to children and, 157–162; minority participation as means of improving, 151–154; racial balance in, 149; Supreme Court decisions on, 99–102; "two-track" system in admission policies of, 13–14
Public accommodations, 95–96
Public policy, and race, 123–125
Public works law, 12
Pursuit of Equality in American History, The (Pole), 22

Quakers, 26, 28
Quotas, 137, 176, 195

Race: Boas on, 105; classification by, 20, 116–117, 138; group identities and, 168; public policy and relevance of, 123–125; societal advancement and proportionality of, 9–10
Racial balance, and integration, 118, 127–128

240

Index

Somerset, James, 29-30
Somerset case, 26, 29-30
South Carolina, 36-37
Southern states: abolitionist sentiment in, 36-38; Missouri Compromise and, 43; post-*Brown* civil rights movement in, 125-126; racial discrimination in suffrage in, 85-86
Sowell, Thomas, 139, 145, 155, 162, 163, 166, 193, 222 n14, 226 n17, 24, 25; 227 n40
Springfield, Illinois, riots, 91
State government: abolitionist sentiment and, 37-38; citizenship definitions and, 72; education of Negroes by, 92; segregation in public education in, 96; voting rights and, 66-67
Stevens, John Paul, 178, 179, 182
Stevens, Thaddeus, 64
Stewart, Charles, 29
Stewart, Potter: *Bakke* opinion of, 178, 182; *Weber* opinion of, 202
Stoics, 26
Storandt, Peter, 225 n14
Students, minority, *see* Minorities
Suffrage: Fifteenth Amendment and, 66-67; Fourteenth Amendment and, 64-66; Jim Crow laws and discrimination in, 85-86; in mid-twentieth century, 113; states' rights and, 66-67; Supreme Court decisions on, 72-73; Truman and, 110
Summer, Charles, 67, 220 n4
Supreme Court: educational decisions of, 136; emergence of Jim Crow laws and, 71-83; as protector of civil rights, 94-96; *see also specific laws*
Sweatt, Heman Marion, 99-100
Sweatt v. Painter, 99-100, 101, 102, 103, 104, 116

Taney, Roger B., 48, 58
Taxation: poll, 73; slavery and, 38
Tests: in *Bakke* case, 189; as predictors of achievement, 153-154; racial classification under Fourteenth Amendment and, 20; suffrage and, 72-73
Thirteenth Amendment, 115; *Bakke*

case and, 16-17; Civil Rights Act of 1875 and, 75, 76; *Plessy* case on, 80, 81, 82-83; slavery abolished by, 58-59
Tillman, Ben, 87
Tollett, Kenneth, 173
To Secure These Rights (President's Committee on Civil Rights), 109-111
Tourgee, Albion, 80-81
Trade, slavery, 38
Transportation, 83-84, 95-96
Treaty of Guadalupe Hidalgo, 43
Tribe, Lawrence, 175
Truman, Harry S, 109
Trumbull, Lyman, 62-63
Tyler, Moses Coit, 33

UCLA Black Law Students Association, 211 n6
United Steelworkers of America, 197, 198
University of Alabama, 112
University of California at Berkeley, 135-136
University of California at Davis: affirmative action plan of, 3-4; arguments advanced by, 151-163; background to changes in admission policy of, 4-7; Bakke's feelings on policies of, 7-9; explicit quotas at, 137; moral equality belief applied to, 9-10; numerical equality as means to end in policy of, 146-147; "two-track" system in, 13-14
University of Missouri, 97
University of Oklahoma, 97-98, 103
University of Texas Law School at Austin, 99-100, 103
University of Washington Law School, 10
Up from Slavery (Washington), 93
U.S. v. Reese, 72, 74

Van Alstyne, William, 170
Vanderbilt University, 13
Vinson, Chief Justice, 99, 100, 102, 103